SOONER THAN TOMORROW

"Dede Ranahan weaves everyday events into her poignant account of her son's descent into psychosis. She takes readers, with her and her family, on a harrowing journey—there is no guidebook—that too many of us are forced to take. Written in diary form, with entries by both mother and son, *Sooner Than Tomorrow* quietly exposes our nation's shameful failure to help those with serious mental illnesses. It chronicles a mother's unending love for a child and a son's struggles to be well. An important book. A loving tribute. A powerful story that tugs at the heart and leaves readers asking, "Why can't we do better?"

—PETE EARLEY,
author of *CRAZY: A Father's Search
Through America's Mental Health Madness*

"This book about psychiatric brain disease is poignant and painful, but, ultimately, a necessary read. In its well-constructed pages, you'll find a mother's diary of her wonderful son and his terrible illness. Every clinician needs a copy of this, every mental health worker, every doctor, and, certainly, every family. *Sooner Than Tomorrow* is as real as storytelling gets. There are no stories more honest than those of our children who live with mental illnesses. This book tells one such story beautifully.

—LAURA POGLIANO,
mother of Zac, Board Member, SARDAA (Schizophrenia and Related Disorders Alliance of America)

Among the uncountable tragedies of the mental illness sub-nation, is its near-invisibility to its host society. So-called normal people live alongside neighbors—even friends—whose quiet pain, mourning, terror, and desperation would affront the nation's conscience if it were better known. Dede Ranahan is among the heroic witnesses who are breaking that silence. Her memoir of the loss of her son—passionate, eloquent, revelatory, and unspeakably brave—brilliantly takes its place among the beacons of light and truth telling that point the way to the reclamation of our most helpless brothers and sisters, sons and daughters, mothers and fathers.

—RON POWERS,
Pulitzer Prize-winning journalist, author of *No One Cares About Crazy People: The Chaos and Heartbreak of Mental Health in America*

Sooner Than Tomorrow

Dede posted her story in two-week increments at www.sooner-thantomorrow.com. The following are readers' responses.

Beautiful words with an undertone that has caught me . . . carrying me up and down. Such a good writer that I am grateful to be with you. I can borrow some courage here.

—JANET

Dede: Your writing is captivating. I find that I'm waiting for the next post, like when you finish a good novel and can't wait for the sequel. You and Pat have such a wonderful gift for using words in prose and poetry.

—JOAN A.

Thanks for sharing your life, Dede. Seven years after Josh's first psychotic break and two-and-a-half years after he ended his life in the hell of prison where he never should have been, I am still angry and heartbroken. I don't want anyone to suffer like Josh and we have. But there's some small comfort in knowing I'm not alone in the sadness that weighs me down everyday.

—ANNE

Dede, you amaze me with your writing ability and your candor in the face of major obstacles. Kiss the cat for me. I will kiss my dog in return.

—NANCY

Dede, you are such a good writer and have so much to say. Mental illness is a huge problem and getting worse every day. We see it in the many homeless people who live here in Medford.

—BETTE

Dede, I am so enjoying your story. So rich and naked.

—LINDA

I see the intelligence and the illness in Pat's posts. He made me laugh—but also evident is the stress on you. I hope you realize what a gem you have in that diary you kept. Pat really comes alive. I can hear his voice.

—CHRIS

I like the way you've included some funny stories with the thoughtful and frustrating stories. I feel like I can relate to your life, Dede. If this was your purpose, then you've succeeded in writing an engrossing and moving memoir.

—JAN M.

You are a stunning writer. Understatement makes many times more horrible. Awesome—awful, real, deep . . . must read. Beyond heartbreaking, my friend.

—SWANNIE

I love *Sooner Than Tomorrow*. Love it even though sometimes it makes me cry.

—JEAN

I read your latest post, and it's beautifully written. I don't say that lightly.

—RITA

So happy for the readers who will discover you.

—LIZ

I loved your diary entries today and laughed out loud several times.

—J.M.

Dede Ranahan graciously shares her story with us and it is absolutely amazing.

—MARY S.

I can relate to you and your son, Pat. I wish I'd written a journey on Shane but had no idea that I would outlive my son or that I would lose him at 39. Savor your time with your family. Even the difficult times.

—DARLENE

I love how you write—I hear your voice as I read your words.

—SHARON L.

Dede, So many of us thank you for continuing your advocacy work. How brave of you to continue the fight after losing Pat. Hope you receive the highest honors for *A Mother's Diary*.

—KIMBERLEE W.

Good reading.

—CRAIG W., HAWAII

The heartbreaking scenarios you describe here sound so very familiar. Thank you for your eloquent writing. I hope that everyone will read your book when it's published.

—MARILYN M.

Your writing skills are exceptional and I particularly love the way you string words together.

—V.

Dede, every one of your blog posts has a portion that I love so much that I take a screen shot and read it over and over. Your last blog had the reference to the grocery cart, and I used it in my company newsletter. This week my screen shot was your poem, which I will share with my grandkids.

—STACEY

I have always respected your writing talent and now coupled with such an important cause. The way you have turned your own personal tragedy into helping others is remarkable.

—PAM R.

I so much like to share your life. Sometimes I see me. I want more, more, more. So mark my name as an avid reader. How I would have loved to converse with Patrick. Such wonderful people in the world. Pity we don't know each other.

— GrannaAnna

Thanks for your postings, Dede. They make us think.

—IRENE U.

Dede, I anxiously await each posting from your blog/book. You write with such skill, and not easy when it's so personal, but your passion sprinkled with humor are the reasons that this is successful.

—JOAN L.

Hi there, I just wanted to reach out and say thank you. I found your site through FB and the "kismet" is right there. In two weeks I am heading up to a monthly writers group here in Los Angeles. We will be writing about our experiences and emotions. It will be cathartic and healing and I've just sent a link of your site to everyone, to get inspired.

—K.

Best.ever.comment: "Trying to find meaning in the suffering . . . rising each day . . . no matter what."

—NANCY D.

I've done this, the primal scream and the mother animal instinct. There can't be anything more painful, not even death. My son was a normal little boy and a normal young man until schizophrenia came calling. Now I feel so shattered. I love your your diary.

—J.H.D.

Your wonderful Pat was blessed with a beautiful, caring, intelligent, and empathetic mother. From a kindred spirit and mama warrior.

—M.B.

Wow.

—R.K.

I think it's a special kind of talent you have in making people feel what you write. I hope you continue using your writing skills to paint the picture of what life is like for many people with SMI and their loved ones.

—CHANNIN H.W.

I love you, and I have grown to love your son, Pat, as well. It's a part of why I cherish the diary. The other reason is because you speak from your heart, the grief, the anguish, and the love that I feel for my son, Masai, too. Crying with you.

—TAMA B.

Dede, you have put words to heartbreaking loss and frustration with our system failure like no one else.

—JOYCE H.

Keep up the good work on your brilliant diary. When is it coming out in book form, please? I would love a copy.

—DEN P., UNITED KINGDOM

I can so relate to what you and the rest of us mothers are dealing with every day. Twenty-two years for me and it just gets worse year by year.

—DALE P-M.

If only this was all contrived drama. It's so visceral. You're an artist. "I didn't know, as I was writing, that I was capturing the last year of my son's life." This breaks my heart.

—HEIDI F.

SOONER THAN TOMORROW

SOONER THAN TOMORROW

A MEMOIR

*A Mother's Diary About Mental Illness, Family
and Everyday Life*

DEDE RANAHAN

WITH PATRICK RANAHAN

For Patrick and his sisters,
Megan, Marisa, and Kerry.
And for the mothers.

Mothers are the people who love us for no good reason.
And those of us who are mothers know
it's the most exquisite love of all.

—MAGGIE GALLAGHER

Above all, I have been a sentient being,
a thinking animal, on this beautiful planet,
and that in itself has been an enormous privilege
and adventure.

—OLIVER SACKS

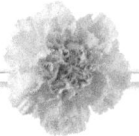

SOONER THAN TOMORROW

Finalist: 2016 San Francisco Writer's Conference
Memoir Contest

Finalist: 2016 Writer's Digest Writing Competition

Finalist: 2017 New Millennium Writings 43rd Literary
Awards Competition: Nonfiction

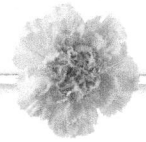

CONTENTS

INTRODUCTION

Welcome to my world.

My story is written in diary format. I wrote it from June 15, 2013, to June 15, 2014. I've always wished I'd uncovered a diary or letter written by one of my relatives a hundred years ago. With so much interest in ancestry right now, I decided to pay it forward for my children and grandchildren, and leave a time capsule for them from the deep, dark past of today.

What I didn't know, as I was writing, was that I was capturing the last year of my son's life. Pat died, unexpectedly, on July 23, 2014, in a hospital psych ward where I thought he was safe. Suddenly, my diary morphed into a more poignant record than I'd anticipated, and after he died, I discovered Pat had been making regular posts on Facebook. I decided to add his comments to my own.

I like stories where I can extrapolate from the singular to the universal—that is where I can identify with a common denominator in another person's experience. One early reader of my diary said, "Your story is so relatable." That's what I hope other readers will say.

You may relate to my story if:

You have a child (children) you love more than your own life.

You have a child who suffers from serious mental illness.

You've lost a child—no matter what age.

You're a member of the sandwich generation.

You treasure conversations with children—especially when they're your grandchildren.

Your cat or your dog is in charge of your household.

Your bones are beginning to creak.

You wake up each morning with a huge hole in your heart but you know, somehow, some way, you have to get up and put one foot in front of the other.

You enjoy reading the other side of history—about ordinary people and their daily lives.

You have a sense of humor.

You've been thinking of leaving something for your descendants—a letter, story, diary, song, painting, or poem—but you haven't gotten around to it. Maybe my diary will spur you on.

More notes about format:

I've added a Before section (Scenes from the Trenches). Going in, I want the reader to know "Yes, Houston, we really do have a problem."

I've divided my diary into quarters—Summer, Fall, Winter, and Spring. I introduce each with a poem—three of them are Pat's.

I end with an After section I didn't see coming.

As I was writing, I had no idea, from day to day, what stories were unfolding. I learn, right along with the reader, what will happen next. We're all on a journey. Thank you for going on this journey with me.

"Take your broken heart and make it into art."

—CARRIE FISHER

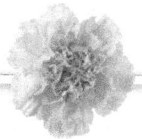

CAST OF CHARACTERS

FAMILY
Dede/Mim—Me
Patrick/Pat—My son
Pop—My Pop
GG—My Mother
Megan (Britt)—My Utah daughter
Marisa (Keith)—My Washington daughter
Kerry (David)—My California daughter
Aidan, Ashton, Sam, Elise, Regan, Ayla—My grandchildren
Jim (Sharon)—My brother
Annette—My Kansas City cousin
Michael (Karen)—My nephew
Jazzy/The Jazz—My black kitty cat
Lexi—Pat's Black Forest Hound

FRIENDS
Grace, Joan, Irene, Helena, Kaye, Deanne, Jan & Jim, Scotty, Bill & Betty, Rose, Jean, other mothers like me.

CAMEO APPEARANCES

Prince George, Warren Buffet, Bill Gates, Vladimir Putin, Linda Ronstadt, Pope Francis, President Kennedy, Batman and Batkid, Nelson Mandela, Dr. Seuss, Malaysia Airlines Flight 370, Wolf OR7, California Chrome, Maya Angelou. Special Guest Star—George Clooney

LOCATIONS

Northern California—My home
Seattle, Washington—Marisa's home
Bend, Oregon—A weekend getaway

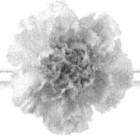

BEFORE

In the midst of winter, I found there was, within me,
an invincible summer.

—ALBERT CAMUS

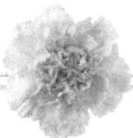

Scenes From The Trenches

How do you react when your 25-year-old son, during what is later seen as his first acute bipolar episode, *kidnaps* his teenage sister, drives her to a hospital, and convinces the emergency room staff to admit her because "she's sick and my parents aren't taking care of her"?

How do you compute when you arrive at the hospital to rescue your daughter—who has a cold—and you find her hysterical and sitting in a hospital bed? You ask your son, who is staring straight ahead with empty eyes, "Why did you bring your sister here?" With logic that reflects his internal confusion, he answers, "Because I knew I needed help."

What recourse do you have when your son's health care providers can't agree on a diagnosis and decide to do nothing?

Whom do you rail against when your son goes through an eight-week protocol at Stanford in a blind experiment for bipolar disorder, is seen for the last time with no follow-up appointment scheduled, and is given a slightly altered dosage of his medication? And, within 24 hours, he's 5150d (an involuntary 72-hour hospitalization) to San Mateo County Hospital in a state of acute bipolar psychosis.

Should you be distraught or relieved when your adult child admits himself to the emergency room of San Francisco General because "Voices are telling me to kill myself"?

Where do you turn when, as the parent of an adult child with severe mental illness, you're told, "You have no right to any information"?

How do you reconcile the fact that the state of New York, at New York taxpayers' expense, hospitalized your son for six months in Bellevue Hospital, and paid his return airfare to the West Coast when he was stable?

In California, on the other hand, where involuntary hospitalizations last 72 hours, on eight separate occasions, judges asked your son, "Are you a danger to yourself or others?" And when he answered "no," eight different judges released him with no money, no medication, and no place to go.

Do you dare find hope again when, a year after leaving Bellevue Hospital, your son has a job, earns an impressive score on the Graduate Record Exam, and receives a fellowship in creative writing at San Diego State University?

Do you give up your newfound hope when, after three months at San Diego State, the attempt to teach, write, work, and conceal his mental disability is too much? Stress causes a Grand Mal seizure and your son spins out of control. He's sicker now than when he was admitted to Bellevue Hospital.

How do you get a fair hearing when, after five years and eleven involuntary hospitalizations, five of which were within one year, Social Security tells you, "Your son is denied SSDI benefits because he does not meet the criteria for severe and persistent mental illness"?

What do you do when your mentally ill family member doesn't have health insurance and can't get a job to access group health insurance?

What do you decide when a California police officer asks, "Do you want me to press auto theft charges against your son for taking your car? Answer 'yes' I send him to prison. Answer 'no' I release him to the street. There's no time to consult a lawyer. Tell me now."

What do you say at three o'clock in the morning, when someone you've never met—a friend of your son's—calls you in California from London and yells, "Get your son out of my house! He's destroying my property!"?

What do you say at three o'clock the next morning when that same person calls back sobbing, feeling so guilty for having his friend forcibly admitted to a London psychiatric hospital? Then he describes the scene as his friend, calm at first, fought ferociously as he was bound into a straitjacket and thrown into a padded cell.

How do you cope when your mentally ill adult child is missing, and your daughter calls you in tears because a newspaper article describes a John Doe who killed himself on the railroad tracks in the vicinity where your son was last seen, and John Doe fits your son's description?

How do you process the hours waiting for the coroner's report to confirm or deny that John Doe is or is not your son? And in those hours, you pray he is not your son and then pray he is your son, to end his pain and to end yours. And when the coroner says, "John Doe is not your son," you take a deep breath but then think to yourself, John Doe is someone's son.

How do you forget the wracked faces and bodies you've seen while visiting your son in locked wards of prisons and mental hospitals? What choices do you have when you realize you cannot, you will not erase from your memory their anguish and despair?

How do you live with your disappointment when, after searching streets for days, you can't find your son and you give up and go home without him?

How do you advocate when the world sees a bum, and you see the little boy you carried in your womb, nursed at your breast, laughed and played with, and knew in your heart was the world's greatest child? And you know somewhere, trapped inside his brain, the world's greatest child is lost and trying to be found.

—DEDE RANAHAN 2001

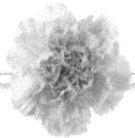

SUMMER 2013

Time dissolves in summer anyway: days are long, weekends
longer. Hours get all thin and watery when you are lost in the
book you'd never otherwise have time to read. Senses
are sharper—something about the moist air and
bright light and fruit in season—and so
memories stir and startle.

—NANCY GIBB

THAT AFTERNOON

That afternoon,
When we had the hot sand
beneath us,
when we conjured
a bottle of Cabernet
from a paper bag,
When sea-life and sky-life
did their respective dances,
that afternoon
when we looked infinity
right in the eye,
when we saw one another
and felt possession,
when words
were unnecessary excess,
that afternoon
still burns hot in my mind,
just like the circle of blue sky
that broke the fog
that fine afternoon.

—PATRICK RANAHAN

June 15, 2013

Beginning

Right foot. Left foot.
Right foot. Left foot.
Footstep after footstep I configure my life.
Right foot. Left foot.
Right foot. Last foot.
Footsteps and life end so soon.

In May 2014, I'll turn 70. I propose to keep a written record of my milestone year. Am I entering a dark, isolating thicket, an evergreen, renewable forest, a gentle but boring shady glen, or something else?

I intend this recounting as a gift for myself, my descendants, and other wayfarers who catch a resonating echo while wandering in my woods. It's later than I'd like but sooner than tomorrow.

Frances Mayes said, "Unthinkably good things can happen, even late in the game."

Let's see.

Patrick's Facebook Post: "Blessed are they who see beautiful things in humble places where other people see nothing."

—CAMILLE PISSARRO

June 16, 2013

What Will Show Up?

Sitting in a swivel chair at a humongous, grey metal desk in Pop's real estate office, I was supposed to be reading. Pop was talking on the phone. "John, it's a new listing. Looks really good. Three bedrooms, two bathrooms, ranch style, in the San Jose neighborhood you're interested in. It's offered at sixteen thousand five hundred."

As a nine-year-old, I wanted to be somewhere else—like outside in the sunshine. My mind began to wander. Staring at a scratch pad with "Moon Realty" printed at the top, I wondered what would show up if I began scribbling one word after another.

I folded my legs into the chair, put pencil to paper, and this poem took shape:

There I sat by the bay one day
I could hear the water far away
I heard the trees humming a song
And I felt the wind rushing along.
I watched the fields across the bay
Where the farmers work hard all day
And I saw the beauty of the land.
I picked a flower growing near a tree
And threw it off into the sea
It floated away like a drifting cloud
And a seagull bird trilled very loud.

There I sat by the bay one day
And that's where I wanted to stay.

I wish I'd kept writing—every single day.

Patrick's Facebook Post: "Sometimes the strongest people are the ones who love beyond all faults, cry behind closed doors, and fight battles that nobody knows about."

—AUTHOR UNKNOWN

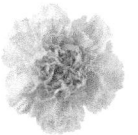

JUNE 17, 2013

MOM

A photograph arrives in my afternoon mail. The inscription on the back reads "1919, Kansas City, Missouri." It looks like a picnic on a summer day, blurry faces, all but one now gone.

In the photo my infant mother, Evelyn, frowns from her mother's lap. Her big sisters, Ruth, Helen, and Margaret—pretty children I remember as old women—sit facing straight into the camera. One is grinning. One is laughing. One, the eldest, holds a stern demeanor as does her mother, my grandmother Josephine. All are attired in complicated dresses—high necks, ruffles, long sleeves—difficult to iron. My grandfather, wearing a white shirt with rolled-up sleeves, sits cross-legged, offering a tight smile through pursed lips.

I never met Grandpa Chance or Grandmother Jo. (I have only her recipe for rosy pickled eggs.) Both died before I was born. I recognize them from previous family photos. I imagine the family still at the picnic, somewhere in time, posing together on the unmown grass.

Tomorrow, when I see her, I must show the photo to my mother. I must send my cousin a note to thank her for sending it.

Patrick's Facebook Post: "I've reached the age where my brain went from 'you probably shouldn't say that' to 'what the hell, let's see what happens."

—AUTHOR UNKNOWN

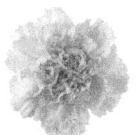

JUNE 18, 2013

PAT

Pat calls and leaves a message on my answering machine:

"Mom, I saw the neurologist today. He wants to do an EEG to test for epilepsy. My psychiatrist is reducing the Depakote I take for my bipolar. She thinks it's the cause of my low white blood count. I've lost eight pounds in the last ten days since she lowered the medication. She also wants me to have a MRI every six months for my brain tumor.

"Oh, and another thing. Lexi needs a water bottle for her dog crate. She knocks over the water dish when I leave it inside the crate with her. The bottle is eight dollars. Can you buy it this week? I have one dollar left until Sunday.

"Lexi peed on the carpet a little while ago. Guess I didn't pay enough attention to her signals. She's being pretty good, otherwise.

"Talk to you later. Bye, Mom."

Patrick's Facebook Post: He's one of the greatest minds in history, and he says nuclear weapons were a mistake. "I made one great mistake in my life when I signed the letter to President Roosevelt recommending that atom bombs be made." Albert Einstein.

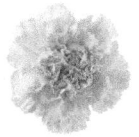

JUNE 19, 2013

I WANT TO QUIT ALREADY

What about days like today? I'm only five entries into this writing project and I want to quit already. What if my stomach, due to circumstances beyond my control, is in knots? How am I supposed to write sensible sentences when I'm distraught.

My forty-four-year-old son has challenges that would bring Goliath to his knees. He calls to say the water bottle he needs for Lexi is fifteen dollars, not eight.

He asks, "Is this okay?"

There's a saying, "When Mama ain't happy, ain't nobody happy."

My corollary to that is, "When her child ain't happy, Mama ain't happy."

My heart hurts. I want to cry. I want to scream. I want to hurl porcelain dishes through plate glass windows.

I won't, though. Pat needs me not to. He needs me to be strong. Especially on days like today.

Patrick's Facebook Post:"Sometimes someone says something really small and it just fits right into this empty place in your heart." (Love, Sex, Intelligence)

JUNE 20, 2013

HELP IN THE MAIL

FIRST LIGHT

Tomorrow a different, darker wing
will brush me, and again
I will tremble with longing and self-pity,
but in this early hour,
with the sun risen coolly
behind mists of morning
and small birds calling
one to another, branch to branch,

I am a mad woman of peace,
gliding through day's bloody tides
as though they were the clearest water.

PUBLISHED IN POTPOURRI, FALL 2003, VOL. 15, NO. 3
USED WITH PERMISSION BY POET JUDITH WERNER

My cousin sent this poem to me in today's mail. Somehow she knew I needed it.

Patrick's Facebook Post: "The only way out of the labyrinth of suffering is to forgive." John Green, *Looking for Alaska* (Love, Sex, Intelligence)

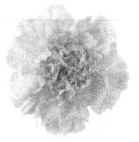

JUNE 21, 2013

INSPIRATION

I'm driving this morning with my friend, Grace, to the Amador Flower Farm in Plymouth. The farm grows thirteen hundred varieties of daylilies. Everyday, in season, more than a million flowers bloom in the farm's growing fields.

We wander on freshly mowed grass through rows and rows of one gallon plants. I read down my prospect list—lilies I've selected off the farm's website—then crumple it up. It's much better to choose from the colors and shapes right before me, giving preference to any lily that seems to bob as I approach.

I choose evergreens with curly, outlined edges—Montage, Hostess, Eloquent Silence, Full Moon Rising, and Call Me Irresistible.

Daylilies come in every hue except true blue and pure white. Some experts say daylilies are edible and have as much protein as spinach, more vitamin A than string beans, and the same amount of vitamin C as orange juice.

Three red and yellow lilies I purchased last year grow in a rear corner of my backyard obscured by denser foliage. I had no idea when I planted them—small green shrubs with spiky leaves—what treasure I was hiding. Now they're blooming. In the morning and evening, I walk out to admire them. I stoop close to inhale their soft, sweet scent.

Daylilies are so named because each flower lasts one day. When one dies, another opens. Each new lily unfolds with fervor—bright face to the sky—whether witnessed or not.

I find inspiration here.

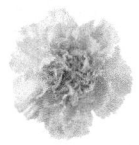

JUNE 22, 2013

CHANGE

This is the year of the big migration. Marisa is moving from a big house in Carlsbad, California, to a little house in Seattle. Kerry is moving from her small house in Roseville, California, to a larger house across the freeway. Her in-laws are downsizing houses, moving from Nevada City, California, to Grass Valley,

California. Pat is moving from his tiny apartment in Roseville to Kerry's old, smaller house.

New jobs, new schools, new homes, new neighborhoods, new routines. Address changes on legal documents. Eleven lives rearranging.

In one year's time, what surprises might appear? What challenges might arise? Everyone is in motion. Change is the constant.

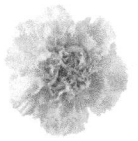

JUNE 23, 2013

MAGICAL THINKING

The sky's been promising rain since morning. I've been waiting, anticipating those first drops of water. But it's early evening and it's still dry. If I take a walk, maybe that will make it rain.

I plop on a baseball cap and head out the door. Dark clouds hover above me. Light clouds hang in the west. A slight breeze feathers my face and trees and shrubs nod to me as I pass by.

What's that? A drop? Another? This is working. A few splatters land on my bare arms.

A woman walking toward me pauses. "It's raining pretty hard over on Snapdragon," she says. "It may stop by the time you get there. Funny, it's hardly sprinkling here."

I walk faster, getting my hopes up. Snapdragon is three blocks up and to the left. I round the corner. No droplets shimmer on leaves. There are no sprinkles. There is no rain. Did I imagine that other woman in the street?

Back home I take off my cap. I turn on the weather report. Enough with magical thinking. At least for today.

JUNE 24, 2013

RAIN

What a marvelous, overcast, wet, summer day. It's such a relief from the ninety degree weather. Leaves are glistening outside my windows. A gentle rain pitter pats.

Jazzy's curled up in a ball. We snuggle together under a soft blanket on my bedroom chaise. I'm reading a cooking magazine that came in the afternoon mail and marking recipes for broccoli cheese, tangy tomato, sweet onion, asparagus, and zucchini vegetable pies.

The article says, "This is savory and unexpected comfort food, to serve warm or at room temperature, and perfect for both cool and hot days."

More rain is expected tomorrow and then, on Wednesday, the summer weather returns.

If I had a fireplace, I'd start a fire. If I had a marshmallow, I'd roast a marshmallow. Instead, I'll light a few candles, listen to the rain, and wait for evening to cross the patio and slip in through the sliding screen door.

Patrick's Facebook Post: When we realize that we're all under surveillance, we can behave like Shakespeare's characters who knew "all the world's a stage, and we are merely players."

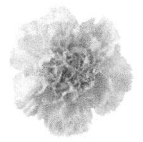

JUNE 26, 2013

A QUESTION

I receive an unexpected email from our community administration:

"There's not enough interest in a family mental illness support group for us to announce it in our monthly magazine."

Not enough interest according to whom? Twenty-two people attended the first support group meeting at my house. They squished together on my red sofa and chairs.

Now group emails are flying back and forth. Group emails are WMD (weapons of mass destruction). They target heavily populated areas. Open a group email at your own risk—they can fry your computer. People send out-of-sync statements and responses. Tempers flare. Defenses surface.

I send an email to request a cease-fire.

"Can we please have an in-person meeting to resolve any issues?"

I have to ask twice. There's resistance. How does trying to do something constructive get so freaking complicated? That is the question.

Patrick's Facebook Post: Summertime and the living is easy.

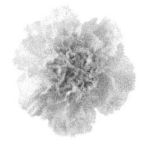

JUNE 27, 2013

ANOTHER QUESTION

I'm at Kilaga Cafe having lunch with a new acquaintance. She's a widow. She thinks when you're a widow, people treat you differently. Differently than being divorced?

"Yes, some think you're more needy."

She gives me an example. "A week after my husband passed, I went to a birthday party. I sat down at a round table in the one empty chair. I chatted with the men on each side of me. You know. Small talk. I thought we were having a good time. Then we all got up to go to the buffet. When I returned to the table, the men were gone. Their wives, one on each side of me, now guarded their turf. This seemed so funny, I couldn't help myself. I started laughing and no one knew why."

I tell my new friend I have to leave to go meet with the community powers that be about my mental illness support group. She gives me some parting advice.

"If you have something worthwhile to do and you run into resistance, don't argue. And for heaven sakes, don't get angry and hung up on the principle of the thing. Figure out a way to bypass the obstacle and go around it."

After all the email brouhaha about lack of interest in establishing a support group, the in-person exchange with the administration staff member is friendly, or appears to be.

"Your meeting announcement will be published for three months in the bulletin section of our community magazine. That's standard procedure. Have a good day."

I leave the meeting perplexed. Another question teases. What was the problem in the first place?

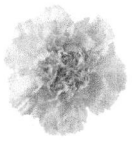

JUNE 28, 2013

HAPPY BIRTHDAY, MEGAN KATHLEEN

Today is my eldest daughter's birthday. I'm thinking about the day she was born. The weather in Rochester, Minnesota, was typical midwestern weather—hot and muggy. In the recovery room, I untied my hospital gown and placed my new daughter face down on my stomach. She clung to me the same way a baby chimp clings to its mother.

The two of us rested bare skin on bare skin. One tired from giving birth. One tired from being born. The nurses let us doze for about an hour. I wanted to hold my baby like that, all mine and all safe, forever. I wanted the clock to stop ticking but Father Time didn't cooperate.

Those birthing moments are memories. Now Megan is forty-three.

JUNE 29, 2013

OLD STUFF

What's this restlessness I'm feeling? I moved into this house six-and-a-half years ago. I must be entering my itchy period. Every once in a while, this over-55 neighborhood gets on my nerves.

Too many couples with lots of money and, at times, insensitive to the fact that not all bank accounts are created equal. Too many singles—including myself—widowed or divorced and wondering how our lives ended up this way. Too many grappling with the distinction between loneliness and solitude. Too many oblivious to the difference. Too many old people talking old people talk.

"She's unhappy because she doesn't have a husband."

"He passed away four days after he was diagnosed."

"The affair's still hot and heavy."

"All my joints are creaking."

"I need a hip replacement."

"I need a knee replacement."

"Where did I put my car keys?"

"I couldn't find my car."

"I couldn't find my driveway."

I'm going to go to bed now. If I can remember where it is . . .

JULY 2, 2013

JUST LIKE YOU

I'm eating lunch with Mom, affectionately known as GG, at her assisted living residence. I feel like a kid when I visit her. I push her in her wheelchair. I hoist it in and out of the trunk of my car when I drive us somewhere.

At her annual physical, the doctor looked at her and asked, "You're not really this old, are you?"

None of us were there when she was born, so we have to take her word for it.

Her hearing is failing. Her legs are weak—a residual effect of childhood polio. However, her blood pressure, cholesterol levels, sodium levels, blood sugar—everything tests in the middle of normal range. Seems all systems are go.

In between bites of an egg salad sandwich, Mom chitchats. I listen.

"See that woman who just walked by? She's one-hundred-and-three. Her boyfriend comes to visit. He's eighty-eight. She's a sparkly little thing. Says she likes 'em young.

"I bid and made a small slam at bridge yesterday.

"Wasn't that a tragedy about the firefighters who died in Arizona?

"Did you read Obama visited the prison cell where Nelson Mandela spent seventeen of his twenty-seven years in prison?

"Do you want to come to the fireworks show tomorrow night? You shouldn't miss it.

"They have such good ice cream here. I don't know what brand it is. Coffee flavor with chocolate sauce. That's the best. Let's have some of that."

I'll have whatever you're having, Mom. Maybe it will get me to ninety-five. Just like you.

JULY 3, 2013

DUPLICATE BRIDGE

My partner and I came in fifth at duplicate bridge today. How is it that this game brings out the good, the bad, and the ugly?

So many egos. So many insecurities. So many agendas.

Must keep it all in perspective. Compete against myself. Try to become more proficient at the game. Make friends in the process. Use bridge to exercise my brain and ward off memory loss. And keep signing up for one more, humble-making round.

Patrick's Facebook Post: A while back I received two postcards from Victoria's Secret for free panties. I went and picked them up (two black pairs) in the hopes that one day there would be a lady in my life to give them to. But alas, it seems I am doomed to be perpetually single, so they're up for grabs. Comment here with why you want them and I'll send them to a lucky winner. They're brand new, tags and everything.

Daniel: If I were a cross dresser, I'd be up for them bro ;)

Patrick: Actually Daniel, I was hoping to send them to a woman, and I swear I've never tried them on :)

Gayle: I love black panties and I will even send you a picture of me wearing them ;-) how's that!

Patrick: Looks like we have a winner!

Gayle: Oh Patrick, I love your sense of humor ;-)

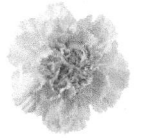

JULY 4, 2013

INDEPENDENCE DAY

On July 4, 1845, Henry David Thoreau moved to his house on Walden Pond. He wrote, "I went to the woods because I wished to live deliberately, to front only the essential facts of life, and see if I could not learn what it had to teach, and not, when I came to die, discover that I had not lived."

I'm not tripping off to Walden Pond. However, I'm trying, through these notes, to catch life lessons I might otherwise miss, and to make each of my days a conscious exercise.

Most of the time, I don't realize what I'm thinking until I write it down. Today, I'm thinking about my country. I'm heedful of its shortcomings and imperfections. I'm appreciative of its benefits and promise. I'm grateful that it's where I was born and it's where I live.

Long may America struggle and summon the political will to be the best it can be. Happy Fourth of July.

Patrick's Facebook Post: Support Art Troops

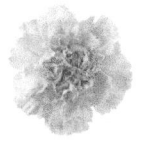

JULY 5, 2013

MARKETING

Things, as we know, are not always what they seem. Note the ads for life insurance, reverse mortgages, and financial advisers. They spotlight happy couples relishing life in retirement.

Check out the Sun City website. It pictures couples smiling, golfing, swimming, hiking, bicycling, playing baseball and pickle ball, dining in the lodge, gathering for happy hour in the sports bar, doing the rumba and the zumba.

Seniors leap over tall buildings in a single bound.

Some of this messaging is accurate. Some is euphemism. Some is denial. Under the gloss, life can get real, real fast. My neighbor phones. Her husband was diagnosed today with esophageal cancer that has metastasized to his back and hip bones.

Besides my family mental illness support group, the Sun City Lincoln Hills community has support groups for bereavement, low vision, glaucoma, cancer survivors, Parkinson's Disease, Alzheimer's, dementia, and pet loss.

I'm thankful I live in a community that provides all kinds of activities and resources—those that help us enjoy engaging moments and those that help us face inevitable challenges.

Sales departments, it seems, don't want to or don't know how to market the latter.

Patrick's Facebook Post: "Let the day evolve without a plan." I stole this quote from Don DeLillo in his book, *White Noise.*

JULY 6, 2013

AIDAN'S POEM

Aidan is our family's eleven-year-old poet laureate. His poem, "Speak to Me," won first prize in the Zion Canyon Arts and Humanities Council—Elementary Poetry Category for 2013.

SPEAK TO ME

As I walk through the canyon, I speak to my father in a soft tone,
"Did you hear that?"
Suddenly I hear my own voice echo back at me,
"Did you hear that?"
I then begin to listen closer;
I hear the river whisper to me,
"Come closer."
"Come closer."
As I take a few more steps, the wind picks up, and the grass
begins to whistle.
Small rocks in the river shift as they crackle and snap,
Crackle and snap.
I can't help but wonder, is the canyon trying to speak to me?
Speak to me!

Patrick's Facebook Post: "I don't know where I'm going but I'm on my way."

—CARL SAGAN

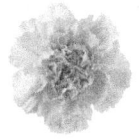

JULY 8, 2013

CRACKING HEARTS

Today's a not-so-good day. My son's sad and that makes me sad. When you're the mother of a child or an adult child who has a serious disability, you walk around with a crack in your heart. Even on good days a heaviness lingers.

Christians revere Mary as the mother of Jesus. They reflect on her sorrow at the foot of the cross. That agony lasted three hours. Sometimes it feels like my son's agony and my agony never end.

If God were to come down and say to me, "Let's make a deal. Your son will be well and lead a fulfilled and happy existence. In exchange you must give up your life," I'd barter a bit.

I'd say, "Thanks for the offer, God. Here's my counteroffer. Let me hang around until my next birthday so I can say thoughtful goodbyes to my loved ones and tie up loose ends."

But God hasn't come down. That's why I've started a support group for people with mental illness in their families. While we attempt to help our loved ones, we need help ourselves.

Some say we have cracks in our hearts so the light can get in. But I see no light. The crack is widening and my heart feels like it's splitting in two.

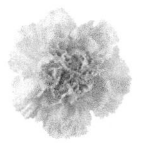

JULY 9, 2013

MYSTERY

There's a spongy little red ball that lives in this house with Jazzy and me. Sometimes it's in the living room. Sometimes it's in the kitchen. Sometimes it's in the den or the bathroom.

I've noticed it prefers to move under cover of darkness. Mornings are when I'm most likely to find it in a new location but, when I stare at it, it plays possum. It doesn't twitch. It doesn't move a muscle. It just sits there waiting for me to go away.

A few weeks ago, the little red ball disappeared. This afternoon, I found it hiding under the living room sofa.

Rarely, but once in a while, I actually see it move. It rolls around the corner from another room and stops at my feet. When I look around the corner, however, no one is there.

Sometimes Jazzy picks it up and holds it between her teeth. She moans as if she's caught a live animal. Eventually, she gets bored and drops it back on the floor. Then we both watch and wait for it to move again.

And now, I have reason to believe the little red ball is reproducing. Yesterday, I saw a little green ball, bearing a spongy resemblance, sitting by the front door.

JULY 10, 2013

% $ ˙ * * * @ # !) %

Megan and Britt and Aidan and Ashton are visiting from Utah. We're gathered at Kerry's house to go bowling. We're waiting for Pat because he has an appointment with a new psychiatrist.

Pat walks in the door. "Things have changed a lot today," he says.

The new psychiatrist has pronounced that Pat's bipolar disorder is an incorrect diagnosis, and his brain tumor is the problem. The doctor's reducing medications and doesn't need to see Pat again unless Pat calls him. This doctor would not sign the approval form for housing assistance we've been trying to get for ten years because, "There is no disability."

I'm in shock. Total shock. Twenty years of Pat's medical history, 5150s, jail time, psychiatric hospitalizations, homelessness, financial dependence, family trauma and heartbreak are all discounted. Discounted by a doctor who's known my son for one hour.

I don't know who this Kaiser doctor is. My son's an adult and I have no legal right to know. It appears my only right is the right to wait for the next crisis.

My son's pleased. He says, "I feel like I've been released from prison."

I understand. A professional's telling him he's fine. We all want him to be fine. We all want to be fine. At the moment, I know I'm not. I feel nauseous, kicked in the stomach, beaten up, spat upon.

This turn of events is sabotaging my visit with my daughter and her family. I don't know what I should do.

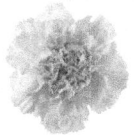

JULY 11, 2013

EMAIL EXCHANGE WITH PAT

"Hi, Mom. My phone died last night so I won't be able to call you after my EEG appointment today. Please email back and let me know if it's okay to come over and do laundry today after my appointment." Pat

"Hi, Pat. Yes, It's fine. When are you coming?" Mom

"Hi, Mom. I just checked my gas gauge and I don't think I have enough gas to get there and back, and then to work on Sunday so I don't think I can do my laundry today." Pat

"Hi, Pat. Okay. In the meantime, can you make an appointment with your oncologist to get the housing voucher signed?" Mom

"Hi, Mom. I sent an email to my primary care physician asking if he would be willing to sign it. I haven't heard back from him yet. Will you do me a favor and call my cell phone company and tell them that my phone is dead, that it's my only phone, and that I need a new battery or a new phone as soon as possible? The phone is insured so this shouldn't cost us anything." Pat

"Hi, Mom. Went online. There's a deductible on the phone. The phone company says it will be $99.99 to replace the phone or battery." Pat

"Hi, Mom. I checked with Radio Shack. They have the battery for $49.99." Pat

"Hi, Mom. I found the battery online at Best Buy for $19.99." Pat

"Hi, Pat. I'm feeling overwhelmed with the amount of financial assistance I'm giving you. I have to check my bank account and think about this before I agree to pay for the phone." Mom

"Hi Mom. While we're on the subject of freeing you from the financial assistance you've been extending, I'm going to begin looking for a housemate. I should be able to rent the extra room for $600 a month, paid to me, and then I'll take over some of the bills you've been paying." Pat

"Hi, Pat. We have to discuss this first and include GG to see if she wants another renter in her house. If it's okay with her, then we have to decide the qualifications required in a potential roommate. Would it be a month-to-month arrangement and how would the rent be assigned?" Mom

"Hi, Mom. I think the rent to GG should stay the same and I should take over some of the bills you're paying and keep the rest to supplement my income." Pat

"Hi, Pat. We really have to go over and sit down with GG and see 1) If she wants someone else in the house and 2) The specifics. GG could be renting the house for twice the amount she's charging you and she still needs income." Mom

"Hi, Mom. Well then, let's go sit down and discuss it with her. While I realize that GG could be getting more for this house than she's getting from me, I'm the one who would have to open my home to a stranger and deal with all the responsibilities that entails. Of course, I'd like you to be free and clear of all my bills but we have to be realistic about the economy, what people can afford, and what I can afford to take over. If we decide that you and GG want all the money a new housemate would provide, then it's not worth it to me to deal with the hassle of it all." Pat

"Hi, Pat. You don't own the house. You're not paying the taxes, homeowner's dues, homeowner's insurance, maintenance, etc. You should be grateful that GG is willing to rent to you at half price. She didn't want to keep the house. She didn't want to deal with renters. She did it to help you. A homeowner is entitled to rent to whom they want and how they want." Mom

"Hi, Mom. If GG doesn't want to keep the house, then I'll look elsewhere. You stated to the Roseville housing division that you were paying $600 a month for my bills. I don't want you to pay my bills any longer than necessary but I don't think I can afford, even with a renter, to pay you $600 a month." Pat

"Hi, Pat. I think this email conversation is not healthy or productive so let's end it." Mom

Patrick's Facebook Post: Mental health treatment is fundamentally flawed. I had a doctor tell me yesterday that he didn't consider doctors and patients to be equals, as if he felt superior somehow to the human beings he was treating. And the building I was seen in had different bathrooms for doctors and patients. Sounds similar to the whites-only drinking fountains of days gone by. He then proceeded to tell me that I had convinced him that I didn't suffer from a mental illness and that I no longer had to take the medicines I've been required to take for twenty-plus years. I'm just supposed to roll over and eat twenty years of my life being shuffled from doctor to doctor and hospital to hospital? Can anyone say misdiagnosis and malpractice?

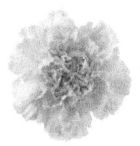

July 12, 2013
Support Group Meeting

Random comments at the Family Mental Illness Support Group Meeting today:

"My child says she's fine. She won't see a doctor. She's forty-five. I can't make her go. We're running out of money to help her."

"If we turn him out, he'll be on the street. I can't live with that."

"My sister has no boundaries. She'll tell anyone anything. She'll tell her social security number if they ask."

"I've lost my other children. They don't want to be around the chaos."

"I have one child. I don't have the experience of a well child."

"My ill son is living with us. It's very difficult. I've just been through surgery and chemo for ovarian cancer. My husband is developing dementia. I have no support."

"My daughter got a traffic ticket for reckless driving. They find her and sentenced her to eighty hours of community service. She doesn't have the capacity to follow through and find an organization that will let her volunteer for them."

"I read something that resonated with me. 'A mother is as happy as her unhappiest child.'"

"My daughter's illness is fracturing the entire family."

"It seems like this illness is very self-centered. Everything is about 'me.'"

"I can't talk about these things anywhere else. People don't understand."

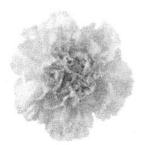

JULY 13, 2013

BREATHING

I'm on overload. I'm facing dilemmas God couldn't figure out. My house phone's ringing. I know it's Pat. He's found a way to call me through his computer. At this moment, I can't deal with his stuff. I'm letting it ring.

Now, my cell phone's ringing. I know it's Pat. I know it's my son and I want off the planet. I'm going to go for a walk. I'm going to put one foot down in front of the other. I'm going to take deep breaths, gaze at the sky, and watch for cottontails.

Patrick's Facebook Post: It's Saturday morning and I should be at my favorite restaurant eating breakfast. But my car is out of gas and I have to make it to the church on time tomorrow. Money is scarce to nothing. I'm thinking of my last lady who could satisfy me by baring her ankles and gazing into my eyes. Still I'm hungry but coffee will have to do. Listening to Mother Hips on Spotify, I'll imagine eggs Benedict and country potatoes, but settle for cereal or toast.

She had a way about her. I find it hard to describe, but she could cock her head in one direction and without saying a word, convey a million thoughts.

When she did speak, she used an economy of language, a thrifty tongue, and she never went on too long.

Grace in her movements, sculpture in her face, she had a way.

I didn't get to spend very much time with her, definitely not the eternity I longed for, but her image and nonchalance is etched in my mind and soul forever.

Man, she had a way about her. I don't know if I'll ever find another who measures up.

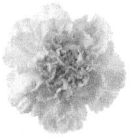

JULY 14, 2013

MORNING HASSLE

Email exchange with Pat:

"Mom, my computer isn't working to make calls and obviously you aren't answering my calls anyway. Will you please get back to me and let me know if you've decided if I can buy a phone battery?" Pat

"Pat, I'm attaching the record I keep of your bills. Do you see why I'm stressing? Use the $25 you got today from your job at the church and buy the battery. I have to start saying no." Mom

"Mom. For Christ's sake, I make $25 a week! That's all the money I have to live on. This is complete and utter bullshit!" Pat

"Mom, by the way, did you ever arrange for the exterminator to come out and spray? The ants were back this morning." Pat

Patrick's Facebook Post: My dog is still hacking up pizza from three days ago. I had the brilliant idea of getting a family size Cowboy pizza from Papa Murphy's and leaving it on the counter while the oven preheated. Damn dog ate the whole pie.

JULY 14, 2013

EVENING STROLL

On my walk this evening, the killdeer nest is empty. It's camouflaged inches from the sidewalk. Brown Mama Bird and her brown speckled eggs blended perfectly with the brown and gray rocks. Mama Bird chose property in a front yard she deemed to be good real estate.

The first time I passed by, not suspecting a nest, Mama Bird charged at me with her tail feathers fanned high.

"Look how big and fierce I am," she said.

The next time I walked by, she led me down the street, dragging her left wing (a killdeer trick) as if she were injured.

"I'm easy prey. I'm easy prey. Follow me. Follow me."

When she saw that I was moving on, she did a killdeer run back to her nest.

I didn't want to disturb her further, so I started walking on the opposite side of the street. Sometimes, I drove by to see how she was. Cars were not scary to her. Not like two-footed monsters without wings or feathers. Monsters who do not fly.

For twenty-eight days in one-hundred-plus degrees, this little bird sat on her nest without sunscreen and without shade. She did what she had to do. She may have had some help. A few times, a second killdeer screeched at me from the garage roof.

Tonight, I walk up the driveway and ring the doorbell. A man holding a small, white Maltese answers. "I'm your neighbor one street over. I've been watching the killdeer nest in your yard. Do you know what happened to the bird and her babies?"

My neighbor explains, "There were four eggs. Two disappeared. One was cracked open in the street. The fourth one hatched and left with Mom."

One out of four. Nature works hard. Hope that baby bird grows up and enjoys a long life. Hope that mom and dad take a well-deserved vacation.

Patrick's Facebook Post: I swear to God, two guys, who looked like George Zimmerman and Trayvon Martin, just delivered some furniture to my house. It was kind of nice to see them working together, carrying a couch upstairs.

JULY 15, 2013

GRATITUDE

I need to laugh. I'm thankful for Maxine, John Wagner's old lady cartoon character, because she makes me laugh, sometimes out loud.

"I believe that everything happens for a reason. Usually, the reason is that somebody screwed up."

"Most stress is caused by three things—money, family, and family with no money."

"There should be support groups for women who can't put their dishes in the dishwasher dirty."

And my favorite—"Let me know if you suddenly become interesting."

Email from Pat:

"Dear Mom, I had an EEG last week and the results just came in. Normal. No brain tumor!" Love, Patrick

"Pat, I'm so glad for your results!" Love, Mom

"Mom, thanks Mom!" Pat

Patrick's Facebook Post: Thank God I'm in the United States of America and not Korea. Thank God I'm in a house and not a homeless shelter. Thank God I have beer to drink and not just water. Thank God I have music to listen to and not just silence. There's so much more to thank God for. Suffice it to say, "Thank God!"

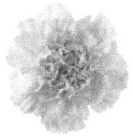

JULY 16, 2013

PAT'S PHONE

Email from Pat:

"Mom, okay, more bad news. Kerry bought me a phone battery and it arrived today but when I plugged it in, nothing happened. The phone itself is dead and the deductible for it is $100 that they will add to my next bill. Problem is, I can't even call to order a new phone. Help!!!" Pat

"Pat, okay, I'm done with this overpriced cell phone server. I'll call them. I want to know when your contract is up and what the penalty is to end it early. I don't see any reason to pay for a new phone with them when I'm hoping to switch cell phone servers anyway." Mom

"Mom, yeah, screw them. I don't know who I can get a phone with though." Pat

"Mom, to tell you the truth, I'd be just as happy with a landline. I've already got a phone I can hook up." Pat

Patrick's Facebook Post: Been without a phone for a week. Thought it was a dead battery, new battery arrived today, no signal, nothing. Computer used to make phone calls but now it won't. Total communication breakdown except for email and Facebook.

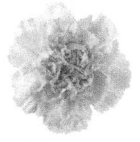

JULY 17, 2013

FINANCES

Email from Pat:

"Hi, Mom. Can I come over and do laundry this morning?" Pat

"Pat, I'm leaving in about twenty minutes to give blood. I expect to be back around one o'clock." Mom

"Mom, okay. See you then." Pat

"Pat, reviewing finances. Expenses I've already covered for you this year total $5,474. I budgeted $6,000 for the entire year. Another six months at $600 per month will be $9,074. I'm over my budget $3,074 for the year.

"This year your income from SSDI, food stamps, your job, and me will be $23,814. If I subtract the $9,074 I'm giving to you, my income will be less than yours. To cover my own bills, I'm using my savings which I may need for another twenty years.

"This is a watershed year, getting you into GG's house. In December, I'll have to reevaluate what I can do in 2014." Mom

"Mom, does this mean if I do get approved for the housing voucher, you're planning to take all the money?" Pat

Patrick's Facebook Post: "Peace is something we can bring about if we can actually learn to wake up a bit more as individuals and a lot more as a species; if we can learn to be fully what we actually already are, to reside in the inherent potential of what is possible for us, being human. As the adage goes, 'There is no way to peace; peace is the way.' It is so for the outer landscape of the world. It is so for the inner landscape of the heart. And these are, in a profound way, not really two."

—JON KABAT-ZINN, *Coming to Our Senses*

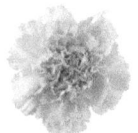

JULY 18, 2013

GIVING BLOOD

I'm giving blood this morning. There's no upper age limit. I can give blood when I'm 101 or 110. You better not try to give blood, though, if you've recently been with a prostitute. That's one of the screening questions.

The technician says, "The most common reason women are eliminated as donors is because they have a low iron count."

My iron count is 14.3. The required minimum count is 12.4. Yay. My blood pressure is 112 over 72. Yay again. The blood I donate will be used locally. In an emergency, it might be shared. Local blood donations were sent to victims of the Boston Marathon bombing. People can give blood every eight weeks. That's a contribution I can make. I'm putting the blood mobile on my calendar.

Patrick's Facebook Post: Life lesson learned on the beach in Hawaii. Sign read: "When in doubt, don't go out."

Shawn: I've always shortened that saying to "When in doubt, don't."

Patrick: We could make it even shorter, "When in, doubt."

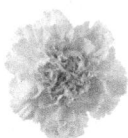

JULY 19, 2013

LIFE IN THE FAST LANE

I'm helping Mom with some paperwork this morning so she invites me to lunch in her dining room. A woman, pushed in a wheelchair by an attendant, stops by our table.

"Hello. I'm Joy. I want you to know how much I love your mother. I wouldn't have survived here without her. She's greatly loved around here. When we're offered dessert, I tell people to say what your mother says, 'What cha got?'"

Joy's wheeled away. I ask, "What did you do for her?"

"What?"

"What did you do for her? She says she wouldn't have survived without you."

"I don't know. I helped her when she first moved in. I told her about the rules and where things are. I didn't think I did much. See that couple over there? They're a romantic item. Lots of rumors buzzing around."

"Do they sleep together?"

"He wants to but her family is adamant. They've told him and the entire staff that he is not to spend the night in her apartment."

"What does she want?"

"She doesn't want him in her apartment at night, either. But during the day, he goes in and out of her room constantly."

I want to ask, "And how do you know this?" but I let it pass. I start a new topic.

"Are you sitting on pins and needles waiting for the royal baby?"

"I'm not sitting on pins and needles, but I bet she is."

Mom changes the subject. "I found out the brand of ice cream they serve here. It's Blue Bunny."

I google Blue Bunny on my iPhone. In this area it's sold at Walmart. That's too bad. I won't shop at Walmart—not until they improve wages and benefits for their employees.

Lunch comes to an abrupt end. "Have to go," Mom announces. "Time for my Friday bridge game. See ya later."

I walk to my car, then turn around. I want to take a peek at the bridge room. Mom's the declarer. She waves her cards at me. I see a flash of black spades and red and black honors.

"Mind if I watch a minute?"

"Absolutely not. Sit down beside me. I bid a small slam. I won't make it but I had to bid it."

Trick by trick, Mom builds her game. She pulls trump. She wins finesses. She end-plays the opponents. She makes her slam—proud vanquisher and queen for the day.

Patrick's Facebook Post: I'm making such a low budget movie there aren't even any cameras.

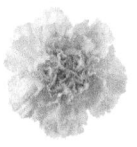

JULY 20, 2013

HAWAII

Email from Pat:

"Mom, you keep asking me, 'Why did you go to Hawaii?' And yesterday you said, 'There's no excuse for what you did when you went to Hawaii.'

"All I can say is, 'I'm sorry I went to Hawaii.' I also need to say that I'd been under a lot of stress, recovering from a near-death brain surgery experience, and hadn't had a vacation in over six years. I needed to do something. I needed a break. It's not like I burned my apartment down or something.

"Please forgive me. I'm sorry that it cost you so much money to bring me back, but you were adamant that I come home and you insisted, melodramatically, that you loved me.

"I feel like you're going to punish me forever for this. Did you bring me home just to rub this error in my face for the rest of my life?

"I'm sorry. You're right, it was an impulsive, irresponsible thing to do, but we have to move on.

"If it's any consolation, I didn't have a very good time there. I was living in a run down, ghetto hostel, and there were crazy people sharing my room, doing heroin in the bathroom, and scaring me half to death. One night, I had to call 911 because there was a madman outside the building banging on everyone's door, demanding a gun, and threatening to kill everyone. He was throwing stones at cars in the parking lot. Ten police and two paramedics were required to subdue him. I was honestly scared for my life. My experience there was punishment enough for taking off at your expense. In your eyes, I can't do anything right, and I'm a horrible person. This is how I feel when we talk. What can I do to remedy this? Will you please forgive me?" Pat

"Pat, I'm off to an all-day meeting in Sacramento. I'll digest this email later. Meanwhile, I'm taking some deep breaths and hope you do the same." Mom

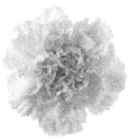

JULY 20, 2013

MENTAL HEALTH MEETING

This morning, I'm attending a mental health meeting in Sacramento. Sacramento is one of the first ten cities to join a national conversation on mental health, an initiative President Obama called for in June.

In my opinion, this initiative process is being erroneously modeled on California's Prop 63, The Mental Health Services Act (MHSA), which was passed in 2004. The MHSA has defects in its design and implementation.

This evening, I've written the letter below to the event funders, to Vice President Biden, and an abridged version to the *Sacramento Bee's* editorial page.

To Whom It May Concern:

I was so disappointed in the meeting today.

I retired in 2010 as the MHSA Policy Director for NAMI (National Alliance on Mental Illness), California. I worked through the early implementation phases of Prop 63 and left the professional mental health community discouraged about our broken mental health system and its impenetrable bureaucratic barriers. I saw waste, cronyism, self-promotion, and political in-fighting.

Today felt like the original MHSA meetings I attended all over again. Too many political appearances, repetitive thank-you's, and personal/professional agendas in play.

The meeting could have been condensed into a morning session. Seven hundred free lunches—many for salaried staff of mental health related nonprofits and provider organizations—wouldn't have been necessary. That money could have been used for critically needed direct services.

There must be a means to deconstruct the multi-layered mental health bureaucracy and the interlinked government bureaucracy. This is the only way more funding will get to the mentally ill who cannot find clinics, beds, or counselors and end up in emergency rooms, jails, or on the street. And that's before we can address needs such as housing and employment.

I don't want our mental health system to be broken. I want it to work. However, productions such as today's variety show, are not the way to fix it. When we stop spending mental health funds on fluff, that will be a step in the right direction.

I'd love to be part of an implementation team that can cut through the hoop-la, a team with the courage to point out the "emperor's new clothes."

Sincerely,
Dede Ranahan
Family Member
Former MHSA Policy Director
NAMI, California

Patrick's Facebook Post: "Another Saturday morning and I ain't got nobody, I got no money cause I never get paid. Oh how I wish I had someone to talk to, I'm in an awful way." With apologies to Cat Stevens.

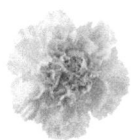

JULY 21, 2013

"TODAY'S THE DAY"

Yesterday, my friend Joan posted a message on Caring Bridge saying she and Beryl welcome visitors. I sent her an email asking her to let me know a good time to visit. She emailed back that today, Monday, would be a good day.

This morning she calls. "The time for visiting has passed. Beryl says, 'Today's the day I'm going to die.' He wants to see family only."

I don't know what to say. I say I don't know what to say.

"Don't worry about what to say. Your friendship is what matters."

Beryl was diagnosed with esophageal cancer on July 5. I've waited too long before. In the future, I'll remember not to assume that there's plenty of time. Upon learning of a serious diagnosis, I'll reach out immediately. Especially with cancer. It's an unpredictable adversary.

Beryl, may your passing, surrounded by loved ones, be peaceful. Joan, may love and peace surround you as you say goodbye to Beryl.

Patrick's Facebook Post: I love to play guitar but I'm without one so I have to go to Guitar Center to get my fix. There I compete with the voices on the intercom, the surf punk frat boys playing death metal, and the wandering shoppers as I play my Lilliputian roar.

JULY 22, 2013

ONE DAY

Mom calls. "I need three refills—amlodipine, omeprazole, and atenolol. Will you order them online? By the way, you made quite an impression the other day. The ladies in the dining room told me I have lovely, beautiful daughter."

"Really? Did you agree?"

"Yes, and I said that you're smart, too. Joy, especially, went on and on about you. Did you order my prescriptions?"

"You mean as we've been talking?"

"Yes."

"No."

"I thought maybe you did. Bye."

Pat's here this morning to do his laundry. Neither of us has mentioned our recent email exchange. Pest control is spraying his house tomorrow. The hot weather is sending armies of ants inside.

Megan's teaching school.

Marisa's hit a bump in the road. She and Keith were set to close on a house in Seattle in a few days. They learned today that their loan agent never submitted their loan application to a lender. They're scrambling to find a lender and a loan at the last minute. A higher interest rate will cost them $130,000 over the life of their mortgage.

Marisa says, "This #$*()# loan agent should lose his license."

Kerry's in San Francisco with Regan and Ayla riding a boat on the Bay.

One ninety-five-year-old mother.

Four children.

One day.

Patrick's Facebook Post: Today I promise to live a little. Today I promise to die a little.

JULY 23, 2013

HOPE AND DESPAIR

England has a new heir to the throne. I stayed up all night to witness the wedding of Charles and Diana on TV in 1981. I remember exactly where I was—in an RV park in Santa Cruz—when I heard the news of Diana's death. I watched the wedding of William and Kate two years ago. And today, I tuned in to catch a glimpse of the new royal, Prince George.

What's this fascination with English royalty? Someone on TV said, "It's a fairytale." Someone else said, "It's hundreds of years of history." And for me, one person nailed it. "With all the sobering, frightening news in the world, royal baby news offers a moment of joy, of normalcy, and hope."

This infant could be the first English monarch of the twenty-second century, or not. History doesn't unfold in straight lines. I won't be around to see what happens but, while I'm here, I wish the little prince and his mom and dad well.

Today, the *Sacramento Bee* published my mental health letter to the editor.

Patrick's Facebook Post: I got me a case of Pabst Blue Ribbon and it's time to tie one on. Walked twenty years of bad news and it's time to tie one on. Nothing ever comes in the mail except for coupons and ads, and it's time to tie one on. Just signed up for Christian Mingle, and there's no frequent drinkers but it's time to tie one on. Identity stolen, Hollywood making bank, and it's time to tie one on. Been captive and hostage most of my days and it's time to tie one on. Cheers.

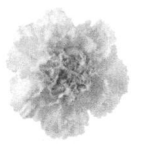

JULY 24, 2013

MISCALCULATION

Beryl didn't pass on July 21 as he thought he would. Joan sent this email today.

"Dede, forgive me if I've already emailed you about visiting, but I can't remember shit! Beryl has limited his visitors to immediate family and a few close male friends . . . part of the withdrawing process.

"Thank you for your offer of a hug for each of us, but I'd like a rain check for me. After he does pass I'll be on my own for the first time in thirty-five years. I'll need lots of hugs. Thank you for your caring concern." Luv and hugs, Joan

"Joan, I'll be here for you. Love and hugs back." Dede

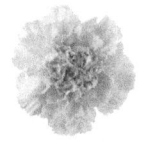

JULY 25, 2013

ONE WISE OLD WOMAN

I'm at lunch with a friend. She's a little younger than I am and starts a new job on Monday, mostly for health benefits. We exchange stories of friends who've deserted us. Seems we're never too old to experience friendship pain.

I no longer believe that growing older necessarily makes us wiser. I no longer believe in wise old women. I'll focus on finding one wise old woman.

My credit card fraud department calls this evening. Seems someone used my credit card number a few hours ago in Burnaby, Canada. I'll get a new number but I have to update all the accounts where I use this card. What a pain.

The customer service associate says, "Have a wonderful night."

Hope the perpetrator of this credit card theft isn't a crafty old grandmother. That's not the kind of wise old woman I'm looking for.

JULY 26, 2013

LEAVING HOME

One day, in the month of July 2000, I left home. I was fifty-six years old.

I loaded clothes, papers, photos of my kids, books, make-up, a hair dryer, and other personal items into my dark blue Infiniti G20 sedan. I paused and inhaled the image of my rustic, ridge-top house nestled among black oaks and bay laurels. Then I drove down the long, winding driveway to go to work.

At work, I parked my "moving van" in the university parking lot and rode the elevator to my ninth floor office. For the next eight hours, life appeared to go on as usual. At 5 p.m., however, I didn't go home. I drove to Marisa's and pulled a blouse and skirt out of the trunk of my car to wear to work the next day.

During the week, on my lunch hours, I scouted for a house to rent. I found one a few miles from the university. With a place to stay, I went back home to pick up my aging Rottweiler. Schatze had hip dysplasia. She was losing the ability to use her rear legs. I pushed and pulled and got her into the front seat of my car. With my best friend on board, I drove down my winding driveway one last time, thirteen years ago this month.

A psychologist I went to for counseling told me her rule of thumb. "In my experience," she said, "it takes a woman approximately half the length of her marriage to fully emotionally recover from a divorce."

By the time my divorce was final, I'd been married for thirty-four years.

If that therapist's correct, it will take me seventeen years to get back to being myself. According to her calculus, I have four more years to go. I wonder how I'm doing?

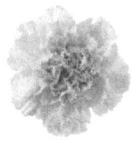

JULY 27, 2013

THE JOURNEY

Mary Oliver is one of my favorite poets. Her poem, "The Journey," is one of my favorite poems.

I carried a copy of Mary's poem in my wallet when I was leaving home. I took it out and read it whenever I felt like I was waffling in my decision to leave. Her words described what I was experiencing and gave me courage.

Mary's poem begins, "One day you finally knew what you had to do, and began . . ."

To read Mary's poem, go to www.peacefulrivers.homestead. com. Click on poetry by Mary Oliver.

JULY 28, 2013

DAILY CHALLENGES

Saw Marisa, Keith, Elise, and Sam yesterday. They drove from Carlsbad to Roseville, spent the night at Kerry's, and left early this morning for Seattle. I hope they'll arrive in Seattle safe and sound, and close on their house without another glitch.

The message on Caring Bridge today about Beryl: "Friday night and Saturday he was out of it, today he's with it! I know it's an emotional roller coaster for those around him and he says it's confusing for him, too. He says, "I've never died before, and I don't know what to expect." We'll enjoy spending the day with an alert person and I'll post again tonight. Thank you for sharing this up and down difficult journey with us."

Beryl says, "I've never died before, and I don't know what to expect." What a brave, honest thing to say.

Daily challenges—some for the living, some for the dying. Seems they continue right up to the moment of passing.

Patrick's Facebook Post: Peace through music.

JULY 29, 2013

FOOD AND HUNGER

I receive an email request this morning from Placer County Food Bank:

"This summer has been extremely hard on Placer Food Bank as rising hunger and decreased donations have left children and families in desperate need. Your quick action will mean so much to our hungry neighbors at this critical time. Children are out of school, without the benefit of school meals. Seniors are struggling to put food on the table. And our area's weakened economy is still putting a heavy burden on everyone."

Pat's here to do his laundry. He shops in my refrigerator and makes himself a quesadilla.

I'm reading an article on the internet about McDonald's McDouble one-dollar cheeseburger. It provides many with a whopping dose of protein and calcium along with 19 grams of fat. According to this article, junk food costs $1.76 per 1,000 calories, compared with $18.16 per 1,000 calories for nutritious fruits and vegetables (2007 University of Washington study).

No wonder hunger and obesity problems exist in our country. For many, healthy foods are luxury items. I'd donate to Placer County Food Bank, but right now, all my food donations go to my son. If each of us feeds one hungry person standing right in front of us, our entire village will be better fed.

JULY 30, 2013

LOSING IT

I'm losing it. I ask Pat the status of the document he needs in order to receive housing assistance. He's been on a waiting list for 10 years. He was so close to getting help. Close as melted butter on toast. Then a psychiatrist, who's known Pat for one hour, decides he's not disabled and refuses to sign the housing papers. This same psychiatrist is not monitoring Pat as he reduces his medications. He says to Pat, "Call me if you need something."

In the past, Pat's been reactive to med changes. More than once, he's been 5150'd within twenty-four hours of a med increase or decrease.

Pat says, "Rejoice with me. Don't worry. Be happy for my health. Don't stress about money. I should sue every hospital that ever hospitalized me and ruined my life."

Pat's managed care provider has a multi-million-dollar fine levied against it. They're charged with denying reasonable access for mental health services and for discharging mental health patients too soon.

I want to write a letter to Membership Services, but Pat doesn't want me to. "I didn't write a letter to your doctor when you were psychotic," he says. "And, by the way, you've made a lucrative career out of my misfortune."

Trying to stand by this adult child and intuit proper parental action is not always easy or clear. Meanwhile, a morning email from a local mental health organization asks, "Can we print your letter that appeared in the *Sacramento Bee* in our upcoming newsletter?"

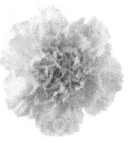

JULY 31, 2013

DIVERSION

A good day at duplicate bridge. My partner and I came in second. Bridge provided thee-and-a-half hours of diversion. I focused on bidding, play of the hand, and defensive leads. No time to think about housing vouchers or screwed-up real estate transactions. Thank goodness for weak two's, strong two-club openings, Stayman, no-trump transfers, new minor forcing, cue bid raises, Roman Keycard, reverses, negative doubles, takeout doubles, and other bridge conventions. When I use them or, more accurately, try to use them, they demand my full attention. They keep me from ruminating about circumstances beyond my control.

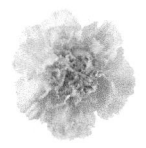

AUGUST 3, 2013

DILEMMA

Today is Pop's 117th birthday. Happy Birthday, Pop. On a cloud or a star or wherever you are, I love you.

Email from Pat:

"Mom. I received a letter today from the housing office denying my request for reasonable accommodation. Their reason is this—'We are not able to approve your request since there is no apparent disability related modification that is unique to this unit.'

"They're advising that if I want to use the voucher, I have to find another place to live. I don't want to move again. I can't handle that kind of stress right now. Their decision is not based on whether or not I'm disabled, it's based on the fact that the house isn't equipped with disability modifications like ramps or machines that move you up and down stairs.

"I've done everything in my power to try and make this voucher work here but it doesn't look like it's going to and it's time to cut our losses. Again, this has nothing to do with what the doc stated on the form, it has to do with the house itself." Pat

"P.S. Are you coming over on Monday for the air conditioner inspection and tune up?"

AUGUST 4, 2013

GOTTA LOVE 'EM

Email exchange with Pat:

"Pat, I'm flying to Seattle on the twelfth to visit Marisa. Can you take me to the airport on Monday and pick me up on Friday? I'm thinking I'll drive to your house. You can use my car and park it in your garage. Will this work?" Mom

"Mom, you don't want to take my car? I think last time you gave me $60 for gas and time." Pat

"Pat, I don't remember why I did that last time. My Prius gets better mileage than your car. As for time, this is something you can do for me." Mom

"Mom, yes, of course I'll take you." Pat

I call my mother:

"Hi, Mom. I have Marisa's new address* for you. Ready?"

"Ready."

"It's twenty-five-ten. Got that?"

"Yes, twenty-five-ten."

"10th Avenue."

"Two-hundred eight?"

"No. 10th. The number ten."

"Twenty-ten?"

"No. 10th. The number ten."

"T-e-n-t-h?"

Now, I'm shouting into the phone.

"No. Not t-e-n-t-h. 10th. As in 9th, 10th, 11th."

"10th."

"Yes."

"10th what?"

"10th Avenue."

"10th Avenue."

"Yay. 10th Avenue West."

"10th Avenue what?"

"West. Capital W. for West."

"10th Avenue little w?"

"No. Capital W."

"10th Avenue capital W?"

"Yes."

"Tell me again. Was that a little w or a big W?"

"That's it. Between you and Pat, I'm checking out. I'm selling the house, closing my bank account, and boarding a cruise ship until the money runs out."

"I'd come with you but I'd get seasick. Bye."

(*For privacy, Marisa's actual address isn't used.)

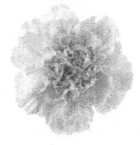

AUGUST 5, 2013

FIRST LAW OF AWESOME

Email from a reader:

"Dede, thank you for the letter to the *Sacramento Bee* regarding 'fluff.' I'm always encouraged when someone else is watching, having worked at the State Department of Mental Health (DMH) for thirty-four years, and having a mentally ill son.

"I'm amazed at the number of women in their 60s unable to find resolution in the mental health system for their loved ones. My phone rings and I know it's another mom with a missing son.

"My worst fear is leaving my son trapped, sedated, and in a board and care warehouse. He's homeless and terrified. This morning, I'm on my way to the shelter to search for him so he doesn't walk to his clinic in the heat. He's done nothing wrong but suffered the misfortune of a brain disease.

"When I worked for DMH, we were trained on how to interact with family members, counties, legislators, and consumers. In fact, I wrote what was known as the 'Five Laws of Awesome.' They were the result of my observations on how we, as bureaucrats, would handle anyone outside the DMH.

"The 'First Law of Awesome' was 'Never Wise Up a Dummy' and was dedicated to dialogue with legislators. I created it during the time I was implementing federal block grants which required seven annual reports to the legislature. One of the reports described the direct and indirect (administrative) costs at federal, state, and county levels.

"I quickly realized that the Feds were charging 8 percent, the state 15 percent, and the counties 26 percent for a total of 49 percent of mental health funds. Fifty-one percent of available funding was going to mental health clients.

"Not only that, there were different definitions at each level for administrative costs, which would have been an attachment to the report of fifty pages. The result would have been legislators screaming at me and hours of explanation.

"I backed out the 8 percent Fed because it was only a first year charge to the state, got my bosses to not charge the state 15 percent, and wrote a one-page report for 26 percent.

"My report flew through the agency and the Governor's office and received approval in three days. The Department of Alcohol and Drugs wrote a seventy-five-page report and, six months later, they were marched to the legislature and kicked. Bottom line—don't give people information they don't understand."

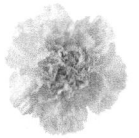

AUGUST 6, 2013

PLANNING

I looked death in the eye today and didn't flinch. I signed up for a prepaid cremation package with trip insurance. This means, if I die while traveling anywhere outside California, I'll be shipped home without additional expense. Cheery thought, but nice to know I won't be left dangling between this world and the next in a foreign country.

I signed Mom up for local coverage as she has no plans to leave California while she's still breathing. We each received a $100 discount because I signed us up on the spot. Think I'll go shopping. I'll buy a $100 outfit to celebrate living this long.

Other features and benefits of the cremation package include the following:

Today's payment will be put in a trust accruing interest. If we seek a refund, we'll be reimbursed ninety-nine percent of the interest. Hmm? Maybe this is a viable investment idea. At the time of passing, we'll receive a titanium ID bracelet to prevent mistaken identity.

Ashes can be co-mingled with the ashes of loved ones, including pets.

What I like is that everything is pretty much taken care of in advance and there'll be less stress at the time of departure. Kind of like packing your suitcase weeks before a long trip.

The big thing about dying, for me, is not being around to find out what happens next. For instance, in the news today—bitcoins and lab-produced hamburger grown from cow stem cells. I want to know about new developments like these. On the other hand, I'm glad I won't have to hear about future wars, murder, and mayhem.

As I think about my final transition, I grapple with Teilhard de Chardin's quote, "We're not human beings having a spiritual experience. We're spiritual beings having a human experience."

It's not clear to me why my spirit needed to have a human experience in the first place. Why didn't my spirit self simply stay where it was—in the great flowing river of infinite consciousness—or whatever? I mean, once I'm back in that realm, it will take a lot more than news of virtual money and hamburger helper to propel me to earth again.

If it's as good as it's cracked up to be, I think I'll like being a human being having a spiritual experience. I'm leaving it at that.

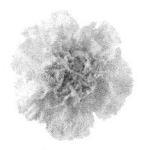

AUGUST 7, 2013

A POSTING ON CARING BRIDGE
PEACEFUL AND POIGNANT PASSING

Beryl had not spoken Monday or Tuesday. Nor had his eyes been open except for brief moments. On Tuesday around 3 p.m., he opened his eyes and saw and felt his daughter holding one hand, his son holding the other and Joan stroking his face. They all said, "I love you." Beryl mouthed what they think was, "I love you," closed his eyes and passed away. There couldn't have been a more poignant and beautiful—while tragic and sad—passing.

Thank you for caring about Beryl and his family. Knowing of your concern and compassion helped them cope with this journey.

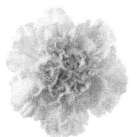

AUGUST 8, 2013

THE MEAN ONE

Well, you never know what might come in the mail or, as today, from UPS. A huge package, four-feet-by 32 inches.

I peel off the packaging tape and open one end of the box. I push and pull to release a heavy object, sliding it out of the box and onto the floor. Dozens of white styrofoam puffs float through the air. I slice through layers and layers of bubble wrap.

It's a frame. Turning the frame around, I'm staring at a mounted piece of cloth. It looks like it's been cut from a larger piece. It's a red and blue abstract design on a neutral background mounted on a Hunter-green mat.

My eyes scan the lower left side of the fabric. Printed in block letters it reads, "Maria Hollinger 1841."

Who was Maria Hollinger? I call my mother.

"Who was Maria Hollinger?"

"Maria Hollinger was my grandmother—your great-grandmother."

"Did you know her?"

"No, she died before I was born. She was my father's mother."

"Do you know anything about this fabric?"

"No, I didn't know it existed."

I call my cousin in Kansas City because her return address is on the box.

"Thank you for the gift. Where did it come from?"

"I found it in Aunt Marg's trunk after she died. It looked like a bridge-table size tablecloth. I think I should share these treasures with you so I cut it up to remove coffee stains and framed what was left—a half for each of us."

"Do you know anything about Maria Hollinger?"

"She was our grandfather's mother. She may be the one who everyone said was the 'mean one.'"

"Really? Why?"

"I don't know. Maybe it wasn't her. I'll try to find out who the 'mean one' was."

Maria Hollinger is now a ponderous presence in my dining room. The framed handiwork sits on the floor and leans against three dining room chairs. I've nowhere to hang this. It's too big, too red, too blue, too green. Maybe one of my daughters will want it.

It is intriguing that I'm looking at something used by a relative in 1841. This was sweet of my cousin, but I'm starting to chuckle. Some people inherit a million dollars. I inherit half of a piece of a tablecloth. Framed.

Now I'm laughing out loud. I'm snorting. I'm glad my cousin isn't here to hear me. I hope Maria Hollinger can't hear me, either. Especially if it turns out that she was, in fact, "the mean one."

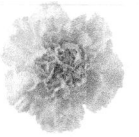

AUGUST 10, 2013

FOR A REASON

Email from Megan:

"Mom, the framed tablecloth looks interesting to me on Instagram, especially with your story. Don't you want to hang it in your garage? Then, in 150 years, you might be perceived as the 'mean one.' LOL.

"Maybe Grandma would want it in her place until my next visit. I'll take it if it's up for grabs. I think it made it all the way to you for a reason." Megan

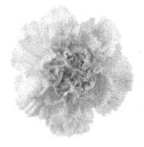

AUGUST 12, 2013

SEATTLE

I'm on Alaska flight 373—Sacramento to Seattle. Seat 24A, window seat. Departs 10:20 a.m. Arrives 11:59 a.m.

I'm going to visit Marisa, Keith, Elise, and Sam. Their furniture was supposed to be delivered from Carlsbad on August 2 but it hasn't arrived. They're staying in an apartment paid for by Keith's employer. They've booked a hotel room for me paid for by the moving company.

I'm taking a pink fuzzy ball with a face on it to Elise for her birthday. It's on her birthday wish list. Both Sam and Elise have new Seattle library cards so I'm bringing magnetic bookmarks for each of them and a book, *Noah Webster and His Words* by Jeri Chase Ferris. Jeri lives in my neighborhood. She's signed the book, "For Elise and Sam—Have lots of fun learning all about Noah! From a friend of your Mim."

We're taking off.

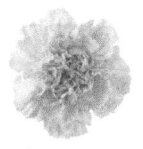

AUGUST 13, 2013

MORNING COFFEE

It's Tuesday morning in Seattle. I'm in room 405 of the Ballard Hotel in the suburb of Ballard. I open double glass doors to a black, wrought iron, eighteen-inch by three-foot balcony. Crisp air stings my face.

My view is of the street below and an alley that dead-ends in a parking lot. The parking lot backs up to the Stimson Marina. I hear street sounds—cars, bicycle bells, and human voices. I hear sky sounds—birds, helicopters, and airplanes.

I watch a crane in the marina hoisting giant crates off a salmon-colored barge. There's a klatch of blue and black garbage containers lined up in front of the restaurant across the street.

The coffee—Coffee Umbria—I made in the room's coffee maker is just right. I know Seattle loves its coffee and this cup is robust.

I'm waiting for Marisa to call or text. We're driving to Snoqualmie Falls. This may be our one day to explore because her furniture is coming tomorrow. That is, it's supposed to come tomorrow. Nothing but problems with this moving company.

But no worries. I didn't come to see the scenery. I came to see Marisa and her family. Yesterday, we visited the empty new house—a 1906, 1400-square-foot Craftsman-style bungalow. Marisa's looking forward to experiencing in-town living as opposed to suburb living in Carlsbad.

Darn. I'm getting those pesky feelings I sometimes get when I visit my daughters and their families. I'll ignore them for the moment. I know I'll have to write about them, sooner or later.

Right now, I'm making another cup of coffee.

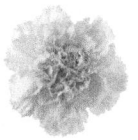

AUGUST 15, 2013

AS THE WORLD TURNS

I'm sitting in a Starbucks on the corner of NW 57th St. and 24th Avenue NW. The sky is overcast, promising rain. The sign on the table says, "As a courtesy to all our customers, we ask that you limit your stay to 30 minutes." I'm the only one here. Maybe my California vibe is scaring people away.

Marisa's and Keith's furniture arrived yesterday. I sat on the back porch as chief inventory clerk. Each box was numbered and the moving crew yelled out numbers as they carried the boxes into the house. I crossed each number off the inventory list. All 367 of them.

At the end of the day, the movers ran out of time to unpack boxes and to assemble a jungle gym—services that were paid for in advance.

The special crew that was required to move the old washer and dryer out of the house and install the new washer and dryer didn't show. There seems to be a communication problem between this moving company coordinator and the rest of the known world.

This move is giving me flashbacks to moves during my marriage—San Jose to Chicago; Chicago to Rochester, Minnesota;

Rochester to Guam; Guam to San Jose; San Jose to Pleasanton; Pleasanton to San Ramon; and San Ramon back to Pleasanton.

And then the moves after my marriage—Pleasanton to Castro Valley; one house in Castro Valley to another house in Castro Valley; Castro Valley to Rocklin; and finally, Rocklin to Lincoln.

In the middle of moves, I always felt hopeful, thinking physical changes would manifest progress and improvement. Sometimes things were better in new locations, sometimes not.

Pleasanton to Castro Valley was traumatic. I was leaving my marriage, my home, and the community I'd lived in for twenty-six years. I moved into an old house in an ethnic neighborhood. I never saw any neighbors, only heard the couple next door screaming in Russian. Sounded like four-letter words.

Not long after moving in, I called a mobile vet to the house to put Schatze to sleep. Kerry and David slept on the floor with her the night before. None of us wanted to say goodbye. (I have her ashes in a box on a shelf over my computer as I type this.)

On top of that, I lost my job and a meaningful mental health project I'd started at the university. This whole period seemed to be about one personal loss after the other. I held on tight to the rattling time machine I was traveling on—not sure where it was headed or how long the bumpy ride would last.

Meanwhile, back at the ranch, I'm still the only person in this Starbucks. Guess I can stay another 30 minutes.

At a table right outside the window, a large human being just sat down. I say "human being," because from the back, I can't tell if this is a man or a woman. The head is covered with a black scarf pulled on like and cap and wound around the neck. He or she is talking on a cell phone.

On the left hand, holding the phone, the fingernails are long like a woman's, but the plaid shirt looks like a man's. Whoops. The right hand just scratched the head, moving like a guy's hand.

Little does he or she know that the lady sitting on the other side of the window is writing about him or her.

A woman has claimed the table behind me and is typing on her laptop. I wonder if she's writing about me.

A big black crow is poking around under the outside tables, gobbling up cookie crumbs. A new fellow, with dirty hands and stringy hair, sits down in one of four leather chairs. He may be homeless. He closes his eyes and mumbles to himself. Two young boys run by the heavyset mystery person on the patio.

I've been here 45 minutes. I could sit here all day on this corner in Seattle—or on any corner anywhere—and watch the world go by. I'm walking outside now, past the object of my curiosity. He's definitely a guy.

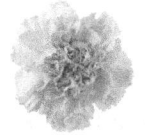

AUGUST 16, 2013

GOODYBYE SEATTLE

I'm back at my table at Starbucks. There are more people here today—five men and two women. One man is busy on his laptop. I wonder what he's writing about. The same crow—I can tell it's the same crow—is back for his Starbuck's breakfast. A small brown sparrow is working the opposite side of the patio. The woman at the table in front of me is wearing a hooded, turquoise sweatshirt with the words "Bhakti Chai" on the back. A rugged looking guy with greasy brown hair sits down at the table with the woman in the sweatshirt.

"Mind if I sit down here? I need to plug in my phone."

The woman stands up and leaves.

Marisa texts. She and the kids will be here soon to pick me up. It's time to go home already.

Yesterday we took a twenty-minute bus ride into town and scoped out Pike's Market. We drooled over fruits and vegetables in every color—red tomatoes, green zucchini, white onions, white garlic, purple eggplant, yellow summer squash, pink peaches, crimson plums, red apples, yellow bananas, and red and green grapes.

Other market items for sale included breathtaking bouquets of dahlias and Queen Anne's Lace, monster slabs of halibut, salmon on ice, mussels, Dungeness crabs, giant scallops, spot prawns, and handmade pastas in varieties like herb and garlic, red pepper and chives, sweet potato, and chocolate.

If I lived in Seattle, I'd be at this market at least once a week.

Marisa bought a dozen white dahlias with lavender centers for her dining room table. The table is surrounded by boxes, packed and unpacked. I'm proud of Marisa's home-making efforts. Martha Stewart would be proud, too.

Last impressions of Seattle on the way to the airport—a sign on a small marquee outside a bar: "Be bold about what you stand up for. Be careful about what you step into."

Another is a sculpture on a random patch of lawn beside the freeway. Marisa says, "It looks like a jettisoned airplane wheel."

I know what it is, but you have to be of a certain age to even have a clue. It's a large tree-size reproduction of a typewriter eraser—the round eraser disc attached to a brush to whisk away eraser debris.

Goodbye, Seattle. Goodbye, dear family.

AUGUST 18, 2013

MAKING AMENDS

Home again. I'm doing laundry and reading *Catching Fire*. The book belongs to Sam. He says, "You should read it, Mim."

I have to hand it to Suzanne Collins. She's written a page-turner. Age doesn't matter. Young and old are among the book's raving fans. I plan to see the movie.

Jazzy's sitting in front of my computer screen with her back to me. She's swishing her tail on my keyboard.

"Stop typing. You left me for five days. Five days. You went to visit Butters. I hate to be a bad news bear, but Butters is a dog. A yappy little froufrou dog. What were you thinking?"

"Sorry, Jazz. Let's go outside and explore the backyard. For the next hour, I'll watch you chase lizards."

Once in a while, I'll look away and read book number two of *The Hunger Games*.

AUGUST 19, 2013

BRIDGE AND BILL GATES

It's Monday and I'm still basking in my Saturday duplicate bridge score. My partner and I came in first in our section with a 60.74 score. We earned 1.69 OA BLK points.

I'm not sure what those points mean—they go toward life master points. To be a life master, you need 500 points. I have 25 points so life master status isn't happening for me in this incarnation. But this is my second best score and I'm trying to improve my game.

Bridge isn't easy. My partner and I review hands from Saturday's game. We talk about leads—leading the fourth down from the longest and strongest suit in a no-trump contract, and leading the top of a two-card sequence in a suit contract.

Warren Buffet plays duplicate bridge. So does Bill Gates. Sometimes they play together as partners. When Bill showed up at a youth bridge tournament, the kids asked him why he likes playing bridge.

He said, "Because I think I'm getting better at it."

If that's a good enough reason for Bill Gates to like bridge, it's a good enough reason for me. Today, after my Saturday game, I think I'm getting better at it.

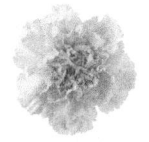

AUGUST 22, 2013

THE MORNING NEWS

Horrific news in today's paper. Photos show bodies of small children in white sheets lined up on a street. They look like they're sleeping. They're not sleeping. They're dead.

Parents point at small figures and claim their sons and daughters. Unbelievable loss in Damascus, Syria. It may have been a chemical attack. It's not yet clear.

Some people live in violent areas. Some people live in safe ones. Who gets to live where?

I'm sitting in a comfortable chair in my den surrounded by family photos, books, and my grandchildren's artwork. It's a small, quiet haven. Everyone deserves a small, quiet haven.

Pat calls. "Mom, Monday's my birthday. Can we go to that sushi place for lunch? I have a coupon for one free lunch if another person buys one."

"Yes, we can go."

It's Pat's 45th.

Mom calls. "I can't go to Regan's birthday dinner tonight."

It's Regan's 7th.

"I'm attending a fashion show. I signed up for it weeks ago. It's sold out and I don't want to lose my place."

"Who's putting on the fashion show?"

"One of the employees owns a wonderful collection of period clothing. One year the theme was the 1890s. That was when Pop was born. Another year it was depression era styles—flappers and stuff. The dining room staff model and serve us fruit salad, coffee, and dessert. It's a very good event."

"Guess we need to give you more notice next time."

"Yes, give me a month's notice so I can get it on my calendar. Bye."

"Bye, Mom."

Her calendar is busier than my calendar. She's my antidote to the morning news.

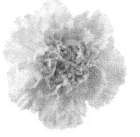

AUGUST 23, 2013

RACE

This morning I saw *The Butler*. This film presents an account of a black butler in the White House. He served eight presidents from 1952 to 1986.

In the car, on the way to the movie, I listen to Capital Public Radio and a discussion about a new school program in Oakland, California. Volunteers and staff, in the African Male Achievement program, mentor young black students to help them navigate the academic and cultural hurdles they face at school and at home.

In Oakland, in one recent year, according to the reported statistics, eight hundred black males were killed by gang and drug violence. In the same year, eight hundred black males graduated from high school ready to enter the California State University and University of California systems. In other words, in that year, black males in Oakland were as likely to be killed as to graduate from high school and go to college.

And tonight, I'm watching a television special about the 1963 civil rights march on Washington, DC. I was in college in California, removed from the march, and naive about race and racial issues. Growing up, I'd had limited encounters with African-Americans or with any ethnic group.

My first African-American friend was a young man who worked at IBM, as I did, during our college summer breaks. We bantered when we found each other in the copy room. While he changed toner in one machine, I ran copies on another.

I believed in God. Michael wasn't sure. He bragged about his college, San Jose State. I bragged about mine, Santa Clara University. We were both sad about losing President Kennedy. We were both hopeful for the Civil Rights Act of 1964. We each thought that interracial dating was okay, although neither of us knew anyone in a bi-racial relationship.

When we left the copy room, Michael opened the door and waited for me while I gathered up my copies. In retrospect, I think we had some chemistry.

Michael came to my wedding in 1967, our only African-American guest. I encouraged him to bring someone with him but he came alone. After my marriage, I moved to Chicago and lost touch. I wonder where Michael is today. I'd like to know his thoughts and talk with him again. But fifty years later, I can't remember his last name.

I regret that I haven't had close, longtime friends of color. I know my life would have been richer. I have a Japanese friend, now, who exposes me to a culture dedicated to the preservation of family history, respect for elders, and traditions that honor the deceased. She expands my world.

I hope it's a two-way exchange.

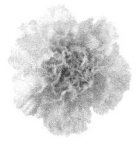

AUGUST 24, 2013

LAST STEPS

I'm at Beryl's Celebration of Life this morning. The room in Kilaga Lodge is packed—a testament to Joan and Beryl's impact on this community, and a testament to this community's supportive network.

Beryl was an artist. His stone and bronze sculptures serve as the table centerpieces. A family friend presents a slide show. It's fun to see Joan and Beryl smiling and waving when they were young. It's inspiring to see them, older and heavier, with their arms still around one another. They were married thirty-five years.

Beryl's children are present and grateful for Pops. His daughter-in-law, Lisa, acts as mistress of ceremonies. She introduces each member of the family, including Beryl's daughter, Jennifer, Lisa's new bride.

Lisa moves across the room. "Among his passions," she says, "cars, art, bowling and football, Beryl loved rocks. So I've left the best introduction to last."

Lisa introduces Joan. "Joan was Beryl's rock."

I believe it. Joan is quiet and often stands in the background. When you talk with her, however, you find a person of substance. Tonight will be Joan's first night alone without family present. She says reality hasn't hit her, yet. In a few days, I'll go for a walk with Joan—a walk without Beryl. Beryl's taken his last steps. Footsteps and life end so soon.

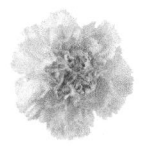

AUGUST 25, 3013

OVERSTATING THE OBVIOUS

I'm starting out the door to go for a walk but it's too hot and, anyway, I'm stalling. I don't want to do what I have to do— complete the paperwork for my prepaid cremation. It's not that it's about cremation. It's that it's about paperwork. Always there's so much paperwork, including online paperwork. I have a stack of bills to pay—mine, GG's, and Pat's. I have to start an Excel file for GG's rental house. It's time to update my revocable trust.

Mom calls to give me her grocery list. She's very specific:

1 package 60 watt light bulbs

2 packages dental tape, NOT floss

3 packages super-maxi pads, 48 count, Safeway brand

2 boxes Kleenex, 200 count, white

2 packages toilet paper, 24 count, double ply

I add her list to the pile.

Now I'm staring at the Authorization for Cremation and Disposition form. A notice at the top, capitalized and in bold red letters, says:

CREMATION IS IRREVERSIBLE

This is not self-evident?

"All the information requested is required by the state in order to file a death certificate. Incomplete information could lead to delays in the processing of permits in time of need."

Oh-Kay. I'll give you guys complete information. Co-mingle my ashes with my pets' ashes and return them to my family.

Marisa asks me to forward the cremation information to her. My brother and his wife request the web address. My hairstylist thinks she should give a brochure to her parents. My mother's following my example. I must be good at this—selling cremation. Maybe I could get a referral fee :-)

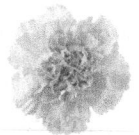

AUGUST 26, 2013

HAPPY BIRTHDAY, PATRICK SEAN

August 26 is a complicated day. It's Pat's birthday. It's also my wedding anniversary. If I were still married, it would be my 46th anniversary. I open one eye this morning, not two. Before I'm awake enough to remember what day it is, I'm hesitant. What is this? Am I still not over my divorce?

I don't mourn the marriage. We were both young, inexperienced, and immature. If we'd lived together first, as all my daughters did with their spouses, I'm guessing each of us may have said, "I love you, but this doesn't seem like a good fit."

In our defense, we were trying to be "good, Catholic kids." And when it became clear how different we were, the wedding certificate had long been signed and the bed made many times.

We never know what goes on inside a marriage, but from outside appearances, my three daughters have solid partnerships. They and their spouses work as teams. They make joint decisions. They parent together. They support each other. When I'm visiting them, I sometimes get those pesky feelings like I did in Seattle.

I watch my daughters and their spouses interact and I experience opportunity loss. I touch base again with the loneliness I felt in my marriage. I'm sure my daughters wish their mother would find a new relationship.

I give myself a pep talk. "Get a grip. Get over yourself. Rejoice in your daughters and their families. Give thanks for them."

A therapist I saw when I was first separated, kept telling me I was stuffing my feelings and pushing them down. What if I'm still doing that? What if that's why, this morning, my stomach's churning like an overloaded washing machine?

Maybe writing about my feelings of loss will bring them to the surface so I can dismiss them. "Go away. I have no need of you." Maybe next year, on August 26, I'll remember only that it's Pat's birthday. Maybe next year, August 26 will be an uncomplicated day.

Patrick's Facebook Post: FORTY-FIVE AND STILL ALIVE!
Ryan: Happy bday
Laura: Happy Birthday Pat! And many more to follow.
Brad: Happy Birthday Pat!
Robert: Yo Patrick! Happy Birthday brother. Hope you're doing well.
Donna: Happy Happy Birthday Patrick. Hope you had a good day.
Scott: Happy Birthday from Berlin, Mr. Ranahan! I send you an ever full stein.

Patrick: Thank you Mr. Shepard. Happy travels!

Lisa: Happy Birthday, Pat!

Merideth: Happy Birthday Pat from all of us! Pam, Dennis, Kevin, Mickey and me!

Urs: Happy Birthday Pat. Wishing you a useful B-Day & many more

Tiffany: Wishing you a very Happy Birthday Patrick!

Jay: Happy Bday!!!

Jen: Happy Birthday Pat!

Cory: Happy Birthday Patrick!

Lara: Happy Birthday Pat! Have a wonderful day.

Keith: Happy Birthday and many good wishes to follow.

Brandi: Happy, happy birthday to you!

Roger: Happy Birthday Pat!

Tanya: Happy Birthday!

Connie: Glad to hear it!

Kim: Happy birthday my friend. I hope this year brings you much happiness and good fortune.

Patrick: Thanks Kim, good to have reconnected with you on here.

Amy: Happy Birthday, Pat!

Kate: Sending more birthday love your way! Wishing you happiness today and everyday!

Kim: Happy Birthday Patrick!

Steph: Wish you a happy birth day/week/month!

Paul: Happy Birthday Pat!

Angie: Happy Birthday Patrick. Hope you have a great day.

Kelly: Happy Birthday to you. Hope you're having a great day!

Erin: Happy Birthday Pat! ROCK ON!

Chris: Happy Birthday! Have a great one buddy!

Steve: Happy Birthday Pat. Hope you have a great one!

Molly: Happy Birthday!

Jordan: Happy Birthday, Patrick!!
Cheryl: Happy Birthday!
Mark: Happy Birthday!
Annie: Happy Birthday, Patrick!
Geoff: PaRana! Hope you have a great day!
Cara: Happy Birthday, Pat! Enjoy!
Veronica: Happy Birthday Pat! Have some fun!
Alex: Happy Birthday!!!
Janet: Happy Birthday Pat! Have a great day!
Patrick: Thanks everyone for the birthday love and good
    wishes. All in all, a good day.

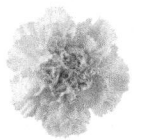

AUGUST 27, 2013

PART OF THE UNIVERSE

I'm picking through my mother's papers looking for the plot number of Pop's grave. Mom wants her ashes scattered there. I come across a poem I've not read before. I google the first line. The poem was written by Mary Elizabeth Frye in 1932.

According to Wikipedia, a German-Jewish woman, Margaret Schwarzkopf, was staying with Mary Elizabeth. Margaret's mother was ill in Germany, but told her daughter to stay away because of Jewish persecution. When her mother died, Margaret said, "I never had the chance to stand by my mother's grave and shed a tear."

Mary Elizabeth composed the poem on a brown paper shopping bag to console her friend. She didn't published the poem but shared it to some privately. In 1995, the father of a soldier killed in Northern Ireland, read the poem on BBC radio. The soldier had left the poem in an envelope addressed "To all my loved ones." Requests for the poem began immediately.

> *Do not stand at my grave and weep,*
> *I am not there; I do not sleep.*
> *I am a thousand winds that blow.*
> *I am the diamond glints on snow.*
> *I am the sunlight on ripened grain;*
> *I am the gentle autumn rain.*
> *When you awaken in the morning's hush*
> *I am the swift uplifting rush*
> *Of quiet birds in circled flight.*
> *I am the soft star that shines at night.*
> *Do not stand at my grave and cry.*
> *I am not there; I did not die.*

I email the poem to Joan. Joan emails back.

"I'm making a copy. It's something I want to remember as I think Beryl is now part of the universe."

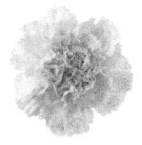

AUGUST 29, 2013

RUSSIAN DOLLS AND BLUE DRAGONS

I'm at a meeting of a new group that's trying to get off the ground—the Lincoln Lollies—or Lovely Older Ladies Laughing, Loving, Interacting, Enjoying, Sharing. Fifteen women have joined so far. Nine are present this evening. We meet in the waiting room of a small counseling office. The organizer is a therapist.

I recall a scene in the Richard Dreyfuss film, *Close Encounters of the Third Kind*. People are scrambling from every direction to get to a mountain top without knowing why.

The women here responded to an email and came from all over Lincoln to the first meeting of the Lolllies not knowing why. Obviously, the invitation tapped into some needs.

This meeting, as the others, is free form. We go around the room and each of us talks about whatever we want to bring up.

Yvonne, the therapist, has shelves in her office filled with miniatures—angels, animals, houses, cars, tools, rocks, children, grown-ups, and mythical creatures like fairies and unicorns. When everyone has spoken, Yvonne asks if we would like to try sand tray therapy. She rolls out a box of sand on wheels—three feet by two feet by two inches deep.

"Pick two figures from the miniatures on my shelves and place them wherever you want in the sand tray."

I can't decide at first.

Yvonne says, "Don't think too much, just choose."

I pick a Russian matryoshka, or wooden nesting doll, and a blue dragon.

"Why did you pick these?"

I'm not sure. From all the miniatures, they jumped out at me. I know the nesting doll has many dolls inside. It suggests the peeling back of layers. The dragon isn't scary. It isn't breathing fire. It looks protective and magical. The doll, as I placed it in the sand tray, is gazing at the dragon with big, wide-open, unblinking eyes. She's unafraid and very close to the dragon. What am I feeling when I look at the doll and the dragon? I'm feeling that they're telling me something. They're telling me to follow my muse.

Patrick's Facebook Post: One year ago today I reported for brain surgery. One of the scariest days of my life. Today I can say that things are back to normal, going out to dinner with my dad to celebrate my 45th birthday.

Lara: Wow, Pat I'm shocked to hear this, and yet happy to hear you're doing well.

Patrick: Normal in a relative sense.

Julie: We are thankful Pat. Have a great time at dinner.

Veronica: You ROCK Pat! Prime example of living life!

Scott: Normal? Who needs it? My relatives aren't normal either.

Katie: Stay strong Pat! Have a fantastic dinner and say hello to your dad from us!

Pam: Happy Birthday Pat! I remember first meeting you when you were about 3 years old.

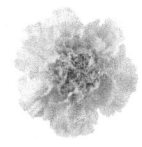

AUGUST 30, 2013

BEAUTIFUL FEET

I had a pedicure this morning. By coincidence, a vet tech, Becky, is coming to the house to clip Jazzy's nails. I can't do this myself. One cat plus one set of nail clippers plus one pair of hands equals total chaos. I ask Becky to call me on her cell phone when she arrives. Jazzy will run and hide if she hears the doorbell. With faked nonchalance, I shut the doors to the bedrooms and the laundry room, closing off escape routes. When Becky calls, I answer with my usual phone voice.

"Be right there."

But, damn. Somehow Jazzy knows. She knows something's up. She sprints for my bedroom where she can hide under the bed but the door is shut. I scoop her up.

I open the front door and Becky comes in. She's only been here once before but Jazzy remembers. She squirms in my arms. Becky grabs her by the scruff of her neck and places her on her side on the dining room table. She shows me how to hold her neck and how to brace her back with my arm.

Jazzy relaxes. She doesn't fight as Becky clips her nails. In less than a minute, the nail trim is finished. I let go of Jazzy's fur and she dashes under the table.

Becky leaves. Shortly, all's right in our world again. Jazzy's sprawled in front of the computer as I type. She's gazing at me. She's purring. We're still friends. And, we have six beautiful feet.

Patrick's Facebook Post: R.I.P. Seamus Heaney, Irish poet extraordinaire.

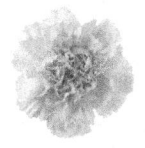

AUGUST 31, 2013

QUANDARIES

The Syria thing is heating up. Russian President Vladimir Putin urges the US to reconsider a military strike against Syria. Russia is a Syrian ally and Russia-US relations are strained, among other things, over Russia's giving national security leaker, Edward Snowden, diplomatic asylum.

Putin challenges the United Nations: "Present evidence that proves it was Assad's military that launched the chemical attacks in Damascus, and not Syrian rebels trying to draw the US into the conflict. Remember what happened, in past decades, when the US initiated armed aggression in different regions of the world. Did US involvement resolve even one problem in those instances?"

Some of our elected representatives in Washington are asking different questions. Is it our mandate to monitor and vindicate international norms? Is military action required in Syria to protect our national security interests?

I try to process foreign positions and US positions the same way. Are the people in power trustworthy? Do they really know the proper course of action? Are hidden personal and political agendas in play? Of course they are. Answers are not easy to sort out.

Across the world, the people I'd like to sit down and talk with are sixty-nine-year-old Syrian grandmothers. What's their take on the situation? What are their ideas to stop the killing of innocent children and grandchildren? Like me, they lack the power to make the killing stop. I'm guessing, though, that they'd be willing to join hands and say a prayer for humankind. I bet that, after prayer, they'd agree the next best steps are to take care of our own families and friends, and to root out the weeds in our own backyards.

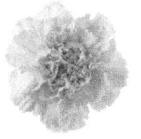

SEPTEMBER 1, 2013

COOKIES I

For some, I hear, baking is meditative. Sinking hands into flour, sugar, eggs, and butter, one can connect with one's higher self. This has not been my experience.

I'm not a baker. I'm more of a souper, or one who makes soups. A pinch of curry instead of salt, Italian sausage instead of ground beef, kale in place of spinach, navy beans for kidney beans. You get my drift. Souping is flexible. It leaves lots of room for error.

On the other hand, baking is precise. You need to attend to exact measurements and baking times or you court disaster—pathetic pie crusts, cracked cheesecakes, and sickly soufflés.

A recipe I've come across for caramel corn cookies has broken my resistance to baking. I love caramel corn and I need a dessert to take to a Labor Day get-together tomorrow.

The recipe sounds straightforward enough. Nothing too complicated here. First step: Preheat the oven to 375 degrees. Check. Second step: Line two baking sheets with parchment paper. Uh-oh. I'm in trouble already. The sheets of parchment paper I've torn off are too long and too wide for my baking pans.

I press one side of the parchment paper up against the rim of the baking pan. I'm trying to put a crease in it to make it fit. It doesn't want to crease. I turn the paper over and try to crease it from the other side. No luck. I fold the paper and force creases into the folds. Now the paper fits but it's ballooning in the middle. I need those pie bead thingies to hold it down. Not a good idea. They'd end up in the cookies.

I'm 10 minutes into this project and not yet working with ingredients. I grab the kitchen scissors and cut the parchment along the folds I've made. I gather up the parchment scraps to put them in the waste basket under the sink. The basket's too full. The parchment scraps fall all over the floor. I'll take care of that in a minute.

Next step: Beating and mixing go okay but this cookie dough seems really dry. I double-check the recipe. I haven't missed anything. I continue on faith.

I bake the cookies for ten minutes, as directed. I let them cool five minutes on the baking sheets, as directed. I transfer the cookies to racks to cool, as directed.

Meanwhile, the parchment scraps need to be picked up. Flour and oats have drifted everywhere—on countertops, on the floor, on my blouse, in my hair, in Jazzy's fur.

I used half the bag of caramel corn. Someone has spilled much of the remaining half into the sink. Flakes of coconut are swimming in puddles of almond extract.

How did this happen? Who made this mess when I wasn't looking?

The directions don't state how long to wait before sampling the cookies. I decide it's time. I take my first bite. I eat the whole cookie. I give it another shot and eat another cookie.

These cookies are okay, but they're not good enough to take to the potluck tomorrow. They're not dry, as I feared. They're flavorless. They don't add up to the sum of their parts. I can't even taste the caramel corn.

This hasn't been a zen experience. I'm not in the right frame of mind to close my eyes and focus on my breathing. What to do? It must be five o'clock somewhere. The cleanup will have to wait.

SEPTEMBER 2, 2013

COOKIES II

Time's getting short. The potluck's at 4 p.m. I go to my recipe book and flip to a proven recipe—Peanut Butter Cup Cookies. All the ingredients are on hand except the peanut butter cups.

I'm at the market to get the candy. Standing in the cake mix aisle, I spy a peanut butter cookie mix. This would be so simple.

The good angel on my right shoulder says, "No. That's cheating. You must make the cookies from scratch."

The bad angel on my left shoulder says, "Naw, go ahead. Stop worrying. No one will know the difference."

I buy the peanut butter cups and the cookie mix. I can decided what to do when I get home.

I'm home. I'm reading the recipe. It involves flour, salt, baking soda, butter, white sugar, peanut butter, brown sugar, eggs, vanilla, and milk.

I'm staring at the cookie mx. It involves the mix, oil, water, and one egg. It's a moral dilemma. It's a no brainer. I go for the cookie mix.

I roll the dough into 36 balls, coat them in sugar, and put them in mini-muffin tins to bake for eight minutes at 375 degrees. I remove the muffin tins from the oven and push one peanut butter cup into the center of each cookie. All done. One dirty bowl and not a trace of flour anywhere.

I'm testing a cookie. It's perfect. It's delicious. The baking is successful. After yesterday's fiasco, one might even go so far as to call it a "zen experience."

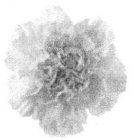

SEPTEMBER 3, 2013

A TEACHER'S TIRADE

Megan calls. She's at the vacation rental house she and Britt own in New Harmony, Utah. She's cleaning toilets, changing bed linens, and getting ready for the next guests to arrive. She's wound up.

"I may quit teaching. I think I've had it."

These words are spoken by the daughter who knew in third grade she wanted to be a teacher and never wavered from that career choice. She's been teaching first, second, or third grades for almost twenty years. This year, she's teaching third grade. What's happened?

"My class size is getting bigger and bigger. I have more and more children with ADHD, autism, or some other learning disability. I can't move the whole class forward because these children occupy most of my time. Some of them are abusive to me and the other students.

"I told the principal about one boy and his disruptions in the classroom. She said, 'Handle it. Nothing can be done unless the student hurts someone.'

"Yesterday, he gut-punched another child at recess. The vice-principal asked the little guy to stop and he sneered, 'Try to make me.'

"I was glad, actually, that someone else was witnessing what I'm dealing with every day.

"Two years ago, our school scored high on the required student tests. Last year, our scores weren't as good. This is to be expected depending, in part, on the quality of students coming to the classroom. Some of our children are transient or homeless.

"The principal says, 'You teachers must have rested on your laurels from last year. You must have let down a little.'

"I didn't rest on any laurels. I didn't let down a little. I worked as hard as I always work. What's worse, we're required to teach like robots. We have to put the same posters in the same places in each classroom. We have to teach to the tests.

"The principal wants us to stay later after school and monitor the kids while they do homework. I said, 'I won't do it. I have my own children and I'll be at home helping them with their homework.'"

What can I say to my daughter to make her feel better?

"Megan, you have many skills."

"Yes, but there aren't many career opportunities here. Women are either nurses or teachers."

Why does this conversation seem like one out of the 1950s? Have women made career progress in only certain sectors or geographic locations? Are teachers and students trapped, like hamsters on a wheel, in unmanageable educational bureaucracies? In my experience, bureaucracies are scary beasts that dwell in dark places, feed on greed and incompetence, and suck human spirits dry.

My daughter is a seasoned, dedicated, teacher but she's burnt out. Wish I had a magic wand or a brilliant suggestion. I say all I can think to say, "Megan, listen to your own voice."

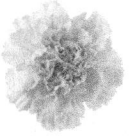

SEPTEMBER 4, 2013

WHICH END'S UP?

The phone rings at 7:30 a.m. It's Pat. I need a cup of coffee before I answer.

"Mom, call me as soon as you get this message."

Not the way I want to start my day. Pat was here yesterday and made an announcement. "I need six hundred dollars worth of dental treatment."

I'm afraid to hear what today's call is about. It's 9:15 a.m. Pat calls again This time I answer. "I called you earlier," he says.

"I know. I needed a cup of coffee first."

"Okay. I need to see the dentist today. My jaw is aching and if we let this go on it will get worse."

"I'm sorry, Pat, I've run out of funds. You'll have to ask someone else to help you."

Mom calls, "Pat phoned. He says he needs six hundred dollars for dental work."

"Did he say he needs to see the dentist today?"

"No, I said I'd think about it and get back to him."

I go to bridge and I'm unreachable for five hours. When I get home, I check my answering machine. My son's called four times.

Pat's trying hard. He's had two job interviews this month but no luck. His resume is full of holes and I don't know if he presents himself with energy. I wish I could meet all his financial needs, but I can't without ripping a hole in my financial safety net—a hole we'd both fall through.

Where's this psychiatrist who's told my son he doesn't have a mental illness and doesn't need medication? Maybe he could pay for Pat's dentist. On the other hand, what if he's right? Maybe I'm the one who needs medication.

An email pops up on my computer. It's from a member of my Family Mental Illness Support Group: "Hi Dede! I announced to my classes today about your wonderful group and what a great resource it can be. I invited those who are interested to attend the next meeting to hear the MediCal speaker. Save me a seat for the 13th. God bless you for your talents and leadership for all of us! Cheers."

Thank you. I need this feedback. Maybe I'm not losing it after all. But things feel topsy turvy and it's hard for me to tell.

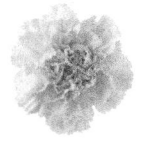

SEPTEMBER 5, 2013

HOMEMADE BOOKS

I'm babysitting Regan and Ayla while Kerry and David attend Back to School Night. These redheaded granddaughters are super cute. Four-year-old Ayla yells, "Mimmy," and gives me a hug. She's wearing a new headband with a big, glittery red bow on top. "I'm going to wear it every day."

Seven-year-old Regan is typing on the laptop. She's writing a letter. "Mim, show me how to print."

Regan prints her letter: "Regan Ayla Kerry David I love you. Because we have fun. And it is awesome. I am excited to make cookes with mim it is going to be fun and the cookes or going to be yummy because it's peanut butter. Love, Regan."

We start making cookies. We crack an egg and Ayla tries to dump it into the mixing bowl. Most of it ends up on her arm. She says, "I have to go wash."

She comes back and adds the chocolate chips. Regan and Ayla dip stray chips into the cookie batter. They lick the beaters. Cookies are an afterthought. They're into the here and now.

I ask, "Where are the toothpicks?"

Regan's looking. "I'm the one who usually knows where Mommy keeps things because Ayla is younger than me and my brain is bigger than hers."

Ayla runs off to play with Kerry's iPad. Regan is assembling treats for Mommy and Daddy—three carrot sticks, five blueberries, and a tablespoon of peanut butter for dipping. She pours lemon water out of a jar from the refrigerator into two paper cups.

"Mommy made it yesterday. Mommy and Daddy love their lemon water."

The cookies are done and cooling. Regan and Ayla are modeling their new Taylor Swift t-shirts. They show me tiny frogs in their goldfish bowls.

"The fish died," Regan says. "I want a bunny but we can't get one. Piper might chase it. Daddy wants a lizard and a snake. My room's messy because Ayla let her friends in while I was at school. I put a 'stay out' sign on the door but she still comes in."

Chatter, chatter, chatter. I want to bottle it.

David and Kerry are back. It's time for me to leave. Regan and Ayla charge out of the den. They've printed Regan's letter dozens of times and stapled pages and pages together to make three books.

"Mim," Regan shouts, "these books are for you. You have to take them home."

"Thank you, Regan. I will take them home."

I most certainly will.

Patrick's Facebook Post: Her last words to me were, "No hard feelings," but I'm beginning to think she meant, "Know hard feelings."

SEPTEMBER 6, 2013

TOURNAMENTS AND WARS

I played in an all day bridge tournament today that was held in an uncomfortable community recreation center. An outmoded air conditioning system froze our hands and feet. Cold, hard, folding chairs stressed our bottoms. Worn cards and bidding boards strained our eyes. The tournament started late and ended late. My partner and I were rummy by the end of the day. We came in third in the morning session, but were too tired to hang around and see the results of the afternoon session.

During the tournament, I look around the room at people playing an intense, competitive game and think about Syria. I wonder what news I'll hear when I get home.

I don't want to find out that we're committing our military. My heart is breaking for the Syrian people, but I believe that violence begets violence. I don't know what we can accomplish with more bombs and bloodshed. So many factions are involved we really don't know whom we might be helping. We can't anticipate unintended consequences.

Call me a skeptic. I don't trust power players anywhere. Not because they're bad people—they may be—but because they're people. In armed conflicts, humans have always made, and will always make, tragic mistakes.

The international decision makers in the Syrian situation are mostly men. They move bodies around in war zones like trump on a bridge table. They set up strategies and signal their partners. They make bad calls and play bad hands. They win some and lose some. Men have been playing war, like bridge, a game of errors, forever.

It's time to forget scores and put egos aside. Everyone, let's call it a millennium. Like leaving a bridge tournament, it's time for all of us to go home.

Patrick's Facebook Post: Went to Papa Murphy's yesterday to get a pizza with my food stamps. (Only place you can use your food stamps to buy prepared food.) Food stamp machine was down. Owner said, "You're in here all the time, we're not gonna worry about it," and gave me a free pizza and even threw in a jar of hot red pepper. Still some good people around.

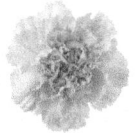

SEPTEMBER 7, 2013

GETTING REAL

I call Megan. It's been another stressful week at school. One of Megan's students is the son of a teacher Megan has co-taught with in the past. A few days ago, the boy's father was riding with his cycling group, practicing for an upcoming marathon. His was the last bike in the line. Traveling around a curve, the sun blinded an oncoming driver. He hit the boy's father and killed him instantly. No charges were filed.

Yesterday, teachers and students attended a Celebration of Life held in the school auditorium. Megan gave cards to each of her students so they could write notes to their sad little classmate. Megan can hardly speak on the phone. She chokes up.

"My trouble-making student is on medication and has calmed down. He's not as combative. He wrote the kindest note out of the entire class. He wrote, 'I know your father will live in your heart forever.'"

Now I'm choking up.

After the memorial service, everyone turned out for the first flag football game of the season. Selected by his peers, Ashton, my grandson, is quarterback for his 4th grade team. During yesterday's game, he threw a touchdown pass, made an interception, and completed an impossible catch. His team won 12-0.

Ashton has Perthes disease, a serious degeneration of the hip socket and femur bone. He's had surgery and time will tell if it's successful. Meanwhile, one leg is longer than the other and Ashton walks and runs with a limp. No problem in his mind, especially when he's on the football field.

"I wish he could play every day," Megan says. "People tell me, 'Quite an athlete you have there.'"

So many powerful emotions crammed into one day. Life doesn't get more real than this.

Patrick's Facebook Post: I'm not even going to look into the game Candy Crush Saga. It seems a lot of my friends are lost in deep candy space.

SEPTEMBER 8, 2013

GRAVY

Linda Ronstadt's no longer singing because she has Parkinson's disease. She says, "People with Parkinson's can't sing."

Linda is of my generation. I remember her top hits—"Blue Bayou," "Desperado," "When Will I Be Loved," and "You're No Good."

In a *New York Times* interview, she's philosophical. "By the time you reach your late sixties," she says, "it's all gravy from here on out, you know?"

I haven't thought about my late sixties like this before. Passing can happen anytime—the cyclist in Utah was a young father. Just because you're old doesn't mean you'll die tomorrow. Just because you're young doesn't mean you won't die tomorrow. There's probably a German word for this that I don't know. Like *bildungsroman* or *schadenfreude*. A word that means the perception of one's inevitable demise can be variable. It can be meaningful. It can be sobering. It can be ignored. Or it can be denied until the last minute.

My perception is colored by the fact that I have a ninety-five-year-old mother. She's the old one. I'm still her young daughter. I'm not going to die yet. Parents die first. This rationale seems to work in reverse for my mother. "I'm not old. I still have a young daughter. I'm not going to die yet."

Thanks to both my mother and father, I have good longevity genes. These genes may or may not get their chance to show off.

I could slip on the proverbial banana peel this evening. Linda Ronstadt's statement is a timely reminder. As I approach seventy, tomorrow can't be taken for granted. Every tomorrow, from here on out, is "all gravy, you know?"

Patrick's Facebook Post: Poetry is essentially not even the printed page anymore. It's the everyday conversations we have as we go through our days, at the grocery store, at the dinner table. It's the social media tweets and updates, the threads on Facebook. It's the glimpses of beauty and synchronicity in our everyday lives, the recognition and utterance of this beauty and so it is more fleeting than ever, like dreams we struggle to remember, and rarely capture in verbal description.

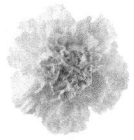

SEPTEMBER 9, 2013

HAPPY BIRTHDAY, JAZZ

Today is Jazzy's birthday. She's nine years old. I'm a little sad. A cat's average life span is 12 to 15 years. Of course, some cats live much longer. Mom's outdoor/indoor cat lived to be 23. I hope Jazzy is primed for the longer end of the age spectrum.

When I adopted her from the SPCA, Jazzy was two. Her biography said she was there because the older woman who'd owned her had fallen and broken her hip. The bio said, "The woman fell because Jazzy tripped her."

What a fluke, I thought. Poor lady.

As I read Jazzy's history, she stuck a paw out of her cage and waved it in the air. "Notice me," she said. I took it as a sign.

My previous kitty, Kitty, was also a black cat. I'd put her to sleep three weeks prior to my visit to the SPCA and I wasn't doing too well. I was observing a mourning period. I decided I'd simply look at the shelter and not make any decisions. I asked to take Jazzy—then known as Katie—into an observation room. She was curious. She was purring. She was in my arms. I took her home.

One year later, while getting ready to go to a business meeting in Los Angeles, I walked into my bedroom to get my suitcase. Jazzy came charging into the room at 30 miles an hour. She ran headlong, with the force of a 12-pound bowling ball, into the back of my right leg. I heard a sound like a tree branch splitting. I looked down to see my right foot pointing to the right and my right leg pointing to the left.

At the end of the day, I'd had surgery and a steel plate and six screws implanted in my right ankle. I'd be out of work for three months. Another elderly lady felled by her black kitty. Some people, like my mother, said, "Get rid of that cat."

Jazzy didn't break my ankle on purpose. I know she didn't. Anyway, it was too late to get rid of her. We'd already bonded. She was and is a steady companion. In the morning, when I wash my face, she washes her face in the second sink. I let the water drip from the faucet for her. When I'm at the computer, Jazzy rests in front of the screen or rides on the back of my swivel chair. When I eat breakfast, she eats breakfast. When I watch TV, she sprawls on my glass coffee table and watches TV. When I come home, after 10 minutes or 10 hours, she greets me at the door.

Most afternoons we take a 45-minute break in the backyard. Jazzy swats at butterflies, glares at hummingbirds, and basks in being an outside cat. When it's time to come in, she comes in because there's an agreement. "We'll go back outside again tomorrow. I promise."

I used to be a dog person. At different times, I've owned a Boston Terrier (Cinderella), a Winchester Terrier (Wimpy), a Cocker Spaniel (Buster), a Bassett Hound (Joy), a Norwegian Husky (Yoda), a Lhasa Apso (Snickers), a Rottweiler (Schatze), and a stray mutt (Scraps).

For some reason, I seem to love the most recent animal best. Of course, Jazzy's the most recent animal. As all my pets have done, she increases my awareness of a different kind of consciousness, a different kind of soul. Some people scoff. My darling brother, when he's visiting, brushes Jazzy out of his way. Should she come between him and whatever he's doing, he says, "Get that damned cat out of here."

My brother's an engineer. What can I say?

I can say, "According to an article in *Scientific American,* a cat's brain has 1000 times more data storage than an iPad and works a million times faster. Please show some respect."

Please stay well, little black cat. You're a special kind of friend. Happy Birthday, Jazz. And many, many more.

Patrick's Facebook Post: I just made chicken stir-fry with a chicken that said use or freeze by 9/7. Wish me luck tonight.

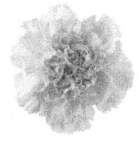

SEPTEMBER 10, 2013

MULTIPLE SCLEROSIS

This morning I'm at the public library for an author presentation and book signing. The SCLH Multiple Sclerosis (MS) Support Group is sponsoring it. A Santa Rosa resident, Ronda Giangreco, has MS. In 2008, back from a cooking school in Italy, Ronda's life was good. She was healthy, had a solid marriage, four grown sons, a comfortable home, and lots of friends. Then she woke up one morning numb on her left side. She was diagnosed with MS and was told she might not walk much longer. She asked herself, "Then where should I walk now?" Her answer was, "To the place I feel most grounded—to the kitchen."

Her book, *The Gathering Table*, recounts the challenge she laid out for herself. She would prepare dinners every Sunday for eight people throughout 2010. The caveat was that everything— bread, pasta, dessert—had to be homemade. Ronda would defy MS one week and one meal at a time.

Thinking about my friend Irene, who has MS, I'm here to learn more about this illness. National MS Society brochures are on the front table next to copies of Ronda's book. I flip through the brochure before the program begins. There are different categories of MS. Irene has secondary progressive. People with this type of MS experience a slow but nearly continuous worsening of the disease. There can be variations in rates of progression and temporary minor improvements.

Ronda is a relaxed speaker. She shares a few, well-chosen slides. Her husband's mother died of MS when he was a teenager. Ronda's diagnosis was devastating for him. Ronda asks, "How many of you have MS?"

The majority of people in the audience raise their hands. They all shake their heads in recognition of the travails that Ronda shares. She says it's important for people with MS to have friends who are knowledgeable and understand what they're going through. I buy a copy of *The Gathering Table* for Irene and ask Ronda to sign it. She writes, "Irene, stay strong."

I'll read the book to learn more about MS. Then I'll send it to Irene. Maybe something in the book will resonate. At least, she'll know I'm thinking of her.

Patrick's Facebook Post: Sometimes I feel like I'm living in a Far Side comic strip, like when I go to Walmart and see morbidly obese people puking in trash cans in the meat department. Problem is, nothing about it is even remotely funny.

Lara: Really? This happened?
Patrick: Yep, a woman was coughing and hacking her way up the meat aisle when she hunched over a garbage can and vomited.
Lara: Wow! I guess this is why my mom refuses to shop there.
Patrick: There are a lot of good reasons to refuse to shop at Walmart and every time I have to go there I swear I'm never going back, but I get lured in by some of their prices.
Greg: Doesn't sound like a Far Side to me, just sounds like Walmart.

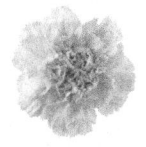

SEPTEMBER 11, 2013

9/11

This is the 12th anniversary of 9/11. I'm flying the flag in front of my house. I'm pausing to remember. I'm saying a prayer for those who were lost and for those who remain. That includes all of us.

Meanwhile, I haven't talked to Pat in a week. I don't know what's happening with his teeth. I'm trying not to call him. Waiting, always waiting, for the other shoe to drop.

Patrick's Facebook Post: Getting mail is pretty much the highlight of my day so every time I open my mailbox and there's nothing in it my heart sinks a little.

Meredith: I say nothing is better than bills.

Patrick: That's true Meredith. I'm usually hoping to get a check.

Angie: What's your address? I'll mail you something so you have something to look forward to.

Lara: Hey Pat, message me your address and I'll send you something. Don't worry I won't stalk you . . . LOL

Angie: Unlike Lara, I might stalk you though. J/K

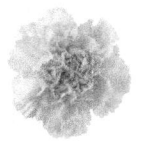

SEPTEMBER 12, 2013

WHERE IS WARREN BUFFET?

Mom calls. "Now that you're finished with all the cremation stuff, I have another project for you. That CD I cashed is sitting in my checking account earning no interest. I want you to find a better place for it."

I don't remember at what point I became Mom's financial adviser. She's a tough client. She's never participated in the stock market. She's adamant, "I lived through the Depression and I don't trust Wall Street."

At ninety-five, Mom doesn't like complicated investments. Her current stash is mostly the result of doing nothing. She and Pop bought a modest tract home in San Jose in 1959 for $16,000. In 2004, she put the house on the market and sold it in three days for $600,000. Mom says, "I want another deal like that one."

Mom owns the house she rents to Pat but times have changed. This house is underwater. More and more, she's dipping into principal to cover her expenses and, like many of us, she's worried about outliving her resources. My mission, should I choose to accept it, is to go out there and find a risk-free, no-fail, get-rich-quick scheme Mom can put to work immediately.

Cremation planning was a cinch compared to this. I'll go online and do some research, but I'm not holding my breath. I need help big time. Where-oh-where is Warren Buffet?

Patrick's Facebook Post: I love sleeping when I'm not having nightmares and I love eating good food, but dammit wouldn't it be great if we didn't have to eat and rest so much? No more endless worrying about the next meal, no dirty dishes, just go, go, go.

SEPTEMBER 13, 2013

HOLDING IT TOGETHER

This afternoon, a new woman joins our Family Mental Illness support group. She's in tears telling us about her son and daughter. They both have schizophrenia.

When she was 47—she's now 73—this lady left her native country and came to the US "to escape Communist oppression and to escape my husband, who also has schizophrenia."

Her daughter has returned to Europe. Her son lives in the Bay Area in low-income housing. "My son's been with me for the last week," she says, "and sometimes I'm afraid of him. He's struck me in the past."

The woman refuses to call the police because, "In my old country, police make irrational arrests of innocent people." She's sad. "I love my son, and there's no help in this country for people with illnesses like his. I'm angry and frustrated. I've been trying to hold it together for a long time. I can't do it anymore."

As the woman leaves the meeting, I tell her, "I'll call you Monday and we'll meet for coffee or lunch."

God bless my mother. She adds some lightness to the day. She sends Jazzy a birthday card: "Dear Jazzy, I wish you a very Happy Birthday with an extra sardine for dessert. I also wish you a Happy Year ahead with Dede. She needs a lot of furry hugs and a lot of TLC. With love, GG (Great Grandma)."

Patrick's Facebook Post: It occurs to me that for each and every one of you on my friends list, I catch myself looking at your pictures, sharing jokes and news, as well as support during good and bad times. I am also happy to have you among my friends. We will see who will take the time to read this message until the end. If you appreciate your friends from all over the world, go ahead and copy this into your stats too, even if it's just for a minute. I'm going to be watching to see who takes care of the friendship, just like me. Thank you all for being a part of my life. Copy and paste please, don't share. If no one reads my wall, this should be a short experiment. This is a Facebook game to see who reads and who just scrolls. If you read this, leave one word on how we met. Only one word, then copy this to your wall so I can leave a word for you.

Kristiyn: Thriftway!

Emma: SF Christmas Eves

Kerri: Poetry

Danielle: Your sister

Pam: Aunt

Ray: Squint

Lara: School

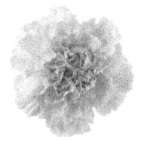

SEPTEMBER 13, 2013

FOCUS

Headlines on my cellphone this morning:

- "Four men sentenced to death in gruesome India gang rape."
- "Man kills wife behind Texas school, shoots self."
- "Wrongly convicted man released after 12 years."
- "Bride who says she pushed husband off cliff released."
- "Man accused of planning to kidnap, eat children."
- "6.6 million children under 5 died last year."
- "Report will show chemical weapons use."
- "Suicide bomber kills 21 at a funeral in northern Iraq."
- "Catholic priest sentenced to 50 years for child porn."
- "Man who burned woman's corpse charged with rape."

I have no way to process this information. Nor do I want to. I wonder, with a daily news diet like this, what are we doing to our collective psyches? We need to focus on what's uplifting in our world and in our lives. Some days, with horror and trauma coming at us from all directions, it feels like keeping that focus is almost impossible.

Patrick's Facebook Post: Shhh . . . don't tell anyone. I love my life.

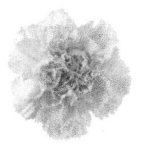

SEPTEMBER 15, 2013

GEORGE CLOONEY

Oh, my gosh. This is kind of embarrassing. For some reason—I've no idea where this came from—last night I dreamt I was out with George Clooney, *the* George Clooney.

We were at a fancy cocktail party with hundreds of movie stars. I didn't know a soul, other than George. Sounds exciting but he kept disappearing. The last time he left me stranded on a grand, sweeping staircase. In the disjointed way that dreams make perfect sense, I found George crouched in a coat closet. He was gnawing on chicken wings.

I said, "You were rude to leave me like that."
He said, "I needed to hide from all the gawking guests."
I said, "I want you to take me home."

CUT.
I see heads shaking. You cannot believe I told George Clooney, *the* George Clooney, to take me home.

NEXT SCENE:
Somehow we ended up in a bedroom. We ended up in a bed. Me and George Clooney. And, in this unbelievable dream, we did the deed. Then darn. I woke up. Right in the middle of our private little orgy.

I told a friend about my dream. She said, "All women dream they're in bed with George Clooney. No big deal."

Well, no big deal for her. I, for one, am getting in bed early tonight to dream again. George might be waiting for me and, with luck, we'll pick up where we left off.

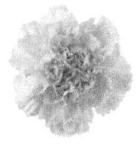

SEPTEMBER 16, 2013

THE MILKMAN

Marisa posts a photo of her house on Instagram and writes, "Sometimes Keith and I joke that it feels like we've time traveled with this Seattle move, but I'm not sure what year to say it is. We have one shower for the four of us, little doorways, creaky floors, random light switches downstairs that turn lights on upstairs, high speed internet, and now, a milkman."

kikishivers: Thumbs down on one shower. Thumbs up on the milkman.

chiamy: Love that you have milkman! That's hilarious! Wish he delivered to Encinitas!

suzyj6: I'm so jealous of that milkman!

I remember the milkman, the Fuller Brush man, the knife-sharpening man, and the Encyclopedia Britannica man. Memories are tumbling all over my page. Each one cries, "Pick me! Pick Me!"

I remember competing at hopscotch. For a long time it was my favorite game.

I remember climbing to the highest branch in our big, old fig tree and singing, so the neighbors could hear, "On top of old Smokey all covered with snow, I lost my true lover for courtin' too slow." I thought Smokey was a train engine and I had no idea what courtin' was.

I remember making up skits and dances and putting folding chairs on the patio for my one-woman talent shows. The show stopper was my rendition of a Patti Page song:

How much is that doggie in the window?

The one with the waggly tail,

How much is that doggie in the window?

I do hope that doggie's for sale.

In addition to being producer and star, I was also the concessionaire. I sold home-popped popcorn, with butter, for five cents. The price of admission was ten cents.

I remember running up and down mounds of dirt in the torn up lot in our backyard, building forts with rocks and cardboard boxes, and yelling, "Davy Crockett, King of the Wild Frontier."

I remember how good it felt to lie, spread-eagled, on warm cement with sunshine burning on my back.

I remember the first one-act play I wrote, "The End for All." One by one, each of the characters (portrayed by my neighborhood friends) ended up dead in the middle of my living room floor.

I remember listening to conversations on our telephone party line. It was fun because we weren't supposed to eavesdrop.

I remember walking home from school at lunchtime for mom's homemade vegetable-beef soup and her homemade apricot pie.

I remember Moon Fairies, a game I made up. My friends and I played it in my front yard after sundown. We sat on the porch steps and took turns doing cartwheels on the grass. When someone spotted the headlights of an oncoming car, we had to run and hide behind a bush or a tree or a telephone pole.

Mortals weren't allowed to see Moon Fairies. When the car and its passengers, unaware of the night's hidden creatures, drove out of sight, it was safe for us to come out again.

Yes, I remember the era of the milkman. Just yesterday, really, yet it seems like a long time ago.

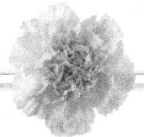

FALL 2013

In fall, nature reflects on itself and summons acceptance.

—DEDE RANAHAN

FROM CALIFORNIA

When Pat was in college on the East Coast, his friend Gary Thompson, was living on the West Coast. Gary was homesick for the fall colors of his native Michigan, so Pat mailed him a package of New England leaves. After Pat died, sorting through two cardboard boxes that contained the sum of his earthly possessions, I found Gary Thompson's book of poems. Suddenly, perusing Gary's work, I stopped breathing. In 1999, he'd dedicated the poem on page 49 of his book to Pat. Slow-streaming tears tempered the rest of my day. I share Gary's poem here with his permission.

Your package of east coast
autumn leaves arrived
just as my life
needed connection to the seasonal
reds of my earliest falls
in Michigan.
I confess, young migratory friend,
the western dogwood beside my porch
is a stunning welcome
flame,
but I miss the maples more
each November spent

here where mostly oafish yellow bigleaf
and tiny imitations
drop their uninspired leaves.
I like to say maple,
my grandpa's eastern kind: mountain, silver,
red, and best of all—the sugar
he coddled as a seedling
and loved until the budless spring
he died. Later, in forbidden Snow
Woods, I gathered red leaves
in my lunch box, afterlives
I spirited home in the childhood dusk.
Your airmailed leaves spill from a basket on my desk; my thoughts
blow east. I'll send along a single heart-
shaped California
redbud leaf I've kept around
to ignite a day,
a fragile western find I found
might make me cry.

—GARY THOMPSON
ON JOHN MUIR'S TRAIL
BEAR STAR PRESS 1999

FOR PATRICK RANAHAN

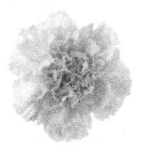

SEPTEMBER 18, 2013

AGING CAN WAIT

Morning:

I'm in the Orchard Creek parking lot. I'm looking for the blood bank's mobile van. I have a 9:30 a.m. appointment to give blood, but I see no mobile van anywhere. Do I have the wrong day? I call the 800 number for the blood bank. It's 10:00 a.m. and the message says, "It's after regular office hours."

I call another 800 number. A real person answers. "I'm sorry. I don't know the van schedule."

She puts me on hold to check the calendar. "You have the right day," she says. "The van had a flat tire this morning. That's why it isn't there."

Thank goodness. Glad to know it's the van and not me.

Evening:

I'd planned to attend a physician's lecture tonight about aging and what to expect. I'm not at that presentation, however. Something's come up. Earlier today I found a copy of *Mockingjay* in the library. It's the third and final book in the *Hunger Games* series. I'm already on page 58.

Marisa sent a text this afternoon. "Do you still have the copy of *Catching Fire* we gave you? Sam's decided he wants it back."

I send a reply text. "You're in luck, Sam. I still have the book and I'll mail it back to you. We *Hunger Games* fans have to stick together."

Aging can wait.

Patrick's Facebook Post: Well, I've been wrestling with my power cord for 45 minutes and it's not charging my computer. About to lose power so if you don't hear from me for a while, you know why.

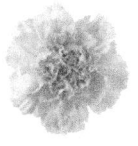

SEPTEMBER 19, 2013

REAL CHANGE IN THE AIR?

Good news in the paper this morning. Pope Francis is making sense. I've not experienced this much emotion about the Catholic Church since the day I walked out of mass 37 years ago.

During the sermon that day, an 80-something Irish priest—from the old country—ranted on and on about birth control. In a thick brogue he declared, "Birth control is a mortal sin. Women are made to have children. Lots of children. Women cannot deny the will of God."

I glanced down the pew at my four tow-headed offspring—Patrick Sean, Megan Kathleen, Marisa Elizabeth, and Kerry Colleen. Every day I felt overwhelmed—torn between being the mother I aspired to be, and being the mother I had the stamina to be. My husband was no longer attending mass. Finding four matching pairs of shoes and socks, blankies, the prerequisite stuffed animals, and getting four reluctant little kids to the church on time, was a struggle week after week. The old priest's blathering on about birth control was my tipping point. In that moment, I lost all connection to the church I'd been born into. I was done.

"Come children," I whispered. "We're leaving."

Alas. A quiet exit was not to be. My little kids toddled down the aisle, bobbing like ducklings behind their mother duck. They chirped in high-pitched voices.

"Mommy, why are we leaving?"

"Mommy, are we going home?"

"Mommy, can we go get donuts?"

I've not been back to mass since. Today, however, Pope Francis delivers a different kind of sermon. He says, according to the *Sacramento Bee,* "The Catholic Church cannot focus so much on gay marriage, contraception, and abortion. The moral structure of the church will fall, like a house of cards, if it doesn't find a better balance.

"Religion has the right to express its opinion in the service of the people, but God, in creation, has set us free—it's not possible to interfere spiritually in the life of a person.

"A person once asked me, in a provocative manner, if I approved of homosexuality. I replied with another question. 'Tell me, when God looks at a gay person, does he endorse the existence of this person with love, or reject and condemn this person?' We must always consider the person."

When asked who he is, the Pope says, "I am a sinner."

Whether the Pope's humanity will filter down to the diocesan level, remains to be seen. Whether rigid church doctrines will catch up with the human condition isn't clear. But, for the first time in years, I feel a God-like presence in the pope who's leading the Catholic Church.

I'm not returning to the church or to mass, but I'll pray that real change is happening. And I haven't prayed, in the Catholic sense, in a long, long time.

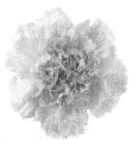

SEPTEMBER 20, 2013

WHO'S ON FIRST?

A woman from the blood bank leaves a message on my answering machine. "We're sorry for the mix up the other day. Thank you for your donation a few months ago. We have a location in Roseville. We're hoping you'll come in there. We won't be in Lincoln again until December. Thank you and have a great day."

My confidence in this organization is not as strong as before. Are they good stewards of blood donations? Are there problems in management? Is our misconnect a random occurrence? I'll give them another chance in December.

Meanwhile, the ladies' bridge group is here. It's my turn to hostess. We're waiting for a member who's always on time. I call her to see if she's coming.

"Is this you, Dede? I went to the wrong house. I had to come back home to find your address. I'll be right there."

Jazzy strolls through the living room. One of the ladies pulls a small, smooth stone out of her pocket. "I don't like cats," she says, "especially black cats." She rubs the rock until Jazzy disappears into my bedroom.

Another woman, whom I've met a half dozen times, is calling me "Betty." I'm embarrassed to correct her. We haven't started playing bridge, yet. When we do, I know we'll forget which suit is trump, whose turn it is to deal, what our partners bid, where we're supposed to sit—Table One or Table Two—and where we left our drinking glasses.

Good thing representatives from the blood bank aren't here. They might begin to question the quality of my blood donation. They might decide to give me one more chance in December.

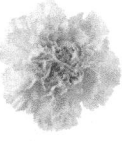

SEPTEMBER 21, 2013

SILENCE

A quiet, rainy day. If someone were to walk into my home right now, they'd hear silence. The TV's turned off. The radio's turned off. The washing machine and the dishwasher are idle. When I left my marriage, I felt uncomfortable with silence. No one in my house, besides me, made noise. No one said, "Let's go to a movie," or asked, "What shall we do tomorrow?" No other voice responded to mine.

At first, I felt lonely, very lonely, even when I was out and about. In the grocery store, for example, I'd hear other people talking to each other.

"Shall we get apples and bananas?"

"Does that recipe need basil or oregano?"

"Let's have soup on Monday and fish on Tuesday."

No one was asking me about menus for the week or about having pork chops versus lamb chops. All I heard were my own thoughts. Shall I have salmon for dinner? It's on sale. Sounds like a good idea.

Over time, however, something unexpected happened. I grew used to silence. I welcomed it. I craved it when I found myself in angry gatherings filled with too many grating voices and too many clashing opinions.

I'm sitting at my desk in my small, quiet haven. I'm watching raindrops slide down the window pane. I'm thinking. I'm reflecting. I'm listening to the inner core that is my soul.

Stillness swaddles me like a warm blanket as I soak in the hush of a soft, rainy day.

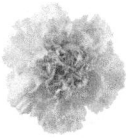

SEPTEMBER 22, 2013

OLD AND CRANKY

Wow. I'm getting old and cranky. I turned off the Emmy Awards. One half-hour was all I could take. What other profession, outside entertainment, has so many narcissistic award shows? Shows that are too frenetic, too cheesy, too political, too much run by the "good old boys." I don't watch television often so I don't know most of the actors receiving awards anyway.

This afternoon, I started reading the novel *Sally of Monticello* by N.M. Ledgin. The author recounts the 38-year affair between Thomas Jefferson and his slave, Sally Hemings.

A quote on the title page: "In reality, the nation should recognize Sally and Thomas as its founding parents and abandon the idea that the United States was a white nation from its inception." Clarence E. Walker, *Mongrel Nation*

This will be an interesting read. Sorry Emmys. You've lost out to a low-tech competitor—a 363 page book. No sleazy jokes. No rambling acceptance speeches. No in-your-face commercials.

No way around it. I admit, without any self-judgment, I'm of another time.

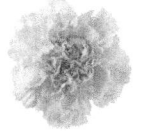

SEPTEMBER 23, 2013

OFF

Ugh. Worst day. I've been at this computer for four-and-a-half hours doing—what else?—paperwork. Paying my bills, Pat's bills, and Mom's bills. I forgot some of my online passwords, IDs, and pin numbers and had to prove I am my own self to get into my accounts. I needed to get info from my dear brother, Jim, in order to add him to a Power of Attorney document.

He calls. He's not happy. "I don't like giving out my Social Security number, my address, my work address, or any of the rest of it. Why do they need this information, anyway?"

Like I know. I'm simply trying to fill out the damn forms. "It's for our mother," I remind him. "Also, what do you think about an immediate annuity for her? Any thoughts?"

"I want a day or two to think about all this," Jim says. "And I'll research annuities."

This is good. I have a two-day reprieve from filling in the blanks on the POA documents. Maybe Jim will come up with a better idea than annuities.

Pat's here to do his laundry. He needs 10 dollars to buy dog food for Lexi. I ask, "How long will I be paying for dog food?"

Pat shrugs. He's trying to get a restaurant job. His dad is providing the $600 for the dental work he needs.

That's a relief. Do I sound crabby? I do. I am.

I look at all the papers on my desk. I'm shredding this stuff. I'll probably shred something I shouldn't. I don't care. Shredding is therapeutic. Shredding is good for my mental health. I'm turning this computer OFF.

Patrick's Facebook Post: I used to enjoy a can of pork and beans but when you've been staring down a lonely can for two weeks, as a last resort meal, they really lose their appeal. Thanks to my sister, Marisa, for gifting me a new power cord for my computer so I'm back online. And thanks to all my generous friends who have offered to send food, money, cook me dinner, send uplifting messages, etc. Feeling Grateful! I get by with a little help from my friends.

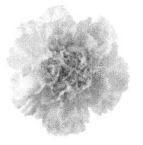

SEPTEMBER 24, 2013

HELENA

I'm having lunch with Helena, the woman who came in anguish to the last family mental illness support group meeting. She's invited me to her home. Helena's whole house is shades of white—white carpet, white furniture, white pillows, white floral arrangements, white artwork, and mirrors suspended in white frames. Her Himalayan kitty is white and sleeping on a white crocheted throw on a white chair.

I'm feeling underdressed in my jean capris and t-shirt top. Helena is dressed in a white jersey top and white slacks with tasteful jewelry. She's wearing white flats. She's proud of her home and shows me around.

"Everything's beautiful," I tell her.

"Thank you. When I lived in Europe, I decorated all my friends' houses."

We sit down at the dining room table, which glitters with white candles and crystal and white floral napkin rings. Helena serves a chicken-and-rice main dish and a salad artfully arranged on a side plate. She begins her story.

"I'm an orphan. My mother suffered from complications of childbirth and bled to death. My father didn't know how to care for an infant and he placed me in an orphanage. It was 1940 and he left to join partisans in the mountains. Later he was captured and forced to work underground for four years without seeing the light of day. In 1944, he was released but he was frail and didn't survive.

"I hoped one day the door of the orphanage would open and someone would enter and call out my name. But no one ever came for me. I remained in the orphanage until I was fifteen. Then I was sent away to a dormitory to be schooled as a nurse focusing on sports medicine.

"I didn't own anything, but some money from my grandfather allowed me to buy a bicycle. I was so happy. I was rich because I could ride my bicycle and not have to walk everywhere. I was also naive. I couldn't afford to buy a lock and someone stole my only means of transportation."

In her early twenties, Helena met the handsome young man who would become her husband for twenty-four years. "He was an artist. People thought he was eccentric as many artists are. After a while, I realized something was wrong and, as time progressed, his voices became more disquieting. It was clear that he was suffering from schizophrenia.

"When I was forty-seven, I finally got permission to take a vacation to Italy with my teenage son and daughter. It was our secret for six months that we planned to defect. I needed freedom from communism and freedom from my husband. When we crossed the border into Austria, we knelt on the ground and gave thanks. I went immediately to the authorities and asked for political asylum. We lived in a refugee camp, sharing one room with twenty-seven other people. After three years, I was considered legally divorced.

"I went to the American embassy several times to ask for permission to emigrate to the United States. I always wore my one dress and makeup—to look nice. At first, I was denied because I didn't speak English and didn't appear to be employable. But I persisted and, at last, we were allowed to come here.

I came with my two children, our few clothes, and not a penny of my own."

In time, Helena learned English and procured employment in an assisted living facility. She pauses. She looks at her surroundings. "I wanted quiet and peace for myself. A place to feel free and to be who I am. I've always known who I am inside—even when I was in the orphanage. I enjoy each day here. Each moment. I never close the shutters because I've had enough darkness in my life. I'm calm today. Not like I am when my son is here."

Helena doesn't understand why, after everything she's lived through, she also bears the sorrow of having two adult children ill with schizophrenia. "It's better in Europe for people like my son and daughter. They give them medicine and allow them to work. Here, a diagnosis of mental illness makes it extremely difficult to be hired and remain employed."

Helena's son lives in low-income housing. He comes to her home for a week once a month. He can be troublesome and abusive, and sometimes she's afraid of him.

"Should you allow your son to come here?"

"I have to. I'm all he has and I know how it feels to have no door open to you. I can't close my door to him."

Helena thinks she may have enough money to stay in her rented home for a couple more years. "I may have to move and find a two-bedroom apartment for my son and me to live in. I may have to look for a job. I could hostess in a restaurant."

At 73, Helena's a beautiful woman proud of maintaining her figure and her appearance. She shows me several photos of herself, spanning 20 years, wearing the same white dress. "I love that dress and that I can still wear it. I made it myself. Maybe I'll ask to buried in it."

Two hours fly by. Helena has an appointment at the bank in half an hour. Her investments aren't doing well and she's not happy. "I'm asking for some changes," she says.

I hug Helena goodby. "You're a strong, brave, wonderful woman."

As I walk down the steps to my car, I blink back my tears.

Patrick's Facebook Post: Thanks Dad for helping me out with a dental appointment. This morning, I pulled a piece of tooth from the inside of my lower gum. Guess this is what they mean when they say "getting long in the tooth." A huge thank you to Daniel Pettegrew for a very generous gift in a time of extreme need. Hard to ask for help but blown away when it arrives.

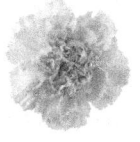

SEPTEMBER 26, 2013

A PLEASANT DAY

Got a haircut and bought a little table at Home Goods for twenty-nine dollars. At Trader Joe's, I purchased two jars of their Lavender Salt Scrub. It's made with apricot kernel oil, almond oil, green tea leaf, avocado oil, Vitamin E, and lavender oil. Love the stuff.

Now, I'm delivering groceries to Mom. I climb over a three-foot patio wall to stack the groceries on her patio and then walk around, through the back gate, to let myself in her front door.

"Some new people moved in," she says. "They're from Lincoln Hills. They play bridge. Do you know them?"

I don't recognize their names.

"He's an interesting fellow. He always sits next to me and pats my hand. If I move my hand, he pats my leg. Yesterday, he stopped me in the hallway to tell me what beautiful white hair I have. He's making me nervous. I don't think he knows how old I am. Next time I see him, I'll tell him I'm ninety-five. That should do it."

I stop at Kerry's to see her newly painted house. Every room is grey except for two special rooms. Regan's room is pink. Ayla's room is lavender. Fresh paint is comforting, clean, and neat. Now Kerry wants to change the carpet and the tile floors. That's the problem with new paint. One thing leads to another.

Home again. The little table works perfectly next to the chaise in my bedroom. It fits under the shutters when I open them with 1/8 inch to spare. I'm settling in to watch a documentary on TV about wild turkeys and enjoying a bowl of my own homemade chili. It's a slow cooker recipe using ground chicken instead of beef.

All in all, a pleasant day.

Patrick's Facebook Post: Went to Walmart at 5:30 this morning to avoid the usual demographic and had a fairly pleasant shopping experience. Clerk who rang me up said, as he handed me the receipt, "Survey on the back. Be sure to tell them how badly we treated you today." And he said it perfectly politely with a huge smile but as I walked out to the parking lot and the lights suddenly went off, I thought to myself that there was something sinister about that.

SEPTEMBER 27, 2013

TODAY'S NEWS/TOMORROW'S REWRITE

NASA's Mars Rover, Curiosity, finds no signs of life on Mars because it finds no methane, a gas that is considered the possible calling card of microbes. On the other hand, it's found unlimited supplies of water. The surface soil is two percent water, meaning every cubic foot contains around two pints that could be extracted to sustain earthling pioneers.

Voyager I, launched in 1977, is the first spacecraft to exit the solar system and enter interstellar space. It's 11.7 billion miles from Earth and hurtling away at 38,000 mph.

On the ground, in a meeting at the United Nations, there's a motion to oversee the removal of chemical weapons from Syria. The president of the US and the new president of Iran speak to each other for 15 minutes on the phone—the first high level contact for these two countries since 1979.

Knowledge of the universe, like the universe itself, is expanding. Historical events keep unfolding. We may not really know what's happening today until 50 years in the future with a contextual look back. Today's good guy is tomorrow's bad guy. Today's hero is tomorrow's fallen hero. What we deem factual this moment may be upended the next, i.e., eggs were bad for us and then they weren't.

At 69, there's one thing I know. The older I get, the less I know for sure.

Patrick's Facebook Post: Needles in the mouth, power tools in the mouth, $625 out of pocket, whole face completely numb. A day at the dentist.

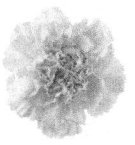

SEPTEMBER 28, 2013

BEFORE AND AFTER

You never know what a day will bring. I'm at duplicate bridge. There's a commotion on the opposite side of the room. I see an elderly man on the floor. People are clustering around him. The club president, a retired doctor, is bending over him.

I don't know this man's name. I'm guessing he's in his late 80s or early 90s. Reports are making their way across the room. He tripped on the back leg of his chair and fell. The paramedics are coming. Everyone seems calm, including the gentleman and his wife. Caution is the order of the day. You have to be cautious at this man's age. You don't know when a little injury might turn into a big deal.*

The paramedics arrive. They're taking their time checking the man out. He has a broken shoulder and a broken hip. They're loading him onto a gurney. We all applaud as they push him out the door. He smiles and waves. His wife follows.

The rest of us resume our bridge game. That's what you do, living each day in a retirement community. You get used to people falling, ambulance sirens, and paramedics. You get used to watching friends and acquaintances, who are fine one minute, being transported to the hospital the next.

One day, you know it will be your turn. Something will happen that alters your projection. There's a major shift and then events will be referenced as "before" or "after." Your life, as it was, versus the way it is now.

I'm trying to get my ducks in a row. I've got my prepaid cremation plan. I really, really need to update my living trust. And mom's living trust. Today is Saturday. Tomorrow is Sunday. Mine might be a whole new story.

*Several months after this incident, the man died from complications due to his injuries.

Patrick's Facebook Post: Every once in a while, you meet someone who shakes you to your core with their authenticity and beauty. And the more you get to know them, the deeper your affection grows. And time goes on, and the mystery continues to surprise you and delight you. Hold on to these people. Cultivate these relationships. They are rare and priceless.

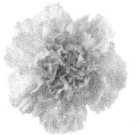

SEPTEMBER 29, 2013

ODDS AND ENDS

I'm updating my library list with new additions:

Levels of Life by Julian Barnes
Sister Mother Husband Dog: (Etc.) by Delia Ephron
David and Goliath by Malcom Gladwell

This Is the Story of a Happy Marriage by Ann Patchett
Zealot by Reza Aslan
Quiet by Susan Cain
The Immortal Life of Henrietta Lacks by Rebecca Skloot
The Casual Vacancy by J.K. Rowling
Still Foolin' 'Em by Billy Crystal
A House in the Sky by Amanda Lindhout
Devotion: A Memoir by Dani Shapiro
I Am Malala by Malala Yousafzai

Weather reports say there's a 40 percent chance of light rain this evening. I'm fertilizing the front and backyards with a shake-and-feed granule fertilizer, the third time this year I've fertilized, and I think it's making a difference. The trees and shrubs are looking greener and fuller.

This evening, I'm having dinner with Joan and checking in to see how she's doing since Beryl passed. She thinks she's going to be okay financially. She's taking pleasure in her pet-sitting business. "I love being with the animals."

I show Joan how to download the Instagram app onto her cell phone. We hover over our smartphones like two techies. Like two techies who know what they're doing.

Patrick's Facebook Post: Got my inner Chicano on at the Latin Food and Music Festival with old friend Carlos Elizalde and Ruckatan, Latin Tribe.

SEPTEMBER 30, 2013

WORTH A TRY

Here we go again. CNN has a clock counting down until the government shutdown tonight. And, in two weeks, we'll be facing another standoff over the debt ceiling.

This is a dangerous routine. When the government cries "wolf" too many times, the public tunes out. Then, really irresponsible government actions take place. The media, of course, doesn't help. Everything is reported at high decibels. Viewer crisis-fatigue sets in. The true bad news is that it didn't rain today. No rain is expected in the next 10 days, either. My fertilizing efforts languish in the warm fall sun.

Meanwhile, I'm making plans for babysitting Regan and Ayla tomorrow evening while Kerry and David go out for an anniversary dinner. I'm thinking up a recipe for gummy worm cookies in honor of October and Halloween, and in honor of the fact that Ayla loves gummy worms. I think we'll put green sprinkles, for grass, on warm sugar cookies. Then we'll add gummy worms inching through the grass, as many per cookie as we want. We don't have to negotiate. We don't have to compromise.

Maybe we should send these cookies to Congress and to the president. Then everyone would be happy and would agree to work together. It couldn't hurt.

Patrick's Facebook Post: The Latin Food and Music festival yesterday in Sacramento was being patrolled by a cute officer with a ponytail and her partner, Officer J. Walker. I kid you not. His name was J. Walker. Can't make this stuff up.

OCTOBER 1, 2013

TOO MUCH FUN

I'm with Regan and Ayla. First, we eat hamburgers and fries. Then Regan does her addition and subtraction homework and I check. Now, we're into cookie making. Sugar cookies are baking and we're waiting to decorate them with sprinkles and gummy worms.

While the cookies are baking, Regan and Ayla are eating the sprinkles. They have to test all the colors. In between, we talk about whatever comes to mind. There are no filters.

Regan says, "I call my father 'Dad' or 'Daddy.'"

I ask, "What do you call your mother?"

Ayla answers, "Muba."

"No," I protest. "You don't call your mother, 'Muba.'"

"Muba, Muba, Muba." Ayla's laughing. This is very funny.

Regan has a question. "Where are your mommy and daddy, Mim?"

"Well, you know GG. She's my mother."

"Where's your father?"

"My father's passed away. He's in heaven."

Regan pauses. "I wish I'd met him."

"You'd have liked him and he'd have liked you. I called him 'Pop.'"

Regan pauses again. "Some Grandpas are Papa and some are Pop."

Ayla's into it. "Papa Poppy Papa Poppy Mim Mimmy Mim Mimmy." This is very funny.

The first tray of cookies is out of the oven. We let them cool a few minutes, but it's hard to wait. Time to put on the sprinkles. Time to pour on the sprinkles. You can't have too many sprinkles on one cookie.

My vision—gummy worms wriggling though green grass— appears to be rather pedestrian. Instead, these gummy worms are cavorting in green, blue, pink, yellow, and orange grass. Some are doing back bends on their cookies. Some are standing on their heads. Some are burrowing through cookies and coming out the other side.

We're making a big mess. We see sprinkles on the floor. Sprinkles in our hair. Sprinkles on the dog. And when we're in our pajamas and reading *Duck Duck Goose*, we find sprinkles in our bed. This is very funny.

"Good night, Ayla." "Goodnight, Regan." Sometimes life is simply too much fun.

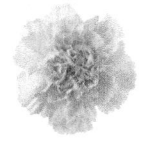

OCTOBER 2, 2013

THE GRANDMA DRAWER

This morning I'm at the Snap It Up thrift shop which is opening October 9. I'm volunteering to work in the store once a week. Proceeds from the shop will benefit FieldHaven's kitty rescue organization. I'm in the back room pricing and tagging clothes. Some are ready to display and some need steaming. Stained and torn items go into a Goodwill bag.

Boxes of clothes and knickknacks are arriving faster than I can sort through them. I'll have nightmares about this. I have a recurring dream about stuff. I'm trying to get somewhere and clothes and toys, that I have to pack, fly at me from all directions and I can never finish. In this store, stuff is coming from every which way while I'm awake. I'll be glad when I'm working the cash register on the shop's out-the-door side.

Two child-size leather purses catch my attention. They're $2 each and perfect for the Grandma drawer in my den. My grandchildren know this special drawer is for them. There they find games, crayons, coloring books, puzzles, hats, magnifying glasses, and stuffed animals. The Grandma drawer needs continual replenishing so it doesn't get boring. It may become one of Snap It Up's best customers.

Patrick's Facebook Post: Thank you Brandi for my first official Rapbay Urbanlife delivery. Enjoying the tasty treats. Delicious! You're so kind.

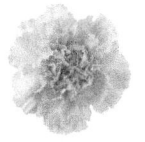

OCTOBER 4, 2013

NAPS

It's windy today and my allergies are kicking in. Antihistamines aren't helping my stuffy nose and itchy eyes. The pills make me sleepy, so I'm about to take a nap on the chaise in my bedroom. It feels decadent to fall asleep in a chair in the middle of the day—like I'm cheating or something. My neighbor takes naps. Friends come late to dinner because, "We fell asleep." Some couples I know take naps together every day.

I never used to take naps. There was no time with little kids and jobs. A nap is a perk of being retired. Or perhaps, napping is simply an innate part of aging. Teenagers take naps. Toddlers take naps. Babies nap all the time. I'm growing backward.

As I drift off, I note my backyard. I think about the birds, lizards, frogs, bees, trees, and shrubs that share my private patch of earth. I give thanks for the sunshine streaming in the window, for the freedom to sleep without fear, for the black kitty purring at my side, for the air I'm breathing in and out, for the chance to dream in the afternoon . . .

Patrick's Facebook Post: The love keeps pouring in. Thanks Lara for the generous and thoughtful surprise in the mail today.

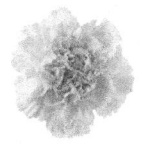

OCTOBER 5, 2013

COURAGE

This week I've learned of four friends diagnosed with cancer—brain cancer, breast cancers, and lymphoma. Three of these friends are my age. One is in her early fifties. Their stalwart reactions move me—acceptance of the situation, determination to meet challenges head on, and energy focused on best possible outcomes. Another word for all this might be "courage."

My colleagues are showing their mettle. They're making preparations. They're reviewing medical procedures and options. They're being honest and humble. They intend to keep things as "normal" as possible. I'm sure they have their moments, in the middle of the night, when they feel overwhelmed and frightened. In the daylight, however, they're sending wishes for a beautiful fall season and for happy holidays ahead.

My friends are making me proud to be old, and showing the heights we can reach when danger looms large and nothing is certain.

OCTOBER 6, 2013

PARALYSIS

Back to square one. It looks like an annuity is out of the picture for my mother. At 95, we've decided we don't want to tie up her funds in a format she can't access right away if necessary. My brother asked his financial adviser for suggestions. He had no recommendations other than CDs or money market accounts.

Today's best money market rate is .90%. Today's best one-year CD rate is 1.05%. These rates are pitiful. Maybe this is a good time to stand still and not get caught in the middle of a Washington stalemate over funding the government or raising the debt ceiling.

Who knows how all this will fall out? It's beginning to feel like we're living in some kind of horror movie. No one can tell the good guys from the bad guys, or if any good guys are left. And no one knows how the movie will end. Maybe it's ending already. Maybe the ending is paralysis—like what I'm feeling right now.

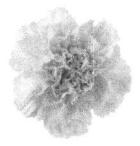

OCTOBER 7, 2013

GOOD ENOUGH FOR GUESTS

It's fall. I'm thinking of my slow cooker and comfort food. Time for tomato basil soup, Father Greco stew, and garlic mashed potatoes. Time for the bouquet of cranberries simmering in brandy and allspice, and pumpkin bars just out of the oven.

Friends say they used to like to cook, but now, not so much. And they say, as a result, they're not eating nutritious meals. For myself, I'm collecting healthy recipes that require little fuss. This recipe meets that standard—good for breakfast, lunch or dinner.

One English muffin split and toasted
Mustard—favorite kind
Canadian bacon slices
Fuji or Envy apple slices
Swiss cheese slices

Place toasted muffin halves, cut side up, on an uncreased baking sheet. Spread with mustard. Layer with Canadian bacon, apple slices, and cheese. Broil for six or seven minutes until the cheese is melted and bubbly. Serve with grape garnishes or orange wedges.

My preference is for simple recipes good enough for guests. And good enough for me when I'm the only guest at my table.

Patrick's Facebook Post: Richard Quest is one of the most annoying correspondents on CNN.

OCTOBER 8, 2013

AGE CALCULATOR

According to an online age calculator, today I'm 69 and 139 days old. I've lived 25,341 days, 3,260 weeks and one day, and 8.33.03 months. Maybe that's why, this evening, I can hardly move. I worked for four hours at the FieldHaven thrift shop this morning. Standing the whole time, I sorted, priced, and placed items on hangers and shelves. My feet were screaming, "What are you doing?" When I got home, I took an aspirin and sat down.

Most days I tell myself I'm younger than I am. Might need to rethink this. Next Tuesday, when I'm at the thrift shop, I'll be working the cash register. I'll find a stool to sit on and then walk around, in between sales, to stretch. Don't want customers mistaking me for one of the antiques.

By next week, I'll be 69.40 years old. The age calculator doesn't stop.

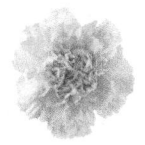

OCTOBER 9, 2013

IN THE BIG SCHEME OF THINGS

There's a message on my answering machine from the window washing folks. It's a woman's voice.

"Hi. We have a problem with your appointment tomorrow. I usually come and work with my husband but I have another job and the person who was supposed to take my place has called in sick, so I can't help clean your windows. I hope we can reschedule. We have five children and, with this business and my other work, it gets a little hectic."

This husband and wife do a great job on windows, screens, tracks, and shower doors. They're running a special for $59— about $40 less than what others are charging. I call the woman back. We reschedule for a week from tomorrow. I hear children in the background. I hear fatigue in this mother's voice.

"Thank you for rescheduling," she says.

"No problem," I say.

"See you next week."

It seems moms and dads are stringing multiple jobs together to take care of their families. In the big scheme of things, my dirty windows are insignificant.

OCTOBER 10, 2013

CONVERSATIONS

I call my friend Irene. Her MS is progressing. Eddie, her husband, is undergoing radiation treatments for a brain tumor. He also needs a kidney transplant. As usual, Irene is philosophical and upbeat.

"We're doing what the doctors tell us and trying to enjoy each day."

Pat calls. "I can't come over to do laundry because I don't have enough gas. Have you made a payment to the bankruptcy attorney for me this month?"

"No. I won't make another payment until the monthly bills I'm paying for you are under five hundred dollars. How's the job search?"

"Nothing."

"You made four hundred dollars a month last year dog-walking."

"I don't want to do that again."

"I have a couple coming out here next week to wash my windows. They have five children and need the income. They probably don't want to wash windows, but they're doing what they have to do."

"I don't want to have this conversation." Click.

Some conversations go more smoothly than others.

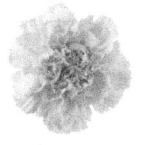

OCTOBER 11, 2013

GETTING IT

Random comments at the Family Mental Illness Support Group Meeting:

"My son's an alcoholic, but I think he has mental health issues, also. He won't see a doctor to get a diagnosis."

"My daughter was sentenced to eighty days of community service for a rear-ender. I wrote a letter to the public defender and the judge to explain that carrying out this sentence is beyond her capability. In court, the judge had my letter but said he couldn't use it because it hadn't come from the public defender. In the end, the prosecuting attorney and public defender agreed to sentence my daughter to ten days of house arrest. I can make sure she fulfills that sentence."

"My son's entering another cyclic period of his schizophrenia. He's less and less able to handle routine situations. We visit him for maybe thirty minutes and then he has to return to his residence. He won't eat with us. We go to the drive-through and get a hamburger and fries, but he won't eat in the car and saves it for later."

"My son's coping. He's working again and his children are with him during the week. He says he's giving up alcohol. We've given him forty thousand dollars this year."

"My grandson and son both have schizophrenia, and they're living together in an apartment. My son has a job and my grandson's taking classes but isn't working. He says he doesn't want to work. I don't know how long this arrangement will last."

"I've spent fifteen thousand dollars helping my daughter. I can't continue. I'm putting my finances in jeopardy."

"We know our ill children can be manipulative, but it's hard to know when to help and when to say, 'No.' People who haven't lived with mental illness in their families shouldn't make judgements about what I'm doing."

"I'm glad to have this group. I can talk here and know that the rest of you will understand and relate to the decisions I'm making."

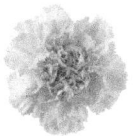

OCTOBER 12, 2013

MISSION ACCOMPLISHED

Yesterday, after sundown and under cover of darkness, I delivered 20 miniature pumpkins—one each to the front door of every neighbor on my street. Today, seven are still where I left them. A few have disappeared. Eight or nine rest in more prominent positions in their yards.

I've done this before. In 1970 in Rochester, Minnesota, my family shared a backyard with eleven other families from all over the globe—Germany, Korea, Australia, France, Mexico, Massachusetts, and Texas. At 3 a.m., I crept from backdoor to backdoor and hung May Day baskets full of flowers, candy, and trinkets—jacks, balls, marbles and stickers—on each doorknob.

In the morning the backyard was buzzing.

"Who did this?"

"Do you know who did this?"

"Did you do this?"

That May Day caper still remains a who-dun-it. Now, the Great Pumpkin has struck on Periwinkle Lane. I hope the over-55 crowd isn't too old to enjoy this. I feel like Ayla and Regan. Sometimes, life is simply too much fun.

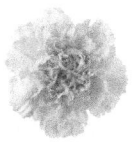

OCTOBER 13, 2013

ALWAYS SOMETHING

Pat leaves a phone message:

"Hi, Mom. A couple of house-related things. It's time to put some foam insulation on the outside water pipes so they don't freeze this winter. I'll install it if we can buy it at Home Depot or Lowe's or something. The floor in the downstairs bathroom is bubbling up in spots and looks like water is leaking underneath it from the toilet. We should probably have someone take a look at it, but I don't think they'll be able to tell what it is without tearing up the floor. Would it be all right if I did laundry tomorrow? Thanks. Pat"

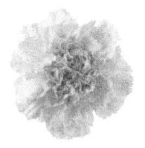

OCTOBER 14, 2013

HOLY MOLEY

I'm at the dentist. With my mouth pried open and packed with dental equipment, the dental hygienist pokes and scrapes and relays pertinent information.

"Your premolars have a nice leaf shape. Your molars have all their bumps. As we age, our teeth move forward, except for a few folks whose teeth move backward. Your teeth are becoming more crowded. They're impinging on your tongue's space and making imprints on it. Have you noticed the change in the shape of your tongue?"

I shake my head. It's hard to talk with a mouth full of metal.

"There's also bone loss around the back molar on the left, which is a wisdom tooth and wisdom teeth behave differently than ordinary teeth. I see from your last visit that the dentist would like to fill about four of your teeth."

"Huh?" I mumble. "I don't remember her telling me I have cavities in four teeth."

"Well, they're not really cavities. They're teeth showing maintenance abrasion, in other words, too much hard pressure brushing. The procedure's to keep the abrasion from getting worse."

"How much?"

"Twelve hundred dollars."

"Is it covered by insurance?"

"You'll have to check at the front desk. Also, it looks like you're snapping your dental floss. You need to slowly insert the floss between your teeth and move it up and down in a zig-zag fashion. Do you sleep with your mouth open?"

"I don't know."

"Well, that probably explains the apparent resistance of the bacteria in your mouth. Saliva pushes bacteria around so they can't do too much damage. But if you're breathing with your mouth open, your mouth is dry and the saliva can't do its job."

I'll try to remember, when I'm asleep, to keep my mouth shut.

"You know, we have an orthodontist here if you want to discuss your teeth moving forward to see if you need orthodontic treatment."

"You're kidding. Braces? At sixty-nine?"

"The consultation is free and she won't push you into anything you don't need."

"I'm not interested. Anything else?"

"Yes, I recommend you use an over-the-counter mouth wash without alcohol because alcohol is drying and we don't want to dry out your mouth more that it already is. And don't use one that will turn your teeth brown like prescription mouthwashes do. I can get the brown color off in your cleaning except in between the places where your teeth are too crowded because you know . . ."

"Yes, I know. My teeth are moving forward."

"See you in six months."

Maybe. I'm heading home. Sooner, rather than later, I'll probably put alcohol in my mouth. And I'm not talking about the alcohol in my mouthwash.

Patrick's Facebook Post: She sometimes shits on the carpet, pees on the floor and the couch, chews up and eats anything she can get her teeth on, jumps on me, scratches my face, wakes me up in the middle of the night after I've had three hours of sleep and absolutely has to go outside only to run around and sniff things and not do any business. And still I love her, my crazy dog, Lexi.

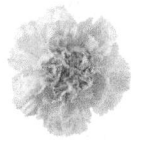

OCTOBER 16, 2013

UNDER CONTROL

The great government shutdown and debt-ceiling crisis of 2013 has been resolved. Sort of. Jack Ohman's political cartoon in the *Sacramento Bee* today captures the situation perfectly.

"We've reached an agreement to create a framework to establish a timetable to pass a bill that allows us to restart talks that will permit this to happen again in a few months . . ."

Couldn't have said it better myself.

Meanwhile, I'm trying to get my own house in order. Yesterday, I replaced cracked rollers in my garage door. Today, I had my windows washed inside and out. I'm looking for someone to clean my gutters. I'm getting estimates to refresh the bark in my front and backyards. Next week, the carpets and the sofa will be cleaned.

Not a fun way to spend money, but taking care of things, as a matter of routine, should limit bigger maintenance problems going forward. And my psyche rests better harboring the delusion that things are under control—which, or course, they never are.

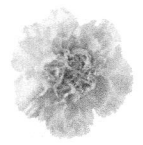

OCTOBER 18, 2013

WILD WOMEN

Yesterday a 96-year-old woman, living here in Sun City with her daughter, locked herself in her bedroom. Her daughter called the police. When they arrived, the elderly woman fired a shot through the bedroom door, missing an officer by inches.

A SWAT team and helicopters were on the scene for thirty minutes. They were able to talk the woman out of the house. She appeared with one hand on her walker and one hand in the air. The 38-caliber handgun was recovered and the woman was taken to the hospital for observation.

Today, a neighbor approaches me for information about my mental illness support group. Her 33-year-old grandson is spiraling out of control and threatening suicide. He can't keep a job, uses drugs and alcohol, and isn't able to abide by the rules in his group home. His family is afraid of him and his mother is caught in the quagmire.

In my experience, mothers are often the one and only hope for their mentally ill children. They hang in with them when the rest of the world writes them off. I have no answers for my neighbor. Our mental health system sucks.

My friend's tragedy is a tragedy for her entire family. If you've not walked in the worn-out shoes of those who are impacted, and if you're judgmental, advise tough love or hint of enabling, you'll see another wild woman—me—go on the rampage.

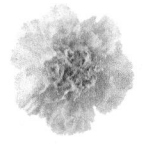

OCTOBER 19, 2013

ONE DAY

Kerry and Marisa are running a 13.1 mile Nike half marathon for breast cancer in San Francisco.

Megan's hiking with her family in Utah's Kolob Canyon.

Pat's working the sound system at Unity Church in Roseville.

GG's attending a tea party in her assisted living facility in Roseville.

I'm playing duplicate bridge in Lincoln.

Four kids.

One mom.

And me.

One day.

OCTOBER 20, 2013

STORIES INSIDE STORIES

I'm taking my Prius in for its 60,000-mile service. The dealership shuttle drops me off at the Galleria Mall while I wait for my car. The shuttle driver tells me to call her when I'm ready to be picked up. Sounds like a plan. The mall doesn't open until 11:00 a.m. and it's 10:30. I find an open entrance next to Pottery Barn. A woman is letting someone inside the store.

"Are you open?"

"No, but we're giving a decorating class and you're welcome to attend."

A sales associate carries a water canister filled with ice, water, and lemon slices out to the desk by the cash register. This is an item I've been thinking about for a while and here it is, right in front of me. And because I'm attending the decorating class, I get a coupon for 10% off anything I buy today. I ask the salesperson to put a water canister and its white porcelain base aside for me while I look around. I love browsing in this store. I enjoy the displays of pillows, candles, artificial flowers, and baskets. As if every home in America looks like this. It's a Norman Rockwell marketing strategy.

I scoot over to Crate & Barrel, which is right next door, to check out their water servers. They have more expensive models but they're not as nice as the one I have on hold at Pottery Barn. This is a shopper's dream. I've found a better buy and I get 10% off. The devil's leading me on. Before going back to pay for the water server, I see white dishes. I'm not looking for white dishes. I don't need white dishes. But dishes and serving ware are two of my guilty pleasures. These dinner plates are labeled a "Best Buy." They're $5.95 each or eight for $41.95. They're oven, micro-wave, and dishwasher proof. They'd look perfect on my table at Christmas. To be an equal opportunity consumer, I buy the plates at Crate and Barrel and head back to Pottery Barn to purchase the water canister. This is turning into a successful shopping trip.

The dealership calls to say my car is ready. They've found some suspicious looking bubbling around the water pump seal. It should be watched.

"How much is the water pump replacement?"

"Four hundred fifty-seven dollars."

"No way."

They're not telling me I can't drive my car off the lot without repair. And a water pump isn't nearly as much fun as a water server and white dinner plates. I call the shuttle driver to tell her I'm ready to be picked up. I get a recording that says, "The shuttle will get to you in the order of your call."

I head over to Nordstrom and sit down on a bench in the entryway between the parking lot and the store. This Nordstrom entrance is where the shuttle driver said she'd pick me up. Half an hour goes by. I call the shuttle service again and get the same recording. I leave another message. I'm in my people-watching mode. A lanky man and a lumpy woman walk through the door.

"I won't wear something like that," she says, "I'm too chunky."

I make up a back story. They're dating. They haven't slept together yet. She's trying to prepare her guy.

Three teenage girls run out the door. One shouts, "There he is. Hey, dude!"

They sprint and scramble into a car. Back Story: The "dude" is the girl's older brother who just got his driver's license. In return for getting to drive the family car, he has to drive his little sister and her friends to the mall.

A Russian family of five charge through the entryway. The mother barks something at the father. Sounds like "$%#!(***". Back story: The husband and wife are fighting over how to spend their money at the mall. She wants to buy a pressure cooker. He wants to buy boots.

A bald man and a long-haired woman enter from the outside door. She races ahead and opens the inside door to the store. "People don't have to open the door for me," she says, "I do it myself." Back story: The woman asked the man to take out the trash this morning and he said, "Do it yourself." She's pissed.

It's two-and-a-half hours since I called the shuttle service. Something's amiss. I call the service tech. I get his cell phone and a recording. I leave a message. I'm tired of people-watching and I'm losing my sense of humor. I call an office number. A perky girl answers.

"Can I help you?"

"I hope so."

I tell her my back story. She puts me on hold. Several minutes later, she comes on the line again. "We're very sorry. The shuttle driver never got your message. She'll be right there."

The shuttle arrives. The driver's apologetic. "It's my third day on the job. I'm so sorry." She apologizes all the way back to the dealership. Inside, the service technician apologizes.

All's well that ends well. I drive back to the mall to pick up my packages. At home, the water server and the white dishes look even better than they did in the stores. I usually hate shopping, but today felt spontaneous and in-the-zone. Next time I go shopping, I'll probably end up buying a new water pump.

Patrick's Facebook Post: I spent a week in my car yesterday. Accepted a ride-share gig to drive a guy to Oregon to bring his daughter to her mother as part of his custody agreement. The ride up, starting at 6 a.m., was narrated all the way by a three-year-old demanding food, water, hand-holding, song-singing, and frequent bathroom stops.

The way back was narrated by a guy (who had a gleam of danger in his eyes) who could not stop talking and would become emotionally agitated every time we saw a policer officer on the road. He pontificated endlessly on how much he hated cops, government, "anything related to social control."

I still hear him babbling. Didn't get home till after 9 p.m. What horrors I have to subject myself to in order to put a few bucks in my pocket. Beware of babblers who can't tolerate silence and who begin almost every thought with, "You know, a lot of people don't know this, but . . ."

If nothing else, the creative material is piling up. I feel a book of short stories coming on.

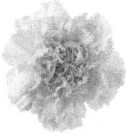

OCTOBER 22, 2013

FASHION SHOWS

It's been 30 years since I've been to a fashion show and, today, I'm at a fashion show put on by community volunteers. Three stores are providing the outfits. The models wear lots of palazzo pants that make everyone look shapeless. Baubles, bangles, and beads remind me of the sixties. Very bohemian.

Ten women are sitting with me at a round table. Four are in long-term marriages. Four are long-term singles. One, who is 70-something, is newly wed. One, who is 70-something, is newly widowed. The circle of life on display in a circle of women.

The woman next to me says, "I hope the show ends soon."

Me, too. I'd like to see a few ensembles put together from the clothing at Snap It Up. At intermission, I ask the woman in charge if they've ever used outfits from a thrift store.

"We don't do that here," she says.

Another 20 minutes and this fashion show will be over, and then I'm good for another 30 years.

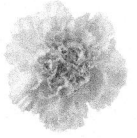

OCTOBER 23, 2013

DISTRACTIONS

This morning I woke up to the sound of someone walking on my roof, the gutter cleaner guy. Talked to a plumber about the faulty garbage disposal in the house GG rents to Pat, and told him to replace it. Now I'm getting ready for the carpet cleaner. I'm moving floor lamps and small tables into the kitchen. With all this home maintenance, my focus is on materials. I'm feeling out of touch with my spiritual side. I take deep breaths and think about how to make cleaning and repairing a meditative exercise. Especially when it's costing me money I'd rather spend on other things.

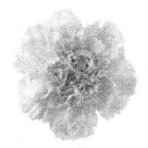

OCTOBER 24, 2013

DAMSEL BRAIDS AND INCHWORMS

Kerry and Regan are attending a Brownie meeting to pack Thanksgiving baskets for people in need, so I'm babysitting Ayla. I pull into Kerry's driveway.

"Boo!"

A pouf of red hair pops out of the shadows.

"Look at the ghosts Mommy hung in our tree. Look at the scary pictures in our window. Want to come in and see our skeleton?"

Inside, Ayla's house isn't as scary as outside. Inside, we're reading books—a Bad Kitty book and a book about a chameleon. While we read, we wear damsel crowns and braids made of corn-yellow yarn and entwined with artificial flowers.

Ayla says, "We must wear them together, Mim."

She looks much prettier in her damsel braid than I do. "It will puff your hair up, Mim, but your hair is shorter than mine so it won't puff it up too much."

We're in the backyard, in our damsel braids, looking for bugs. Right away Ayla spies an inchworm. "I love bugs, Mim. When I grow up, I'm going to work with bugs."

Ayla picks up the inchworm and cradles it in her palm. "This is Bumpy. He's the same worm I found last week."

"The same one?"

"Yes, but this is the real Bumpy."

We pick leaves and grass for Bumpy and throw a couple of pieces of bark into his plastic bowl. Ayla notices a pink flower on a small bush. It looks like a miniature camellia. "Isn't it beautiful, Mim?"

Ayla drops Bumpy on the flower. He's taking a nap.

Still wearing our damsel braids, we're back in the house and using Kerry's iPad. Ayla knows the password. She finds a screen of Halloween games. She's facile. Playing games on iPads is easy—like reading books and finding bugs.

"Show me how to play the games, Ayla."

"It's simple, Mim. Watch me."

I am watching you, Ayla. Watching you is pure joy.

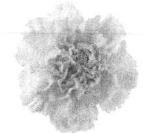

OCTOBER 25, 2013

ODE TO CLEANING

The whole house is torn apart
The furniture's piled high
The ceiling fans whirr overhead
The carpets have to dry.
The cat can't find her litter box
The sofas are still wet
The more I try to clean my house
The messier I get.

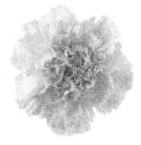

OCTOBER 27, 2013

BUSY DAY

My busy day:

1. I refilled two bird feeders. They've been empty for weeks. The word in the trees is, "Don't bother with that house on Periwinkle Lane. Food's good when you can get it, but the management's unreliable."
2. I put the house back together from the carpet cleaning.
3. I took my evening walk early since it's getting dark sooner. I was happy to note that most of the pumpkins are still where I placed them.
4. And finally, I bought it. Something I've been thinking of buying for a long time. I'll only use this item when it's pitch black outside. I have to work up my nerve and listen to my give-a-shit self and then maybe, maybe I'll say what I've done. Stay tuned . . .

OCTOBER 28, 2013

GRAVITY

Went with my friend Kaye to see *Gravity*. My favorite line in the film is when Sandra Bullock's character says, "I hate space." She's having a really bad day in the universe.

I'm sore and out of shape. Kaye is older than I am and looks great. She gives me the phone number of her personal trainer, Deanne. She can show me what gym equipment to use and how to use it. Paying for a personal trainer isn't in my budget. But being out of shape isn't in my budget, either. This is preventative care.

I know I won't stick with a workout routine unless someone expects me to show up. Deanne will expect me to show up. The time's come. I'm out of excuses and gravity makes things fall. Improving my strength and flexibility is important.

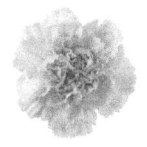

OCTOBER 29, 2013

ANIMAL SANCTUARY

My friend Grace and I are at the Folsom Zoo Sanctuary. The emphasis is on sanctuary. The animals, about 90 of them, are rescued. They're not forced to appear if they don't feel like it. An attendant says, "They can't choose their food or where they sleep, so we let them choose where they want to be within their space."

It's overcast today and some cages seem empty. Time to stay inside perhaps?

A declawed mountain lion, rescued from a family keeping it as a pet, strides back and forth.

A raven sits alone. The attendant explains. "The other ravens were picking on her so we had to isolate her for her own protection. She's very sweet. We talk to her and spoil her."

A tiger is sleeping. A sign on the cage says, "There are more tigers in captivity in the US than remain in the wild."

Peacocks and chickens roam about the grounds with us. A feral cat cage houses four residents. The information says, "An estimated 40 million feral cats live in the US. Their average life span is two years. An indoor cat can live 14 years or longer."

A bear is rooting on the ground for insects. He ignores the fruits and vegetables mounded nearby.

Two condors, a male and female, share an "apartment." Both were found injured and are retired to this compound. The male rebounded from his injuries but suffers from arthritis.

A restless coyote, Maggie, paces in circles. She's anxious. An attendant says, "She's too tame to survive in the wild. She's too wild to be in a cage."

A macaw monkey drinks from a pond. He sometimes has seizures and is on medication. The sign says, "Please alert an attendant if the monkey appears to be in distress."

I'm grateful to this sanctuary for its care of these animals. At the same time, I'm sorry many of them seem to have human-like afflictions and/or afflictions caused by humans. Our relationship with animals is such a mixed bag.

Patrick's Facebook Post: I just got home from a terrible Mexican dinner. I ordered the two-cheese enchilada plate and realized a couple bites into my first enchilada that the cheese wasn't even melted. I sent it back and asked the kitchen to heat it up for me. They brought it back with a fresh, hot melted enchilada which was good, but they returned the original second enchilada with unmelted clumps of cheese. I know, I know, first-world problems, but hell of an aggravation when you spend as much time as I did justifying spending money on dinner the first place.

OCTOBER 30, 2013

ELDER RIDE

Irene calls to thank me for the book on MS. "I received the package last night," she says. "I can't talk long. We have a meeting this morning with the hospice staff."

Hospice? When did Ed's brain tumor move from treatment to hospice?

"He's getting worse. We looked into a hospice facility near our daughter, but it's expensive and we've decided to use hospice assistance in our own home."

As usual, Irene sounds calm and resilient. She'll call me and give me an update when they have more hospice information. Another friend whose husband is dying. My new normal?

My cousin Annette calls. She's bubbly about the packages she's sending. "They'll arrive Monday by UPS. Will you be home?"

"Yes, I'll be here."

Annette, who is 75, is putting lots of effort into gathering, organizing, and forwarding family history and heirlooms. I ask her how she is. "I was really sick in July and August with asthma, but I'm better. My daughter-in-law has to have hip surgery and my son's asked me to come help."

My friends Jan and Jim have invited me to their home in the Bay Area in November. Jan goes to physical therapy for back and hip issues. Nevertheless, she's making plans to go to Yoshi's, a favorite jazz club in Oakland, on a Sunday night. She wants me to join her and Jim and a few of their friends.

I hate the drive from here to there, but I have to go. This elder ride seems to be getting more unpredictable for everyone and we all need to stick together.

Patrick's Facebook Post: What a morning. Met up with some regulars from the dog park and we drove up to Auburn to take the dogs to the river as a treat. My dog, Lexi, who hasn't had lot of experience off leash in the woods, took off in a mad sprint the moment I unleashed her and disappeared into the forest. Three hours of wandering around the woods calling her name, whistling, searching to no avail. Drove around the perimeter of the forest but couldn't find her. I had resigned myself to the fact that she was indeed lost and was dreading the long drive home without her when two guys showed up on the trail with Lexi on a leash. Thanks for the scare you damn dog.

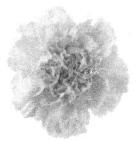

OCTOBER 31, 2013

HALLOWEEN

I'm among that spooky percentage of people who don't like Halloween. I never have. Oh, sure, when I was a kid I went trick-or-treating. I hid my stash from little brother. But somehow, I never got into celebrating ghosts and goblins.

As a mother of four children, Halloween loomed like a gotcha test. Other mothers were creating clever outfits for their children. I didn't sew. I wasn't crafty. I hated the pressure I put on myself. "You must come up with original, complicated, over-the-top costumes for your kids. You can't use costumes from last year. You can't cut holes in sheets for eyes and drape them over small bodies. A black mask does't count as a costume. A witch's hat doesn't count as a costume. A pair of surgical scrubs? Absolutely not!"

As an adult, I don't enjoy costume parties. Don't ask me why. I don't know why. It's one of life's little mysteries. My best year, I made ladybug costumes for me and my husband. My worst year, I went to a costume party without any Halloween attire at all—not even an effing pumpkin necklace.

My daughters send me cute pictures of my cute grandchildren in their cute Halloween costumes. Kerry and her crew gather at an RV campground every Halloween with their friends. The campground sponsors contests for the best decorated camper and best costumes. The children trick-or-treat among the campers in a safe, controlled environment. My grandchildren are being gifted much better Halloweens than I gave to my children. My daughters, their mothers, get mega Halloween brownie points.

In this over-55 community, I don't get trick-or-treaters at my door. I miss them. I enjoy seeing their colorful costumes and their expectant, painted faces. I adore their squeaky little voices saying, "Trick or treat." I like to be the good guy and hand out candy bars. I don't do fruit.

To my credit, perhaps, I have a living, breathing black cat. She sits in my kitchen window every day all year long. Maybe the Halloween committee will give me one or two Halloween brownie points for her.

Patrick's Facebook Post: The last five years I have had like zero trick or treaters. This year I moved into a new house in a nice neighborhood so I wasn't really prepared for the gangs of ghouls on my doorstep. I ran out of candy with the last bunch. Guess I'm not answering the door anymore tonight.

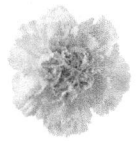

NOVEMBER 1, 2013

OBSESSION

I'm online reviewing recipes—some new ones sent to me by a friend and some sent in a daily email from allrecipes.com. I check my recipe box on that site. I've saved 1,599 recipes. That's 4.38 years of recipes if I were to make a different one every single day.

Not only have I saved 1,599 recipes, I've scanned at least that many more and not saved them. I've read thousands of reviews by other users. I've studied a gazillion photos that accompany the recipes. What is this? It must be some kind of addiction. Recipe insecurity? Recipe obsession?

I get dozens more recipes each week from Pinterest, more recipes than any one person could use in a lifetime. Sometimes GG says, "This recipe is very good. Will we ever get to eat it again?"

Good question. I'm always onto the next, yet-to-be discovered gem—the recipe to end all recipes.

This recipe thing, it has to be genetic. GG never cooks in her assisted living facility. She never shops, but she checks the grocery inserts in the Wednesday newspaper each week. She compares prices and looks for special offers. She doesn't pass the information on. She reads the ads and dumps them in the waste basket.

So what's that about?

I sent a recipe to my friend Grace a while ago. She keeps raving about it. She says, "Every time I serve it my guests love it."

I want to make it again, but I can't find the bloomin' recipe anywhere—not in my online recipe box, not in my document file, not in my cookbooks. I have to ask Grace if she can send my recipe for zucchini ribbons back to me. When she does, I better print it and tape it to the inside of my pantry door. My pantry door is finite. When it can't accommodate one more recipe, that should be it. The pantry door collection will be my one and only recipe collection.

Maybe, then, GG will get something "very good" served to her more than once.

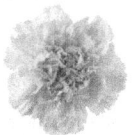

NOVEMBER 2, 2013

A CALLING TO WRITE

In her book, *How the Light Gets In*, Pat Schneider talks about writing as a calling. I think about Pat's words and sit here at my computer because, if I don't, I may miss something. Who knows, it could be something funny, sad, or even brilliant. When I write, words appear on the page and show me things I wouldn't otherwise reflect upon.

To begin writing, Pat says to take whatever comes. Whatever image. Whatever words. Whatever first flashes into our minds. "It's a gift from the unconscious."

Each of us has a unique voice. There never was and never will be another voice like mine. Or yours. We need to find our voices and put them to work. I write so I might think and act with both mindfulness and exuberance, and to tell the stories that are mine to tell.

As I write, I recall Pat Schneider's "Blessing for a Writer," and sprinkle it on myself like holy water:

". . . lost though you may be in the forest,
drop your own words on the path like pebbles
and write your way home."

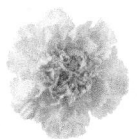

NOVEMBER 3, 2013

HIGH TECH LOW TECH

Another day at the computer paying bills online. Online sites are supposed to be safe and protected by firewalls and other technology I don't understand.

There's a two-page article in today's *Sacramento Bee* about the National Security Agency (NSA) and some of the questions raised since Edward Snowden began releasing the agency's documents in June. According to the article, a former NSA official says, "Without new leadership, new laws, and top-to-bottom reform, the agency will represent a threat of 'turnkey totalitarianism,' and the capability to turn its awesome power, now directed mainly against other countries, on the US public."

This is a scary thought. It sounds too incredible, but is it? Why do I feel apprehensive for my grandchildren? No wonder I'm writing in this journal. The simple, tactile act of putting words on a page is comforting. Old school. Low tech. Connected to that primitive man who drew on rock walls. But wait. What do I know about that caveman? When he wasn't marking his cave, he was probably clubbing his wife. I wouldn't have trusted him anymore than I trust the NSA.

Here's crossing fingers that our collective wills and wisdom prevail, and we'll figure out a way to keep technology and humanity in sync. Here's hoping the NSA isn't tracking my online bill pay, and this is my imagination, stoked by newspaper accounts, needing a time out.

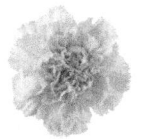

NOVEMBER 4, 2013

SPENDING PLAN

Financial guru Suze Orman would be proud. I'm reviewing my budget spreadsheet for 2013. Heading into the home stretch, I'm coming in $7,000 under budget. I've been cautious all year because I wasn't sure how much financial support I was going to need to give to Pat.

So I cut back. I didn't take a vacation—only a weekend visit to Marisa in Seattle. I didn't make any major purchases. I budgeted

$1,000 for medical expenses and used $150 of that amount. I budgeted for home maintenance and yard maintenance and came in as budgeted. I budgeted for car expenses and came in $500 under budget. With no major catastrophes, I'll end the year in the plus column.

I have no debt. I own my home. I have solid medical coverage. I pay cash or I don't buy it. Where I'm not doing as well as I'd like is in putting what money I have to work. I'm not in the stock market. Own no bonds. I'm still benefitting from CDs earning 3.5%. Once they mature I don't know where I'll turn.

I know the drill. Asset diversification. Asset allocation and reallocation. Percentages in cash, stocks, and bonds. I also know that no one cares as much about my money as I do. I've been screwed by financial advisers in the past.

Meanwhile, I sit on the side lines of the great stock market run since its last downturn. Nevertheless, like the tortoise and the hare, my net worth keeps increasing because I draw less from my saving than it's earning in interest. I'm not rich, but with diligence and luck, I'll take care of myself and not become a burden to anyone. I intend to spend my last dime on the day of my departure.

Next year, I want to include a trip in my budget plan. A trip to somewhere I've never been before. Actually, I prefer the term "spending plan." Sounds less onerous than "budget plan." A trip might be someplace not that far away. There's a whole world, right in my backyard, waiting to be explored.

I'm sending this travel thought out to the universe, waiting to see what exciting proposition it presents for my consideration—within my 2014 spending plan parameters, of course. And the universe knows what they are.

NOVEMBER 5, 2013

EQUANIMITY

Okay. I've changed my mind. I can't be sanguine about my demise. Not on days like today.

The news from NASA, and their Kepler space telescope, is that billions of earth-size planets exist in our galaxy. A planet for every person on earth. These planets don't necessarily have the same biochemical conditions that led to life on earth. The earth has features that are amenable to life—a circular orbit, a good-size moon, and tectonic activity that recycles the planet's carbon. With zillions of planets out there, however, the chances are good that some form of life exists elsewhere in the universe. SETI, the search for extraterrestrial intelligence, thinks we'll find earth-like worlds soon. What is their definition of "soon?" Soon, as in my lifetime? NASA and SETI better get to work. I'm not leaving until we find out if somebody else is out there.

On the other hand, it may not make any difference. We must consider the distances between us and habitable planets. A light-year equals 5.8 trillion miles. Twelve light-years to the nearest possible ocean planet would compute to about 70 trillion miles. The velocity of the New Horizons probe is 35,800 mph. That speed, times 24 hours per day, times 365 days per year means (by my calculation) it would take around 225,000 years to get to the neighbors next door. By then they may not be home. They may be on vacation. They may have moved to another planet.

Then what?

A girl can change her mind. I'm changing my mind. Again. Becoming stardust myself may be the most efficient way to uncover the mysteries of life in the universe and to circumvent barriers of time and space. My equanimity is being restored.

Patrick's Facebook Post: I want to open a pizza place called Failure Pizza. We would have specials like the Power Failure, the Personal Failure, the Marriage Failure, the Nuclear Failure, etc. Employees would answer the phone, "Failure Pizza. Describe your failure."

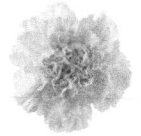

NOVEMBER 6, 2013

INSIGNIFICANT OR NOT?

"Whatever you do may seem insignificant to you,
but it is most important that you do it."

—GHANDI

That's where I am, today, in this writing endeavor. Doubting. What difference does it make?

Meanwhile, my Kansas City cousin keeps sending me family photos and documents. I'm looking at a copy of my great-great-great-grandfather's will written in 1840.

"I, Christian Shelly, of Washington Township, Franklin County and State of Pennsylvania, being weak in body but of sound mind and memory do make this as my last will and testament to wit:

First, I allow that all just debts be paid by my executor as soon as can be done after my decease. Item; I devise to my wife, Magdalena, the use of my plantation wherein I reside and also the part which lies opposite Adam Sesher's building and the improvements which are on both tracts all during her natural life;

And also one horse creature and all the cows and all my household and kitchen furniture, bedstead and bedding, stove and vessels of every description and all other articles which may be in that part of the house which I occupy—all of which my said wife is to have during her natural life."

I'm fascinated by this peek into nineteenth century life. Not because it's family history, but because it's common detail from another time and place. I try reading between the lines. I hear a man, who I'm guessing never cooked a meal or washed a dish in his life, saying, "I'm not sure why we need all these pots and pans." I hear a man saying, "While I'm alive these are my possessions." Not "our" possessions.

I've never heard of Christian Shelly before. The copy of his will arrives because my cousin saved it, packaged it, and mailed it. But when I open the package, it feels like this document time-traveled to get to me. Is Christian Shelly's spirit hovering nearby as I examine his will? Is Magdalena's spirit hovering nearby as I read her name on a 173-year-old document? Are Christian and Magdalena urging me to keep writing?

Will my record of ordinary life, early in the twenty-first century, be interesting to someone in the future? Will a great-great-great-grandchild read it and say, "I wish I'd known my great-great-great-grandmother?" Or will he or she say, "What a crazy old lady?"

For some reason, today, keeping this journal "seems insignificant" to me. Does Ghandi's imperative—"it is most important that you do it,"—then apply?

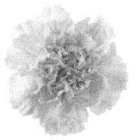

NOVEMBER 8, 2013

FAMILY MENTAL ILLNESS SUPPORT GROUP

Random comments at today's meeting:

"My son's having a difficult month. My brother died. Our dog died. A staff member at a health food store recommended that my son take a certain medication and it can be deadly if taken with the wrong combination of other drugs. My son's new psychiatrist told him he shouldn't take that medication, and he's listening to him."

"Our daughter's really ill. She can be violent and dangerous. We don't know what to do, and we're hoping someone in this group will have a suggestion."

"I'm here because my thirty-three-year-old grandson, who has bipolar disorder, is stressing everyone in the family, especially his mother."

"This has been a really bad month. I don't know if I can talk about it without crying. My son's in Southern California, and I'm glad because I'm afraid of him. He has drug and alcohol problems, and I'm sure he has underlying mental illness. He's living on the street. I don't know how to help him. I can't stop thinking about it."

"I don't know if I belong here. I'm dealing with depression myself and trying to find help before it gets out of control."

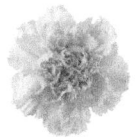

NOVEMBER 9, 2013

MISSING TEETH AND TOO MUCH HAIR

Regan calls on FaceTime to show me her missing front tooth.

"Regan, where is your tooth?"

"The tooth fairy has it, Mim."

"What did the tooth fairy leave you for your tooth?"

"Four dollars and ninety-five cents."

"Wow. That's a generous tooth fairy. What are you going to buy with the money?"

"I don't know."

"Do you have a bank for your tooth fairy money?"

"No. I don't know if the money's any good."

"Why?"

"It's got gold sprinkles all over it."

"Tooth fairy gold dust?"

"Yes."

"That's very special money. Does Ayla have any loose teeth?"

"She has one that's kind of loose. She fell and knocked it loose and chipped it."

"Do you have any more loose teeth, Regan?"

"Yes, see? The front tooth next to my lost tooth is wiggling. Mommy says not to wiggle it. She's afraid I won't be able to eat anything if both of my front teeth are missing."

"You'd have to drink chocolate milkshakes all day."

"I know."

"Can I talk to Ayla for a second?"

"Okay. She's drawing with my art set."

"Hi, Ayla, What are you drawing?"

"I'm drawing a picture of you, Mim."

"A picture of me?"

"Yes, you're holding my hand. See?"

"Ayla, Mim doesn't have long hair. She has short hair. You drew her with long hair."

"I know. I don't care."

"I like your picture, Ayla. I like that we're holding hands. Remind me, Regan, to pay you the money I owe you for your school marathon."

"I walked ten laps."

"Then I owe you ten dollars. A dollar for each lap."

Oops. We're disconnected. This conversation is over. I love my iPhone and FaceTime. They're perfect for viewing missing teeth and original artwork. And for getting on-the-spot reporting from people in the know.

Patrick's Facebook Post: Went to a wonderful concert last night chock full of classic jazz standards from Porter, Gershwin, Cohen, Kern, and others. That incredible and beautiful vocalist, Ann Roach, at the helm backed by master percussionist, Michael Bayard, keyboards, Doug Matson, and stand up bass, by Rob Lemas. The tunes are all echoing through my mind today with the highlights for me being "Dance Me to the End of Love," "Let's

Do it," "Luck be a Lady Tonight," "If I Only Had a Brain," and "Somewhere Over the Rainbow." "Fever" was scorching hot and an amazing encore of "What a Wonderful World." Can't believe I get to work with such incredible talent, awesome.

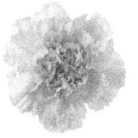

NOVEMBER 11, 2013

THAT'S ITALIAN

Home again. I visited my friends Jan and Jim in San Carlos. We went to Yoshi's on Jack London Square. We ate dinner and attended the evening show—Pasquale Esposito Rendering Italian Jazz. He gave an energetic performance, engaged with the audience, and revealed a flair for comedy.

I think, in a past life, I lived in Italy. I once walked into a 400-year-old farmhouse in Montecatini Terme and got goosebumps. It's the only time I've ever thought to myself, *I've been here before. I remember this room.*

In my next life, I want to live in Italy, *again,* and have a mad, passionate affair with an Italian singer. Not a marriage. I'm not sure Italian singers would be good at marriage. Too many luscious ladies to distract them. But a fling with one would be fine. Then I'll call Jan and tell her all about it. She's alway looking for a guy for me. Remind me to share my Match.com and It's Just Lunch stories sometime. They're not pretty.

If a good guy comes along, that will be great. If that doesn't come to pass, that's okay, too. I'm leaving it up to fate. *Che sara,*

sara. That's archaic Italian for *Que sera, sera.* What will be will be. And this week I'm in one of my Italian phases. Thanks to Jan and Jim and Pasquale Esposito.

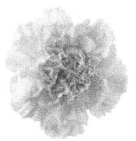

NOVEMBER 12, 2013

SNAP IT UP

I'm at Snap It Up working the cash register. Lots of customers this morning. One lady spends $196.00. "I have five children," she says. She doesn't want her receipt. "I like kitties."

Another woman, her friend, says, "She spends money like this everywhere she goes." They live out of town but I encourage them to come back. "Come back often. Come back soon."

A young woman buys three pairs of jeans for $15.00. Another considers ten etched wine glasses for $10.00. "I'm not going to buy these," she says. "I'm not. I'm not. I'm not. Please ring them up."

A ten-foot artificial houseplant goes for $10.00. Prices are low. The intent is to move merchandise. The strategy is working. Word is getting around that this is a nifty thrift store. I'm not usually a thrift store person. Thrift stores are often crowded and packed with so much stuff I can't see anything. They smell dusty, musty, old. Not this store. Merchandise is displayed with care. Clothes are steamed if wrinkled. Duplicate items are kept in the back until the first item sells. Adoptable kittens and cats swat at strings and balls in an adoption area. People see that their money is being used for a good cause.

I'm not immune. I'm buying a Christmas ornament for $2.00, a Christmas music box with dancing elves for the Grandma drawer for $4.00, and a brand new Westinghouse iron for $5.00. I'm working for free and paying for the privilege. I'm being a very good volunteer.

NOVEMBER 13, 2013

THERE'S THE RUB

An email from AARP is asking for donations to help the victims of Typhoon Haiyan in the Philippines. I click on the "Donate Today" button. I change the designated donation from $50 to $25. That's as far as I get. Will this donation provide food and water to someone who needs it? Or will it be swallowed up by bureaucratic ineptitude? Or worse, will some middleman simply fold my dollar bills and slip them into his own pocket? I'm leery.

On the other hand, I can't mail $25 to someone in the Philippines. There's no means of delivering mail. I can't ship food and water. My donation of a few cans of beans would be eaten up by shipping costs. It would end up where?

It's a conundrum.

Should I simply make the donation to AARP, close my eyes and trust that it will get to someone in need? The message says, "One hundred percent of all funds raised will go to organizations helping the victims of the typhoon."

Ah. There's the rub. The synapse where money changes hands. I'll never know how my donation is used, of course. The other option is to do nothing. The classic approach-avoidance scenario.

The AARP Foundation will match, dollar for dollar, contributions up to $500,000. I guess I'll click again on the "Donate Today" button and then click the "Submit" button to complete the transaction. Why do I have such angst over $25? Because I want the donation to help, and because it's the principle of the thing.

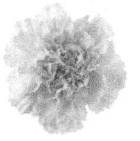

NOVEMBER 14, 2013

PERFECT DAY

I wake up at 8:00 a.m., make coffee, and read the paper. I water houseplants, launder a couple loads of clothes, and vacuum the house. I shower and dress, pleased with my shrinking waistline. I can tuck my top into my jeans. I can wear a belt.

I visit the new Dollar Store near the market. A neighbor's there. We chat and catch up. Her husband died earlier this year. She's doing okay. We give each other hugs.

At the grocery store, I check out tomatoes for a recipe to try for dinner. "What kind of tomatoes are best?" I ask the produce guy. His name is Scotty.

"Sometimes," he says, "tomatoes look good, but then they don't have any flavor. The heirlooms are best. I promise. I don't get a commission."

At the checkout counter, I joke with Scotty, who's now working the register. "You said these tomatoes are free. Right?"

He doesn't blink. "That's what I said. They're free today."

"Really?"

"Yep. I didn't ring them up."

On my way out of the store, I scan my receipt. No tomatoes listed. What a simple little gesture that makes my day. Thanks, Scotty.

At home I make corn, zucchini, and tomato pie. The pie and the tomatoes are flavorful with the help of parmesan cheese, garlic, and salt and pepper. Soon, I'll climb into bed and read more of *The Immortal Life of Henrietta Lacks*. I'm learning about HeLa cells and ethical dilemmas in scientific research.

Nothing happened today. Yet, on many levels, it was perfect. A perfect sort of day.

Patrick's Facebook Post: 10 things you didn't know about me and were afraid to ask:

- I've written two books—a book of poetry and a memoir.
- I was second in line for the starring role in the movie "Lucas" about a kid who plays football.
- I became close friends with Nobel Prize-winning poet, Joseph Brodsky, when I was in college.
- I, too, have been to over 20 Grateful Dead concerts, Tanya Rosa.
- Once met Bob Weir at a house party after an Oakland show.
- I did a solo motorcycle trip through 29 states when I was 24.
- I am a survivor of heart surgery and brain surgery.
- I once lived on the island of Guam.
- I got to sit with Bill King on the radio broadcast bench at a Warriors' game when I was a kid.
- Used to be a teen model for Macy's, JC Penney, & Sears.

NOVEMBER 16, 2013

BATKID

The City of Gotham, a.k.a. San Francisco, is saved today by Batman and Batkid, a.k.a. Miles Scott. Miles is a five-year-old cancer patient whose wish to the Make-A-Wish Foundation was to help Batman.

At 10 a.m., a plea was broadcast on San Francisco public television. The San Francisco police chief asked for Batkid's help in apprehending the Riddler. During the course of the day, Batkid did the following:

- Rode in a black Lamborghini Bat-mobile.
- Locked up the Riddler.
- Saved a damsel tied to cable car tracks.
- Rescued the San Francisco Giant's mascot, Lou Seal, from the clutches of the Penguin.
- Ran the bases in AT&T Park.
- Read a message from President Obama.
- Claimed a key to the city from the mayor of San Francisco.

Twelve thousand people turned out to role play and root for Batkid in his pursuit of justice and the American way. The San Francisco *Chronicle* published 1,000 copies of The Gotham *Chronicle*.

What an amazing display of communal whimsy. Long live Batkid. Long live the Make-A-Wish Foundation. Long live thousands of people, at the ready, to cheer our hero on—with heart.

Patrick's Facebook Post: Gradual Facebook withdrawal: I'm going to go get something to eat and I'm not telling you where and I'm not going to post a picture of my food.

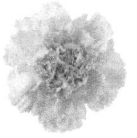

NOVEMBER 18, 2013

WALKIN' THE CAT

I've gone and done it. Didn't want to do it in broad daylight but, the way I figure, it's now or never.

I'm still reading Rebecca Skloot's, *The Immortal Life of Henrietta Lacks*. Last night, I fell asleep readin' the book. That's why this dialect is stickin' in my brain. I love the honesty, the energy, the music in it. As one of Henrietta's relatives told Rebecca, "If you pretty up how people spoke and change the things they said, that's dishonest. It's taking away their lives, their experiences, and their selves."

Anyway, I woke up this morning with a tellin' in my head— as if I spoke like one of Henrietta's relatives. Perfect timin' cuz I'm not sure I want to reveal what I'm doin'. This way of talkin' will be part of my disguise. Not that my inflection or phrasing is accurate. It's not.

So I been pushin' this new cat stroller round my house for two weeks. I been hopin' The Jazz would get curious and want to ride in it so I can take her for walks. She's curious 'bout everythin' else. She jumps in boxes. Jumps in paper sacks. Soon as I open a cupboard door, if I'm not watchin,' sure enough she's in that cupboard. And she ain't comin' out.

Like an idiot, I'm pushing this kitty carriage around in my house, at night, with the shutters closed. The Jazz loves riding on the seat of GG's walker. She loves riding on the back of my desk chair. But she doesn't even sniff at this stroller. She doesn't get near it.

This morning, I decided the time has come. We have to try this thing out or I'll have to take it back to the pet store. Got a good deal on it too—half off. I make sure the zipper on the stroller's mesh covering is aligned and ready to zip. I pick my kitty up using a soft voice to not scare her too much. I plop her in the stroller and zip it shut. Fast as I can. She's not happy but she's not screaming, either.

"We're taking a walk," I say. "Out to see the birds and the bees and the trees and the flowers. Out to see the big wide world you never get to see."

I start down the sidewalk and, boy, am I hoping no one is coming out on the street today. I should have a worn a big, floppy hat and dark glasses to cover my face. Too late. I round the corner and wouldn't you know. Here comes a neighbor from the next street over. Orchid Lane. That's the fancy street. She's out walking her dog. She's coming right at me.

"Well, isn't this great," she says. "You're walking your cat. Makes sense since she probably won't walk on a leash."

My neighbor doesn't know how right she is. Her dog's yapping at The Jazz, who's hissing through the blue mesh covering. She's got a view out all four sides of the stroller.

"You didn't see me," I say. "We never had this conversation," I say.

My neighbor nods and moves on. I round the next corner and the next corner and the next corner. We're in the home stretch for our first outing. The Jazz is turning back and forth in the stroller. Looking out the back at me. Looking out the front at Lord knows what. But like I said, she isn't screaming.

Back to the front door. I push the stroller inside and unzip the cover. The Jazz flies out. She's glad to be free. Guess we'll keep this pet contraption. It wasn't that bad out there—long as I don't catch eyes peeking through curtains as we pass by.

I'll stop trying to pretend I'm not doing what I'm doing. I'll hold my head high and wear bright colors. Don't know why people can walk dogs but not cats. It will broaden Jazzy's life experience. It will be good exercise for me.

Don't tell my kids about this, though. I'll never hear the end of it.

Patrick's Facebook Post: Don't look back. "A mind that is stretched by new experience can never go back to its old dimensions." Oliver Wendall Holmes, Jr.

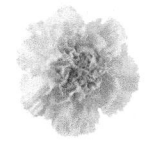

NOVEMBER 19, 2013

IT'S CRIMINAL

More talk in the news today about murders and suicides attributed to guns and mental illness. More talk about the lack of services and beds for the mentally ill who ask for help. More talk about the failure of our mental health system.

I've fought the battle for better mental health care for a long time. Between 2001-2003, for example, in the university system where I worked, I produced seminars titled, "Mental Illness in the Classroom—How to Recognize It and Who Can Help." Teachers, kindergarten through university level, were hungry for this information and came to these workshops from throughout California and from out of state.

For one symposium, Tipper Gore sent a personal video message to the audience. For another, we featured the award-winning KQED documentary, *Hope on the Street.* In the film I narrated our family's anonymous story, which was one of five stories. With the KQED producer, I traveled to the Carter Center in Atlanta, at the invitation of Rosalyn Carter, to show the film there.

In spite of worthwhile projects and sold-out attendance at our conferences, university resistance to dedicated mental health programs was entrenched. Deans were interested only if programs would bring in big bucks for their schools. Some professors said, "Forget it." In a focus group for faculty readiness, one professor told me, "I'm fed up with students making irrational outbursts in my classroom. I'm a professor because I want to teach. I've no time for this other nonsense."

Resistance was widespread. A ranking member of the State Department of Education said to me, "Please don't educate teachers about mental illness. They'll become more frustrated than they already are when they learn there are no resources to make the changes that need to be made."

When my position at the university was cut, my mental health programs languished. I found out, later, that certain administrators and faculty members experienced mental illnesses within their own families. The powers in charge, however, could not or would not connect the dots. Much stigma and shame existed.

In 2013, there is still much discrimination and shame. I get asked, from time to time, to get back in the fray. I say, "My energy, these days, is concentrated on my son."

I know that younger advocates will continue the struggle, but it's sad that getting timely, appropriate, discrimination-free mental illness care remains a huge challenge. For those who suffer from serious mental illness, priority for their care continues to sink to the bottom of the proverbial heap.

It's criminal.

NOVEMBER 21, 2013

FOLLOW THE LEADER

Kerry and Regan are at a parent-teacher-student conference, so I'm with Ayla. We're in the backyard. Ayla's blowing bubbles and Piper's trying to catch them. She jumps and chomps at them in mid-air and makes them pop.

Ayla says, "Popping bubbles is Piper's favorite thing to do. She was born to chase bubbles. She's a crazy dog."

It's windy so we go inside. Ayla has an idea. "Let's play my cherry tree game."

Ayla sets up the game and explains the rules. We start playing, but we're running out of cherries. Ayla makes a unilateral decision.

"This game's too hard for you, Mim. Let's play another game."

We're playing Candy Land. For Ayla, Candy Land isn't a competitive game—it's a team sport. The red, green, yellow, and blue plastic people must all advance toward the Candy Land castle together. If one plastic person draws a good card, all plastic people get the same good card.

"I'll be the leader," Ayla says. "The rest of you come with me."

Now, we're building something—a tower slide for marbles. Ayla knows exactly how to fit the green tubes and purple tubes together. She holds up a silver marble.

"This is the test marble. Let's see if it goes."

The marble rattles down the tubes to the bottom. Our marble tower is a success.

Kerry and Regan are home. Regan got all T's on her report card. T stands for *On Target*. Boy, have things changed. On my report cards, we got E for *Excellent*, S for *Satisfactory* or U for *Unsatisfactory*. If I'd gotten a T, I'd have torn up my report card and run away from home. I'd have thought that T meant *Terrible* or *Terminated*.

Kerry takes me upstairs to Regan's bedroom. She shows me the dresser she's spray-painted white. It used to be my dresser when I was 15. I didn't like it at the time. Made from solid maple with tongue-in-groove drawers, it seemed like furniture for old people, not me. Today, the dresser has been passed down to my granddaughter. It looks modern painted white. It has clean, classic lines. It will, most likely, be in the family when I'm no longer around. I could get sentimental.

Ayla's rolling on the floor. "Look at my butt, Mim."

Kerry says, "Stop, Ayla. you're not being polite."

Ayla's laughing. Butts are funny. One can't get maudlin with Ayla around. If we follow the leader, we'll find lots of fun things to do.

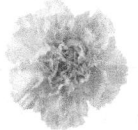

NOVEMBER 22, 2013

NOVEMBER 22, 1963

It's 10:45 a.m., November 22, 1963. I'm in Father Fagothey's philosophy class at the University of Santa Clara. I'm sitting in the fourth desk from the front in the third row from the left. My off-again-on-again boyfriend, Jim, is sitting in the desk next to me on the right. A student enters the room and hands a note to Father Fagothey.

Father Fagothey's reading the note. He's not moving. He's looking down. The room is silent. Father Fagothey looks up and says, "Class is dismissed. President Kennedy's been shot."

There's a collective gasp. Students run out the door. Jim picks up his books and disappears down the hall. I'm walking across campus back to my dorm. It's a crisp, clear day. Leaves are falling. Like the leaves, students are scattering in all directions. Some are gathering in small groups. Everyone's crying. I'm crying. I pass Jim. He's sitting in his white Ford Thunderbird in front of the student union. He doesn't see me. His eyes are closed.

The TV's humming in my dorm lobby. I don't stop to watch it. I go to my room and throw some books and clothes into a small bag. I'll drive home—it's minutes away. I'll watch the news in my living room. I'm praying that when I get home and turn on the TV, the newscaster will say that the president's in surgery and expected to survive. The president's going to be fine. The country's going to be fine. The world's going to be fine.

I know, fifty years from now, I'll recall I was in Father Fagothey's philosophy class when I learned President Kennedy was shot. I hope I'll also recall that, when I got home, TV reports said he was out of danger and receiving good care.

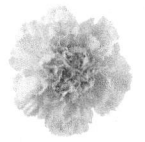

NOVEMBER 24, 2013

HAPPY BIRTHDAY, MARISA ELIZABETH

Tomorrow is Marisa's 40th birthday. This weekend Megan and Kerry have joined her in Seattle for a sisters' weekend. They're posting photos on Instagram. They're all smiles and hugs. A candle is blazing like a sparkler on Marisa's birthday dessert.

I'm pleased that my daughters are good friends. Not all sisters end up being friends. I hear. I don't know. I never had a sister, really. I say, "really" because my mother did give birth to a little girl, Loretta Marie, when I was four. I didn't learn about this until later. She lived a few hours.

I was excited that my mother was having a baby. I couldn't wait to hold it. Then Pop walked in the front door empty-handed. He said, "They were out of babies at the hospital today."

That was it. No further discussion. What? How could this be? The day my mother goes to the hospital to get our baby they're out of them? Could we only get a baby on this one day? What about tomorrow? Will more babies be coming in? I didn't ask these questions. I mulled them over in my four-year-old mind. Thinking about this, now, my chest feels heavy. I've never talked about it.

About six years later, when I was ten, my friend's mother was expecting. I was jealous. Mary Jo was about to have a baby in her house. I knew, by then, that hospitals didn't run out of babies, that babies grew in mothers' tummies. I understood I had a baby sister who died. What if Mary Jo's baby would die? The thought crossed my mind. Then Mary Jo's little sister died during childbirth. Did I wish that and make it happen? The thought haunted me. I was a terrible, terrible, little girl with evil powers. Another thing I've never talked about.

Wow, Marisa's birthday and the subject of sisters has gone in an unexpected direction. Back to my daughters. Once again, I'm jealous. I have a perfectly okay brother. I'd also like to have a sister. And Jim would probably like to have a brother.

I talk to my cousin Annette in Kansas City. "You need to come out here," I tell her. She says she'll think about it. She doesn't like traveling and making trip arrangements. Maybe, if I tell her I have to have a sister and she's it, she'll come.

Meanwhile, Happy 40th Birthday, Marisa. I love you and Kerry and Megan. And Patrick. And Jim. We mustn't forget the brothers. Here's to at least 40 more years—for all of us.

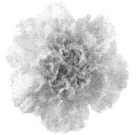

NOVEMBER 25, 2013

LITTLE THINGS

First thing this morning, I called to wish Marisa "Happy Birthday." I asked her about the wine and chocolates I'd ordered for her room. And about the note that said, "Have a Wonderful Sisters' Weekend."

I'm bummed. Marisa didn't get the wine, or the chocolates, or the note. I can't reconstruct the situation. This error can't be undone. I call the hotel and ask to speak to the manager. I'm connected to Edward. "I'm looking at your daughter's hotel record," he says. "I apologize. We totally dropped the ball on this. I can offer a discount on the next booking of our hotel. I'll send you an email to track this offer."

I'm waiting for the email. I'd rather have had an excited text from Marisa at the beginning of her birthday weekend about the surprise in her room. Maybe whoever "dropped the ball" won't do it again. Maybe he or she will remember, next time, that little things can mean a lot.

An email exchange with Pat.

"Hi, Pat. See you Thursday at Kerry's. Can you pick up GG at 4:00 p.m.? Kerry and I will be cooking. I have a postcard here for you. I'll bring it on Thursday." Mom

"Hi, Mom. Yes, I'll pick up GG on Thursday. I think, after the last payment to the bankruptcy lawyer we owe three hundred sixty dollars. I made a little money last weekend and I'm wondering if we could pay off the total if I give you half—one hundred eighty dollars. Thanks." Pat

"Hi, Pat. If you can pay half, that is a huge help. How did you make the money? At the church?" Mom

"Hi, Mom. I made the money helping a friend of mine with his screen printing business at an Irish dance competition at the Sacramento Convention Center. I'll call and verify what the total is. So, if I pay half, can we pay the total and get this over with?" Pat

"Hi, Pat. Yes, let's get this over with." Mom

"Hi, Mom. Thank you." Pat

Patrick's Facebook Post: I just spent two days helping a friend with his vending business at one of the most bizarre cultural events I've ever witnessed. It was called Oireachtas 2013 and was the Western Region Competition of Traditional Irish Dancers. There were about 2000 young girls competing for national and world qualifications and most of them were anywhere from 5-13 years old and they were all done up like beauty pageant contestants in full costume dresses, wigs, and makeup. I might have some serious nightmares tonight.

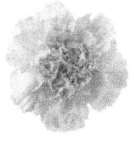

NOVEMBER 26, 2013

GOD BLESS US EVERYONE

Whoa. I just called Irene. She's always the same—calm and grateful. Ed has taken a turn for the worse. Irene says that hospice has moved in full-time. "They're wonderful. And my daughter Eileen who's a nurse, is here, too. I couldn't manage without her. Thankfully, we're able to keep Ed comfortable. And the grandkids have decorated his room with deer antlers and photos to make his room look like his room at the ranch. That's his favorite place to be."

"Is he awake?"

"He comes and goes. He's such a nice guy."

Irene and Eddie have been married 51 years. What a wonderful thing to be able to say after 51 years—"He's such a nice guy."

"I won't keep you, Irene, but I want you to know I'm thinking of you."

Irene wishes me "Happy Thanksgiving." She and her daughters are planning to fix a turkey and celebrate with the grandkids and with Eddie in his room. He won't be leaving it again. More of my friends are dying with grace. I'm thankful for their example. God bless us every one.

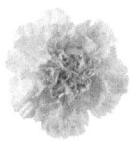

NOVEMBER 28, 2013

THANKSGIVING

First time, ever, that I haven't hosted Thanksgiving. I used to have 25 to 30 people for Thanksgiving. Then it dwindled to ten. Now, I'm passing turkey day to Kerry.

I'm at Kerry's. We decided it would be fun, as long as we're both spending the afternoon cooking, to do it together. I'm preparing a new recipe for roasted Brussels sprouts. They remain attached to the stalk. They'll serve as both the centerpiece and a side dish. My cell phone rings. It's Pat.

"Mom, I'm having a really bad day."

"What's happening?"

"I can't find my wallet. I've looked everywhere. I had the cash in it that I planned to give to you today."

Here goes my stomach. I've already put $360 on my credit card to pay the bankruptcy attorney. Pat is supposed to give me half today. I've been feeling proud that he's earned some money and offered to pay some of the bankruptcy expense. Is this for real? Have I been set up? Why do I never know how to handle situations with my son? They always catch me off guard.

Pat arrives at Kerry's. "Did you find your wallet?"

"No."

I'm home again. We had a scrumptious Thanksgiving dinner, but this money thing is throwing me. Why the drama? On Thanksgiving? I'm forgetting about the things I'm thankful for. I send an email.

"Pat, I'm counting on that $180 for Christmas expenses. I wasn't planning to put $360 on my credit card." Mom

"Mom, hopefully my wallet will turn up soon and I'll have the money to give you. If not, I'll get the $180 to you as soon as possible." Pat

"Pat, I took you on good faith and I'm disappointed. I can't keep being the financial fall guy. I'll deduct the $180 from the bills I pay in December." Mom

"Mom, I had the money set aside to pay you. You don't even care that I am out nearly $200 if I don't find my wallet. Please give me some time to either find my wallet or come up with the $180." Pat

Patrick's Facebook Post: Happy Thanksgiving Everyone!

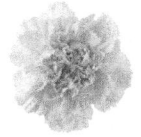

NOVEMBER 29, 2013

WHICH END'S UP?

Early morning email from Pat:

"Mom, I hardly slept at all last night. Not only am I upset and worried that I lost $200 that I intended to give to you and that I worked very hard to get, I'm terrified that you're going to cut off my cable, internet, phone, and renter's insurance.

"I'm already having a terrible time finding work, but without these things it will be basically impossible for me to look for work, send out resumes, or reply to employers via phone.

"Please don't do this to me. I feel like you are punishing me for something I shouldn't be punished for—losing my wallet. I realize that I still owe you $180 and I fully intend to get that to you as soon as I'm able, but taking away my communications with the outside world is not going to help me achieve that." Pat.

No matter what I do, I always feel like I've done the wrong thing with my son. I've been too lenient or too strict. I call Pat. "I'm coming over to help you look for your wallet. Maybe a different set of eyes will find it."

I'm at Pat's. His house, as usual, is in disarray. Dirty dishes in the sink. Dust everywhere.

"The last time I used my wallet was at Walmart. I don't remember seeing it after that."

"Do you think someone took it out of your pocket?"

"I've thought about that."

"Call Walmart and see if someone turned your wallet into lost and found."

Pat calls. No one's answering the phone.

"Okay. I want you to go there and check with customer service."

I look upstairs, downstairs, inside, outside, in the garage, in the car. There's no sign of a wallet.

"I worked really hard for that money. I was feeling good that I could buy Lexi's dog food this month and pay for her shots."

I'm home again. I get an email from Pat.

"Hi Mom. I forgot to ask you if you could drive me to my MRI for my brain tumor on Tuesday? I'm supposed to take an Ativan and not drive. Thanks." Pat.

Everything's so mixed up and convoluted with my son. Every day I question my own judgment.

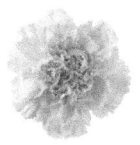

NOVEMBER 30, 2013

TOPSY-TURVY

It's 8:30 a.m. The phone's ringing. It's Pat.

"Mom, I think I'll have some money to give you tomorrow."

"Did you find your wallet?"

"No, I sent an email to the church and told them what happened and I think some of the people are going to help me. I'll let you know, tomorrow, how much I can give you."

Back and forth. Up and down. I'm feeling topsy-turvy. Also, I'm hiding out.

Six months ago, a dermatologist determined that chemicals in my hair products were the cause of my then swollen, itchy eyes. He prescribed a new shampoo and my eyes cleared up. Yesterday morning, I woke up with two bulging eyes. By evening, they were much worse. I called a hospital advice nurse. She scheduled an appointment with the dermatologist this coming Monday.

Meanwhile, trying to think of a clever metaphor or simile but nothing's coming to mind except a cliché. I look like shit.

Not a fun way to begin the holiday season.

Patrick's Facebook Post: I picked up a Christmas tree a few months ago. It's fake with pre-strung lights. I put it up today. Gaping holes in places, two strings of lights don't work, top is broken and leans off to one side. It's a Charlie Brown Christmas. Funny, sort of, because it's unfortunately true.

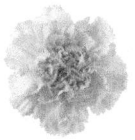

DECEMBER 1, 2013

HIDING OUT

Pat calls. "I have your money for you."

"All of it?"

"Yes, I told the people at the church what happened and they all chipped in and gave me the money. I'll give it to you on Tuesday when you take me for my MRI."

"Stash it someplace safe in the meantime. Don't lose it again."

"I won't."

I'm putting my collection of Thanksgiving pilgrims away and gathering Christmas decorations from the garage. I'm trying to forget that I look like you-know-what. Hope no one comes to the door or calls me on FaceTime. I won't answer if they do.

Good thing about The Jazz. She doesn't seem to notice or care what I look like. She purrs and cuddles with me on good days and bad.

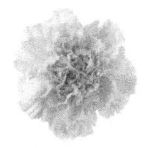

DECEMBER 2, 2013

KEEPING ON KEEPING ON

Irene calls. "Dede, thank you for the beautiful Thanksgiving e-card. I just opened it. Am I calling at a good time to talk?"

"Yes."

"I want to let you know that Ed passed away on Thanksgiving morning. All the family were gathered in his presence. It was very peaceful and he didn't appear to suffer. It's too soon, of course, but I'm glad he didn't linger. He wouldn't have been good at lingering."

"How are you, Irene?"

"I'm okay. Both of my girls are here with me and I couldn't have made it without them. I go in for more MS treatment on the tenth. There are many decisions to be made. Ed will be cremated and his ashes will be scattered beneath his favorite oak tree on the ranch. I'll put the house on the market in the spring. Eileen wants me to come live with her in Grass Valley. I may do that for a while, but I need full-time assisted living. I'll be looking for a facility I can afford that has some residents in my age group. It's a bit overwhelming.

"Irene, when you're in Grass Valley, let me know. I'll drive there to see you."

"I will. How's everything with you, Dede?"

"At this moment? Everything's okay. I try to take one day at a time. Thank you for calling. And please Irene, take good care of you."

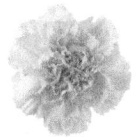

DECEMBER 3, 2013

IT'S COMPLICATED

I'm at the dermatologist's office. He looks at my swollen eyes. "Your eyes are much worse than the last time I saw you. I'm stumped. This problem is more of an internal medicine problem. You should see the allergy doctor."

I'm with the allergy doctor. He's showing me photos of people with swollen eyes on his computer. "We have to figure out if this is an outside-in problem or an inside-out problem. I'm ordering some blood tests to determine your thyroid function. Orbital edema is one of the least understood diseases on the planet."

I have a disease?

"Whatever explanation you offer for your swollen eyes, I guarantee that the theory's already been studied and found lacking. If you want to get a Ph.D. in this illness, medicine will thank you. This occurrence is idiopathic, or of an unknown cause. Meanwhile, another option is to start a course of prednisone. It will be hard on your bones, but if I were in your shoes, I'd opt for the prednisone. You are, medically speaking, becoming a complicated lady."

Hmm? Usually, I think "complicated" sounds interesting. Not this time.

Home again. I'm discouraged. I look like a movie monster with huge, swollen eyes and enormous bags of fluid hanging down my cheeks. Have to keep this in perspective. I'm sure most folks would think mine is a minor problem, compared to MS or to dying.

Santa, all I want for Christmas are two normal-looking eyes.

Patrick's Facebook Post: I know I should take it as a compliment, but getting carded at the bar when you're ordering a beer and you're well into your forty-fifth year is getting a little tiresome.

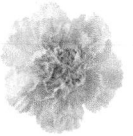

DECEMBER 4, 2013

IT'S IDIOPATHIC

I'm picking Pat up to drive him to Kaiser for his six-month MRI. I try not to think about why we're doing this. It's to check if his brain tumor is returning. I wonder what he's feeling when he goes through the procedure. Fear? Worry? Like a time bomb's about to go off in his head? When he gets in the car, he takes out a wad of dollar bills.

"Here's your money."

"One hundred eighty dollars?"

"Yes."

"All from your friends at church?"

"Yes."

I never cease to be surprised by this son of mine. And by people in his church.

Home again. I'm taking prednisone, Benadryl, and non-aspirin acetaminophen, trying to fix my itchy eyes. I email the allergy doctor. "Anything else I can do for this itching?"

He emails back. "Wash your eyelids twice a day with warm water and no tears baby shampoo to remove any irritants. All the blood tests are coming back normal. As we discussed, it's idiopathic angioedema, or no known cause."

I have to remember this word. Next time I have to explain why something's happening that I don't understand, I'll say, "It's idiopathic. It's occurring spontaneously. I don't know why."

I don't have to know why. It's a foolproof answer for whatever you need a foolproof answer for. It covers all the bases and gets you off the hook.

Patrick's Facebook Post: Tried very hard to hear the music in the industrial noise of an MRI of the head, but there's no music to be found there, it's just horrible noise.

DECEMBER 5, 2013

NELSON MANDELA

Nelson Mandela is dead at 95. One commentator says, "Some leaders are respected. Some are loved. Mandela was both loved and respected around the world."

How long does the influence of a world leader last? Will South Africa remember Mandela's example? Already there's talk that the integrity he modeled is coming undone. Scandal, greed, and political corruption are reported in his homeland. Is it inevitable that we regress when an icon no longer stands before us?

Mandela thought for himself. He was pragmatic. Nonviolent resistance was not an inviolate principle for him. When nonviolent resistance didn't appear to be working he promulgated a course of limited violence. "There is no moral goodness in using an ineffective weapon," he wrote in his autobiography. Yet, when the burden of decision-making was upon him, Mandela often used other tools in his toolbox. He chose forgiveness and reconciliation.

Mandela honed his ideas and his values during 27 years in prison with lots of time to think. A convergence of time, circumstance, and character gave his life historic meaning. He didn't nudge the world. He shoved it.

Patrick's Facebook Post: Glad I had the chance to hear him speak in Oakland. R.I.P. Nelson Mandela.

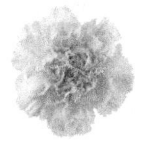

DECEMBER 6, 2013

ABUNDANCE AND HUNGER

I'm stocking up on staples at the local discount grocery outlet—getting ready for Christmas week and the marathon of holiday meals. I'm culling my recipes and making selections.

I'm at the checkout register. My total is $168.83. For this amount, I get black beans, white beans, garbanzo beans, kidney beans, bread, soups, canned tomatoes, assorted shredded cheeses, tuna, evaporated milk, olives, cottage cheese, peanut butter, pasta, Tabasco sauce, Worcestershire sauce, cereal, walnuts, almonds, lemon juice, sour cream, sausage, sugar, flour, baking soda, Canadian bacon, and cat food. The list doesn't include perishable fruits and vegetables, which I'll go back for next week.

I'm heaving eight heavy bags from my car to my kitchen. By the time everything is put away, this will have been a half-day's undertaking.

Pat sends an email:

"Hi, I signed a petition to the United States House of Representatives, The United States Senate, and President Barack Obama which says: 'We demand that Congress cease playing political hunger games that hurt vulnerable families, children, and local communities. Vote against any cuts to the Supplemental Nutrition Assistance Program—Food Stamps. Will you sign this petition? Click here. Thanks.'" Pat

I sign the petition.

It's 10 p.m. and I'm in bed for the night. It's 37 degrees outside and a heavy rain is falling. I hear it thudding onto the bark in my backyard. I pull up the red blanket I throw on top of my quilt. I'm warm and toasty under the covers.

I give thanks for this comfort. As I rest my head on my pillow, I close my eyes and imagine looking through the plaster ceiling, through the cement tiles on the roof, through the cloud cover, and into the dark, endless expanse of the universe. I breathe in and out. I'm one with what is. I fall asleep.

At 2:30 a.m., I'm wide awake. Prednisone is reducing the swelling in my eyes, but it's revving me up and interrupting my sleep. Canadian geese are flying over. They're squawking back and forth. Where are they flying in the dark, in the rain? Are they looking for shelter? Are they looking for food?

I remember the staples in my cupboards. I consider abundance and hunger. I don't go back to sleep.

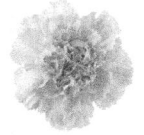

DECEMBER 7, 2013

SNOW

I was supposed to play bridge in an all-day regional tournament today. A new bridge partner has to cancel. Her daughter has bipolar disorder and lives at home. Her daughter's going through a rough patch. She's talking about not wanting to live.

"We can't leave her alone."

This friend comes to the family mental illness support group. Our December meeting will be next Friday. I'll send out a reminder and ask for an RSVP. With the holidays, people may be too busy or out of town. Or, with the holidays, there may be greater need to convene and support each other. Holidays can increase stress, push buttons, pull triggers.

It's still raining. Oh, my gosh, it's snowing. The black bark in my yard is turning white. I'm cocooning. I'm turning on the Christmas tree lights, lighting candles, and heating the oven—getting ready to bake banana bread to put in the freezer.

I'll call my friend, later, to see how her family is doing. Maybe the falling snow will provide a quiet distraction—a meditation on things bigger than ourselves.

Patrick's Facebook Post: First sign of the apocalypse: local grocery store discontinues Heinz 57 steak sauce.

Found a flash drive in my winter coat pocket that I was certain I had lost in a public computer room. It contained some very private data so glad I found it.

It's actually snowing here. Rare.

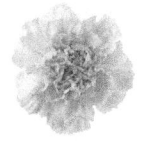

DECEMBER 9, 2013

SHOWING UP

I'm sitting here staring at the computer screen as if something wondrous is about to crash through the glass. A brilliant thought? A novel idea? A 3D-living-technicolor manifestation of my awesome mind at work?

Writing pundits say, "You have to show up." Show up or you might miss the moment an inspiration bursts into view. Right over your head. Like a cloud with a candle in it or something.

So here I am. Waiting. Watching, Wondering. Thinking about that box of dark chocolate marshmallow Santa Clauses stored in the garage. I bought the candy to be Christmas after-dinner treats, but they've been delivered too soon. There were 18 in the box and they're disappearing one at a time. There are nine left. I need twelve. I'm short three. What to do?

I could order more, but I bought them on sale and now I'd have to pay full price. And the timing would still be off. They need to arrive right in time for dessert on Christmas Day. Not a moment too soon.

I could have them delivered to a friend's house. I'd ask her to bring them over with an invitation to join us for dessert. This plan has defects, though. Which of my friends is trustworthy enough? Which doesn't like dark chocolate covered marshmallow? Which has nerves of steel and oodles of willpower?

None of them. We're all wimps.

There's another plan coming into focus. Plan B. I could skip the dark chocolate marshmallow Santa Clauses altogether. It's not like I've announced them already. I could serve peppermint ice cream with chocolate sprinkles, and who the heck would know? And since nobody would know, nobody would be disappointed.

I wouldn't have to bother a friend to store the Santas and deliver them. I wouldn't have to worry about the timing thing. There'd be no reason not to go into the garage right now and take one Santa out of the box. The more I think about it, the more I'm liking this Plan B. It makes a lot of sense.

The writing pundits are right. I'm glad I plopped myself down in this desk chair, glad I sat waiting in silence, glad I didn't let a blank computer screen intimidate me. If I hadn't shown up at my computer today, I'd have missed this inspiration altogether.

Patrick's Facebook Post: You have reached the end of the internet. Turn around and go back.

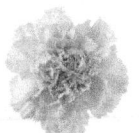

DECEMBER 10, 2013

THE THRIFT STORE

I'm at Snap It Up for my Tuesday morning shift. People come in the door one and two at a time. It's a steady stream this morning. The first customer says, "I'm buying these clothes for my sister. She and her longtime boyfriend broke up. She's wearing his clothes and he's wearing hers."

"Can she go to his house and pick up her clothes?"

"No, it's a volatile situation. I'm trying to stay out of it, but she needs some winter clothes. She's wearing summer stuff."

Another woman's found three strange-looking red cords. I don't know what they're for, but she does. "They're Christmas lights. Please plug them in and make sure they work. I've lost my job and I have to be careful spending for Christmas."

All lights light up. Three light sets sold, fifty cents each.

I show a small, petite lady the dressing room. She's holding a brand new pair of Gloria Vanderbilt jeans. I think they look a little big for her. She'd better try them on.

A woman with a walker hands me a denim jacket, a headset, two Christmas wine glasses, a lavender-and-peach scarf, and a green bracelet. "I'd like to see that lavender beaded bracelet in the counter, too."

The bracelet's three dollars. She clasps the bracelet on her wrist. "I really like it. I better not. I have to make the check I got today last the rest of the month."

I tell her maybe her luck will hold and the bracelet will still be here next month. Damn. Wish I'd thought to offer it to her for half-off.

A young girl asks, "Do you have any ugly Christmas sweaters? My brother needs one for a work Christmas party." We search both the men's and women's racks. No ugly Christmas sweaters.

"Let me look in the back and see what's come in." I find three ugly Christmas sweaters—all large women's cardigans. The girl's eyes get big.

"Let me go get my sister-in-law."

A few minutes later the sister-in-law flies in the door. "Can I see those sweaters? It doesn't matter that they're women's." She's giddy to have three sweaters to choose from. She picks a tan sweater with a green Christmas tree on the front and a brown moose on the back.

"My husband will be so excited to have this sweater for his party."

Another happy customer. I love this job.

A new woman says, "I'd like to look at that Christmas creche in the cabinet."

I pull out a boxed set with 15 pieces—Mary, Jesus, Joseph, the wise men. The whole enchilada. The box is worn, but it looks like Mary and Joseph and crew have never been out of it. The woman inspects the plastic pieces for chips.

"I'd hate to buy this for my daughter and then get stuck with it if she doesn't like it. I'll re-donate it if that happens."

Sold for eight dollars.

Three Hispanic women pile a mountain of clothes on the counter. Most items are one dollar, or *uno*. A few are two dollars, or *dos*. That's our bilingual exchange. I smile. They smile. Everyone's laughing.

An Asian man comes in, inspects some items on the Christmas decor table, and leaves.

The woman with the jeans comes out of the dressing room. The Gloria Vanderbilt jeans are too big, but another pair is perfect. I put the Vanderbilt jeans to the side and ring up her purchase. Those are really nice jeans she didn't buy. They're size eight. Hmm? When was the last time I wore a size eight? Do I dare try on these jeans when I'm through for the day?

The Asian man comes back. He buys two Christmas ornaments. One for fifty cents and one for ten cents, plus tax. He gives me the exact change.

Last sale of the day—a two-dollar Christmas ornament. I hope it's for an ugly Christmas ornament exchange. I don't say that.

I'm in the dressing room with Gloria Vanderbilt. I look in the mirror. I turn around. I look again. I'm so excited I have to tell someone. I tell the manager. "Jennifer, the jeans fit."

Sold for five dollars. And throw in a Christmas scarf for The Jazz.

What a great store. It raises funds for FieldHaven. It gives exceptional value to the community. To me, it feels like home and a breath of fresh air.

Patrick's Facebook Post: Just love the feeling of creeping along in a parking lot, looking to the right at the empty spot you're about to pull into, when you hear the crunch of a collision from a pickup truck backing into you. Which is to say that I don't really like the feeling at all.

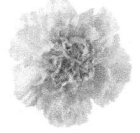

DECEMBER 11, 2013

GIVE THIS MAN A CHANCE

The December surprise arrives. Actually, it's not a surprise. The surprise would have been if there were no surprise. Pat was in an auto accident yesterday.

"Mom, it's a fender bender. It happened in a parking lot."

He's called the insurance company. He's taking the car into a collision center for an estimate. "The other guy says we're both at fault. I might have a thousand-dollar deductible."

Lord. Who might have a thousand-dollar deductible? I'll be the one who has the deductible.

Pat says, "It's bad timing. I have a job interview in Davis tomorrow. I can't drive my car that far with the driver's side rear view mirror torn off."

"Okay. Drive my car to the job interview."

Pat arrives to pick up my car. He's printing forms for the DMV that the insurance company told him to fill out. They think it was the other guy's fault. Pat says his policy doesn't include rental car coverage while his car is being repaired.

"Let me know what the insurance company decides and how the job interview goes."

Pat looks handsome in his tan jacket, white shirt, and polished black shoes. My son's trying hard to get his life on track. I gaze at him in awe. He never gives up. This man, this son of mine, deserves a chance.

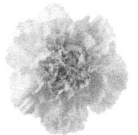

DECEMBER 12, 2013

BACK TO SQUARE ONE

Pat calls. "I didn't get the job."

That was fast. "What did they say?"

"They had fifty-six applicants for five positions."

"Well, it would have been a long commute."

"I know, but I would have driven it."

"What about your car?"

"The other insurance company is saying that we're both at fault. USAA is saying it's the other guy's fault. They may have to get a third-party mediator."

"Okay. Let me know when they make a decision."

"Okay. Bye, Mom."

Patrick's Facebook Post: My dog's defecation clock somehow got set to three a.m. this week. Guess it's good practice if I ever have a child.

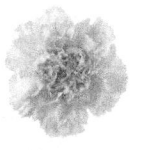

DECEMBER 13, 2013

HIDING IN PLAIN SIGHT

There are 13 people at the mental illness support group meeting today. One new person shares her story—long-standing and difficult. She's trying to get better services for her son. He hears voices. He says, "The voices are telling me I need to help them blow up the world or I need to kill myself."

The woman's been unable to get an appointment for her son to see a psychiatrist. She's trying to get assistance from someone in a state senator's office. She's also collecting gloves, hats, and coats for the homeless. Her son stays in a grungy downtown hotel and she's concerned for those who don't have an inside place to stay in the 20-degree weather we're having.

"Is your son still talking about killing himself?"

"He says, 'Mom, I'm handling it. I told the voices I'd help them blow up the world. I called their bluff. They've quieted down.'"

A marriage-and-family therapist joins the group for the first time. "I've worked with clients who have mental illness and I've worked with many families. I came today thinking maybe I could answer some questions or make some suggestions. I'm aware that everything said in this room is confidential. If I meet you the neighborhood, I won't acknowledge you unless you want me to."

An elderly couple sits close together. She looks frail. He's been here before by himself. "I brought her today so she can listen, and I'm here to support her."

I ask, "Do you want to talk about anything?"

"No, we're observing."

We sit at a U-shaped table in a grocery store that lets us use a conference room once a month. Shoppers walk by the closed, folding plastic doors. They can see us but they can't hear us. Mental illness doesn't exist in this country. We hide it in plain sight.

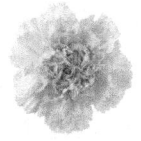

DECEMBER 15, 2013

CHRISTMAS GIFTS

I've ordered *Frozen* dolls, Anna and Else, for Regan and Ayla. Have calls in to Megan and Marisa to see if there's something I can send for Aidan and Ashton and Sam and Elise or if cash in a card is in any way exciting.

"How much do you want to spend?"

I hate this question. It touches on issues behind issues behind issues. It verges into psychology, financial literacy, and emotional conditioning. It's one of the fundamental questions about aging on a fixed income. How do I make sure I don't run out of money too soon? How do I weigh living now versus living later? How do I discern when to splurge and when to save?

I'm on the phone with Marisa. We're each online for hours, trying to find a pair of pink, fluffy slippers for Elise. Who would think that pink, fluffy slippers would be difficult to find? Finally, we find slippers. They're not pink. They're not fluffy. They're brown with chocolate dots on them. Elise says, "They're good."

Sam wants a Golden State Warriors beanie. That search takes a couple of minutes. The slippers and the beanie are both available on Amazon. Shipping times are good for Christmas delivery. Christmas gifts for two sets of grandkids down. One set to go. I'm waiting for a callback from Megan.

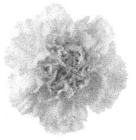

DECEMBER 16, 2013

FROM MY NOW TO YOUR NOW

Megan's on the phone. Aidan and Ashton need rubber bands for their Rainbow Looms. So, I'm sending money gifts to buy rubber bands and whatever else they want.

My cousin Annette calls from Kansas City. Her son, Danny, recently met a man from Wayne County, Pennsylvania. The man says, "The county's crawling with Funks." Funk is my mother's family name. Danny's trying to get more information about possible, current-day relatives.

Annette and I discuss a photo of an 1890s farmhouse. She and I both have copies. An unknown relative wrote on the back of the photo, "This is grandmother's house. On the porch is one brother, and on the lawn is another brother, and another brother is to the left."

A reminder to give more specific information.

This evening, as I slip under the covers, I'm thinking about my descendants. I want you to know dear children, grandchildren, great-grandchildren, and great-great-grandchildren, that I'm thinking of you. I hope my writing will give you a picture of life in the distant past—in the years 2013-2014.

My "rainbow loom" uses words. With words, I'm trying to weave a big, warm hug that will wrap around you in the future.

HERE'S A BIG HUG FROM MY NOW TO YOUR NOW.

Love, Mom, Mim, Great-Grandma, Great-Great-Grandma.
Love, Dede

Me with The Jazz in my kitchen at Christmas (2012)

Pat on the beach (1988)—Before our world came undone.

Pop (1940) with his brand new Oldsmobile.

My mother, Evelyn (GG), and me (1945).

Me and Pat (1969)—I can still feel him in my arms.

Pat (1969)—He was curious about everything.

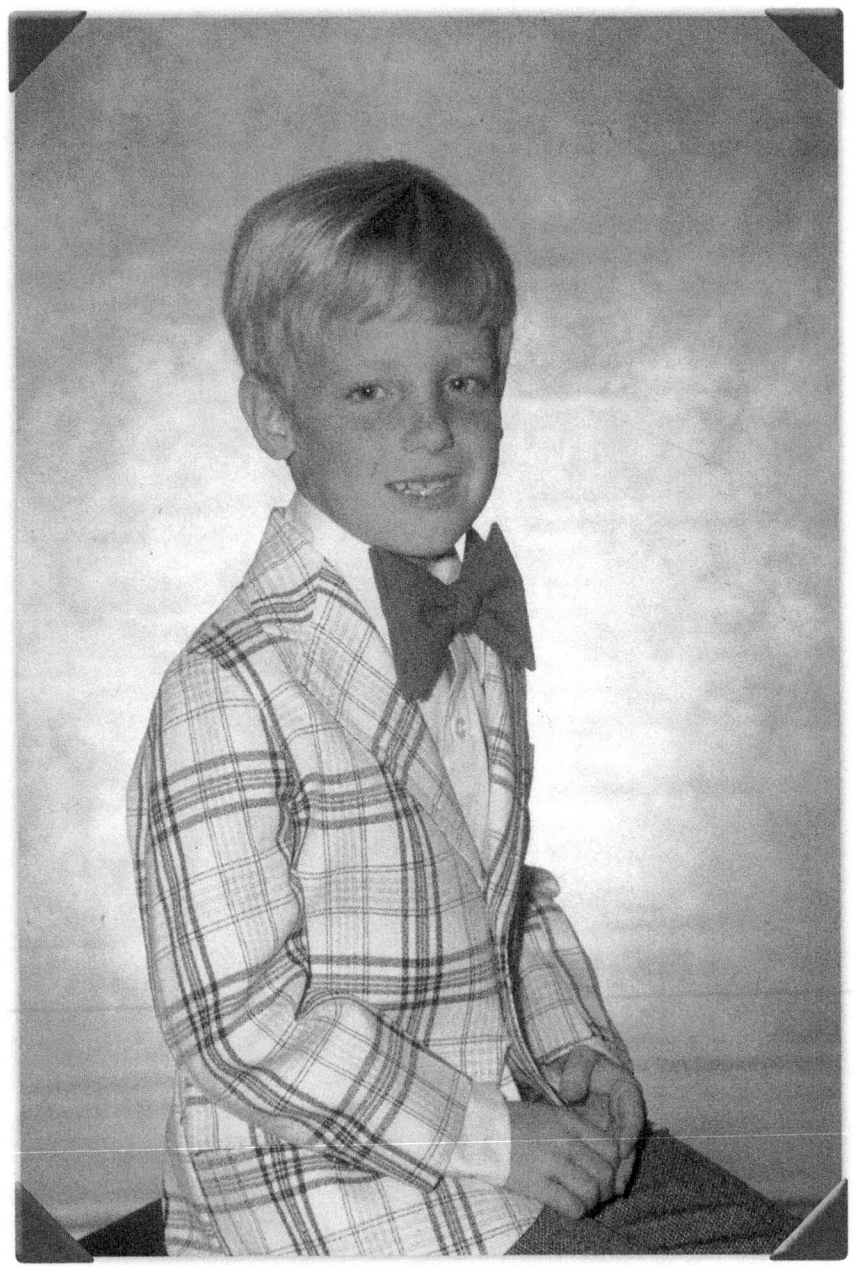

Pat (about 7 years old).

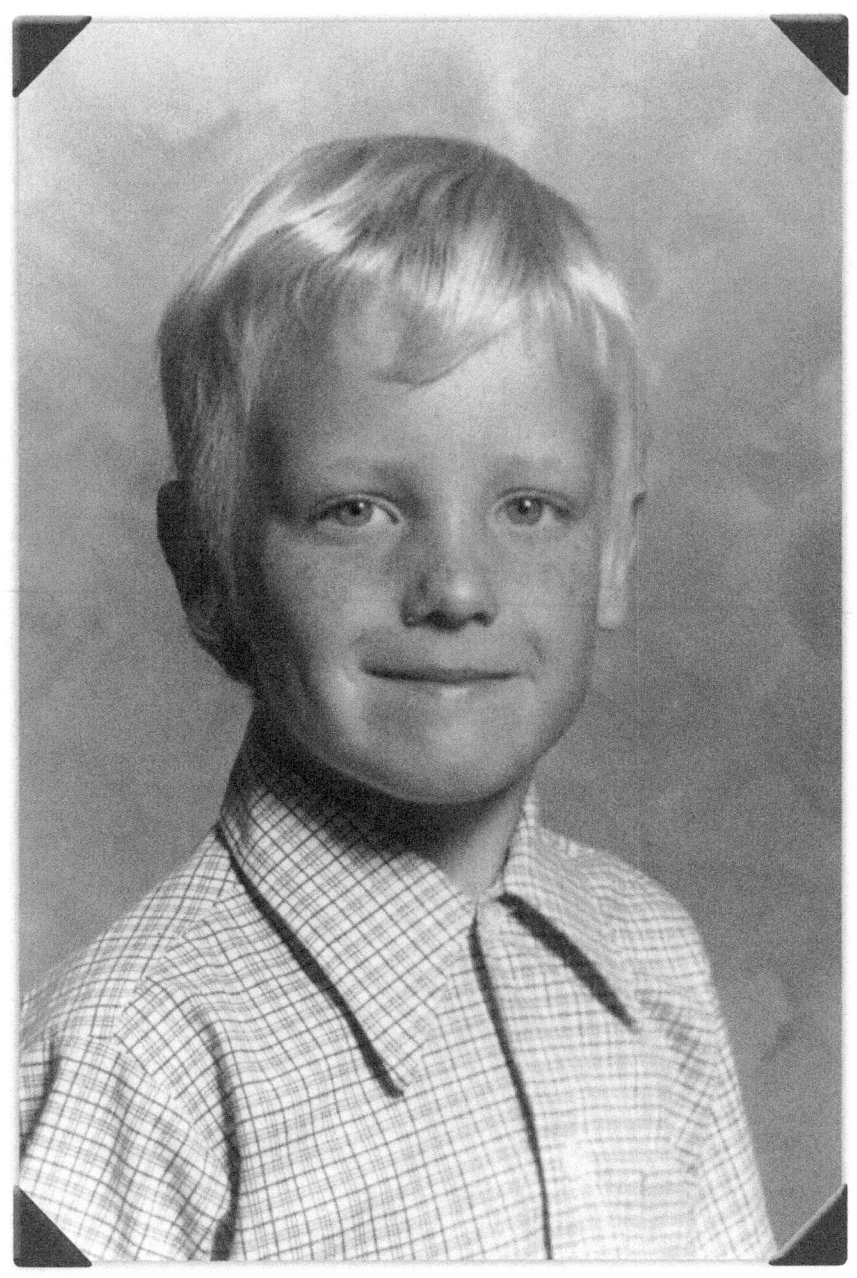

Pat in third grade.

Me at a Writer's Conference (1982)—Proud new author.

Pat in one of his modeling portfolio photos (around 1983).

Pat in another portfolio pose. Modeling was his idea.

Pat in his senior year at Hampshire College.

Megan

Marisa and her family—Elise, Keith, and Sam.

Kerry

Pat & GG (2013)—Pat loved spending time with her.

Lexi (2014)—Pat loved his dog so much.

Jazzy with her red ball.

Megan, Kerry, & Marisa (2004).

Pat in a solo guitar performance at our local deli (2013).

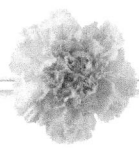

WINTER 2013-2014

I prefer winter and fall,
when you feel the bone structure
of the landscape. Something
waits beneath it; the
whole story doesn't show.

—ANDREW WYETH

TONY'S FINGER

He called the boiler room and said,
"This is John up in the penthouse.
Come on up and crack the steam in."
So I took the cowhide gloves and walked
across the January parking lot
to the main building of the hospital,
stuck my key in the elevator and rode it
to the mechanical penthouse, third floor.
The door opened to show me the tradesmen
all caught up on a different pipe
like kids on the monkey bars.
I put the pipe wrench to the blue valve
and cracked it slow, remembering John's admonition:
"You've got a hundred'n twenty pounds of pressure
coming through there. Open it too fast
and it'll blow you through the fucking roof."
Steam sang through the pipes as the condensate
dripped from the new silver gaskets
onto the concrete floor, scribbling a lazy map.
A man lost his finger here on the original job
putting in the permanent air handlers,
and when I look up to check the steam gauge,

I see where his buddies drew a picture—
a severed digit with the brotherly words:
"Hey Tony, here's your finger."

—PATRICK RANAHAN

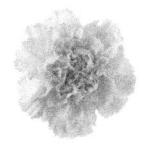

DECEMBER 18, 2013

ON THE BACK BURNER

I'm shopping at Trader Joe's and buying more food supplies for Christmas. Today's items include pecans, dried cherries, parmesan crisps, lemon curd, artichoke hearts, hearts of palm, Spanish Manchego cheese, pomegranate arils, and pico de gallo.

I stop at Macy's to buy two jelly roll pans for Kerry. They're on her Christmas wish list. On the spur of the moment, I call her.

"Are you home? Will you be there for a few minutes?"

"Yes and yes."

I want to give the jelly roll pans to Kerry now, in case she can use them for her Christmas baking. She answers the door in a jacket and scarf.

"Are you going somewhere?"

"No, just keeping warm."

I give her the red Macy's bag with the pans inside.

"Are these the right pans?"

"Yes, thanks."

Regan and Ayla are in the family room. Kerry and I stand in the entryway.

"I had my annual exam today, Mom. I have a lump in my right breast. I found it myself. I've had it for a month. I have to have a mammogram and some other tests."

I observe my daughter. She has a new haircut with bangs and tapered sides framing her face. She looks very cute. It takes a moment for her words to sink in. She's not crying, but close. She's scared. I put my arms around her and we hug.

"They can't see me for the tests until Monday. I don't want to wait that long. They may have another lab that I can get into sooner."

"Call them, now."

Kerry calls the doctor's office. It's closed. She calls another number. She's talking to someone like she's ordering pizza. Matter-of-fact. But her legs are shaking. Her body's shaking. She gets an appointment for 8:30 a.m. Friday morning.

"I'll go with you."

"You don't have to, Mom."

"I want to."

"Okay."

I hug my daughter, again. "We're not panicking yet. There's no family history of breast cancer. It could be nothing."

Kerry was planning to have Christmas Day at her house. She can't think about that right now.

"If you don't feel like hosting Christmas, we can have it at my house. What time should I be here Friday morning?"

"Come at eight and I'll drop the girls off for their rides to school."

Suddenly, getting ready for Christmas is on the back burner.

Patrick's Facebook Post: How do you spell relief? Insurance adjuster calls and informs you that your $1,000 deductible has been waived due to other party's fault.

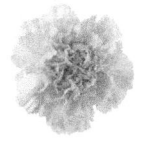

DECEMBER 19, 2013

PLANS AND PRIORITIES

I text Kerry. "How are you this morning?"

"I'm okay. I'm glad my appointment is tomorrow, though."

Me, too.

I get busy. I decide to clean my oven. You turn on the automatic cleaning cycle and let the oven clean itself. Piece of cake.

I press the self-clean button. I set the timer for two hours. The words "lock door" light up. I try to shut the door, but the door latch has protruded without catching and the door won't shut. The "lock door" light is flashing, but I can't shut the door to make it stop.

Hmm? I push another button—"control lock."

Oh, dear. Now everything's blocked. The "clear/off" pad's not working either. I pull out the oven manual. I check the troubleshooting section. No help there. Maybe there's a number to call for assistance.

I need the model and serial numbers. I find them on the left side of the range at the bottom, almost to the floor. I bend over but I can't read them. My trifocals aren't lining up so I can see the numbers.

I lie down on the floor on my stomach so I can get my glasses at a better angle. Who put these numbers in this position? What were they thinking? Did they consider the people who'd be sprawled on floors trying to read them? Were they laughing in the factory? Finally, after five minutes, I've copied the numbers.

I hope they're correct. I call the 800 customer service number. The number's not operative. This is beginning to feel like a communist plot. I don't want to call a repairman. My stubborn oven is not a repair issue. It's an operator failure issue. I call Neighbors InDeed, our neighborhood volunteer help line. I leave a message. It's embarrassing.

Long story short, an hour-and-a-half later a volunteer arrives at my door. He says, "I'm not sure what to do, but I'll take a stab at it."

After 45 minutes of trying this and that and almost giving up, the "lock door" light stops flashing. We push on the door latch and it aligns with its slot in the oven door. Three hours after I began, my automatic oven cleaner is set and functioning.

Now I'm at the local market. Another $89 in groceries. This is never-ending. Oven cleaning and grocery shopping, usually they're routine. Today they're diversions.

I was supposed to join a friend tomorrow to see *Catching Fire*, but instead, Kerry and I will meet. How quickly plans and priorities can change.

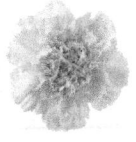

DECEMBER 20, 2013

IN THE MOMENT

I'm with Kerry at Sutter Hospital. She's wrapped in a hospital gown waiting for her ultrasound. She did some research online that makes her feel hopeful.

"There's an eighty-percent chance that I don't have breast cancer. Maybe it's because I'm thinking about it, but my right boob hurts."

"That's good," I say. "I don't think cancer hurts—at least in the beginning."

A nurse calls Kerry into the ultrasound room. Another nurse comes and offers me coffee or tea. She must know I'm a concerned mom. I thumb through a woman's magazine. Lots of yummy looking slow-cooker recipes—chicken soup, tomato sauce, chili, stews, short ribs. Comfort food. I brought a book to read, but it sits on the chair. Magazine articles are better suited to my attention span.

Kerry comes back. So far, so good. The ultrasound looks okay. She's bracing for the mammogram. This will be her first one. The same nurse calls Kerry again. Back to the slow-cooker recipes. I may have to buy this magazine. It's the January 2014 issue. Kerry returns.

"That wasn't bad. It pinched a little, that's all."

Ten minutes go by. The nurse comes out and says, "As soon as the radiologist is finished with another patient, I'll ask him to look at Kerry's mammograms."

This nurse is friendly and considerate. She knows we're waiting for the right report. When she comes back again she's smiling.

"Everything looks good. Call your doctor in six weeks for a follow-up check."

I'm smiling. My daughter's smiling. "I didn't know how that concern was weighing me down," she says. "I was really grumpy."

Kerry texts David. He texts right back. "Yay! I'm so relieved. I was so worried."

It's ten in the morning and, all of a sudden, we're both starving and ready for lunch. We drive to a nearby restaurant for soup and sandwiches. We talk about Christmas gifts and children and decorations.

"Kerry, do you feel like today is kind of another birthday?"

"Yes, wondering, even for a little while, is making me think differently about things."

My tomato-basil soup in a bread bowl is hot and well-seasoned. Kerry devours her beef-dip sourdough sandwich. We're both present in the moment. It feels so good.

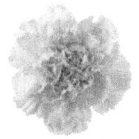

DECEMBER 22, 2013

HOW THE LIGHT GETS IN

I'm rereading Pat Schneider's new book, *How the Light Gets In*, about writing as a spiritual practice. Pat worked seven or eight years on the book. I believe she's close to 80 years old. I don't know her. Nevertheless, I send her an email.

"Dear Pat, I'm rereading your wonderful book, *How the Light Gets In*. I must confess that I'm making a mess of it with underlining, asterisks, and brackets. I'm sad that I've come so late to finding you.

"I'm turning 70 in 2014 and I'm writing my thoughts and reflections leading up to that event. My premise/excuse is that every voice is both average and extraordinary.

"I'm not sure, exactly, where 'my boat, my words' are taking me. I am sure that there's 'a place that I'm imagining, the existence of which I cannot prove, except by going there.'

"When I stare at my blank computer screen, your words will be a neon sign flashing in my mind. 'Take whatever comes.' Thank you so much."

Dede Ranahan

To my surprise, Pat replies.

"Dear Dede, Thank you so much for your beautiful message. I am delighted that my book is meaningful for you. It was a long and important journey for me, and I am thankful that it is helping you to write.

"Be brave, tell the truth, ring the bells that still will ring and let the light get in. My very best wishes for your writing and your life."

—PAT SCHNEIDER

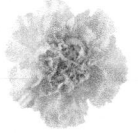

DECEMBER 24, 2013

CHRISTMAS EVE

My brother, Jim, and his wife, Sharon, arrived here on Saturday from San Diego. My nephew Michael and his wife, Karen, arrived on Sunday from Mountain View. It's been nonstop eating ever since.

We're testing two versions of my homemade Irish cream each day. One is made with whiskey and one with brandy. Looks like a toss-up. But it must be good, because everyone wants to test it again. And again.

Tomorrow is a Christmas open house at Kerry's. I'll bring ham and a sesame-noodle pasta salad. Thursday, the day after Christmas, will be my annual crab feed—fresh crab, sourdough bread, spaghetti with David's Bolognese sauce, mixed greens with dried cherries, pecans, and shaved parmesan, and peppermint and egg nog ice creams. And, of course, homemade Irish cream. Friday we'll begin leftovers.

We're hauling GG back and forth each day from her assisted living facility. We pick her up at 4 p.m. and she's ready to go home by 7:30. Pat comes over each night to join us for dinner. We celebrate family being together. This is, I think, as good as it gets.

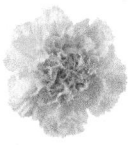

DECEMBER 25, 2013

A CHRISTMAS CARD

Dear Mom,

Thank you for everything you always do.
Akamai777.

Love, Pat

Note: Akamai (ah-ka-my) is Hawaiian slang for wit and wisdom. In spiritual numerology, 777 is a lucky number, a number of God. "Akamai777" meaning "Wit, wisdom, and a big hug from the universe," is one of Pat's favorite salutations. I don't know if he made it up or found it somewhere.

Patrick's Facebook Post: Merry Christmas Everyone! Love and Light!

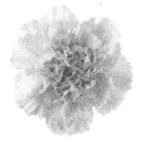

DECEMBER 30, 2013

CLUES

Christmas company's gone. Jim and Sharon left this morning. Jazzy's wandering around. "Where did all the people go? Is it just you and me again?"

I'm listening to music from the movies on my new stereo. It's a Christmas gift from Jim and Sharon. Jim spent two days buying it and hooking it up. It has five speakers and surround sound. When we turned it on for the first time, I caught my breath. My kitchen radio doesn't project and is full of static. This orchestra in my living room sends notes swirling through my soul.

To make the stereo work, I needed to upgrade my ten-year-old television. I now own a TV with DMI1. I'm not sure what DMI1 is, but the images on the screen are bright. Colors are vivid. People are three-dimensional.

When I bought my old TV, it was considered cutting-edge. How long will it take for this new one to be outdated? Six months? Built-in obsolescence discourages making choices. Choices must be made, however, or we live in suspended animation.

Megan, Marisa, and Kerry gave me a Kindle. Now I have more choices—books with covers and paper pages, or books downloaded on a computer-type device. I'll buy books when I want to keep them and underline and write in the margins. I'll read reviews and previews on the Kindle. I'll download books when I want to have one at the ready.

By the time a descendant chances to read this, TVs, stereos, and Kindles will be obsolete. Someone, an older person, will have to explain what the heck they were.

Today, people research their families on ancestry.com. They want to know who they are by knowing who they came from. They look for clues in "the old days." I'm trying to pay it forward by leaving these notes about "the old days" for those who come after.

Patrick's Facebook Post: I find more and more that, when faced with the various daily challenges life throws at me, I am beginning to repeat an old mantra, "Lord Have Mercy."

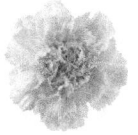

DECEMBER 31, 2013

HAPPY NEW YEAR

It's the last day of the year and I'm working at the kitty rescue thrift store. Goodbye 2013.

Like all other years, 2013 flew by. It gave us a pope from South America, Prince George in England, civil rights advances, worries over national security surveillance programs, chemical weapons in Syria, severe weather, gun violence, health care struggles, water shortages, and government impasses.

Tomorrow, the first day of the new year, offers chances for new beginnings:

We'll try harder.

We'll hold hands and celebrate diversity.

We'll love our brothers and sisters.

We'll be good stewards of earth and its creatures.

We'll cure the sick and feed the hungry.

We'll make the distribution of wealth more equitable.

We'll guarantee gender equality in jobs and politics.

We'll make sure technology is in sync with our human hearts and minds.

We won't fight.

We won't go to war.

By February, the new year's aura will have begun to fade. We'll have failed to keep our resolutions even through January. Politics, economics, and other world woes will challenge us and drag us back into old bad habits. But tonight and tomorrow we have hope. We have breath and life. Help us remember, 2014, every day we have one day to try to be the best we can be.

Patrick's Facebook Post: Highlights from helping Mom to set up her new HDTV stereo system: Getting her to listen to "Holy Diver" by Ronnie James, "Dio Blackout" by The Scorpions, and "Little Too Late" by Nicki Bluhm and the Gamblers. 2013 was a very good year—moved into a new house, had cancer-free MRIs, got a dog, enjoyed myself. Ready for 2014 to be filled with new opportunities for learning, employment, and relationship. Happy New Year everyone!

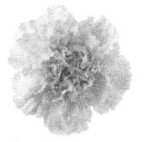

JANUARY 1, 2014

DOING WHATEVER I WANT

I'm putting the house back together—taking ornaments off the Christmas tree, stowing snowmen away, retiring Jesus, Mary, and Joseph for another year. It's fun putting up Christmas decorations. It's a relief to take them down. At first, the house looks bare. Then it begins to look peaceful and uncluttered again.

I'm not making much progress. I keep taking time out to read the first book I've downloaded onto my new Kindle—*Gone Girl* by Gillian Flynn. It's a thriller and a page-turner. I'm still in my pajamas. No make-up. No plans to leave the house. Basking in downtime from nonstop holiday eating and a houseful of guests. A quiet, do-whatever-I-want kind of day.

Patrick's Facebook Post: Unlike many New Year's Eves gone by where I rang in the new year with the Grateful Dead, last night I had a low-key evening of working sound for a burning bowl ceremony at the church (a much different burning bowl than you find with the Dead), went out for beer and appetizers at the Yard House with the minister and a couple of ladies from the church. Yes, church ladies. Then went out alone to a local Irish pub where I found nothing I liked in the drunken crowd, the horrible music, and the incessant noise. Was home and in bed by 11:15 p.m. Hard to believe I'm the same person I was twenty years ago.

Gayle: On the first day of the year I need to tell you, Patrick, that everything you write and say makes me smile or shake my head.

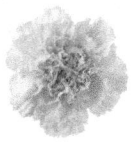

JANUARY 2, 2014

STORIES IN THE NEWS

There's a story in the newspaper today about a marine ecosystem that scientists are calling the "plasticsphere"—a new, human-caused ecosystem of plastic debris. The plasticsphere is a product of discarded plastic items—flip flops, margarine tubs, toys, toothbrushes—that get swept from sewer systems and river systems into the sea. When the debris washes into the ocean, it breaks down into bits that are colonized by microscopic organisms. Scientists fear that chunks of polyethylene and polypropylene then percolate into the environment.

According to the article, about 245 million tons of plastic residue is produced each year. That represents 70 pounds of plastic for each of the 7.1 billion people on the planet. Researchers are studying this trash to determine the damage it does to our oceans. And to us.

Another story is about computerizing people—a movement to outfit people with electronic devices than can be swallowed, implanted, or attached to skin via "smart tattoos." Critics say this pushes the boundaries of what it means to be human. Supporters envision a day when devices, placed in people, will enable them to control computers, prosthetic limbs, and other objects with their thoughts.

A nonprofit organization, Mars One, based in the Netherlands, has the goal of turning the colonization of Mars into a reality show. Over 200,000 people have applied for a one-way ticket to Mars. More than half are under the age of 35, but 26 are over 56. The oldest applicant is 81. The US has the most applicants—297— moving into round two of the winnowing process. In the next four years, Mars One will cull the applicant group down to 40. Those selected will train in groups for seven years. Then, a global audience will vote and choose the first team to go to Mars in 2025.

In 2025, I'll be 81. Body and soul of mine, please stay healthy and together. I want to be around and find out how these stories play out . . .

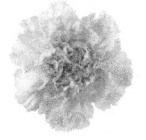

JANUARY 3, 2014

A LIFETIME'S TOO SHORT

I've finished reading Madeleine L'Engle's *A Wrinkle in Time*, which I should have read as a kid but didn't. I'm poking around on the internet, trying to understand what a tesseract is.

I'm looking at interactive diagrams. I get the first dimension— a line. I get the second dimension—the square of the line—a flat square. I even get the third dimension—the square of the second dimension—the flat square is no longer flat. It has a bottom, sides and a top. It's a cube.

This is where it gets dicey. You square the cube, but you can't really draw it. Some people call this the fourth dimension or time. Then, to get to the fifth dimension, you square the fourth. And the fifth is a tesseract—a wrinkle in time or a shortcut through space.

Of course. Silly me. Why didn't I see this before?

One site says in 200 years we may have a different understanding of the fourth and fifth dimensions that will change everything. Great. I don't have 200 years to find out how everything gets changed. I'm feeling frustrated when, in fact, everyone faces the same dilemma. There's more to know than can be grasped in one lifetime.

JANUARY 4, 2014

BABY, IT'S COLD OUTSIDE

Bears hibernate when it's cold outside—and it's cold outside. I think I'm part bear. I know what I'm about to do and I don't want to admit it.

It's 4:30 in the afternoon.

I kick off my shoes and crawl into bed.

I pull the red, velvety throw round my hands and my head. That rhymes.

My bones are cold. They feel like frozen chicken bones. I'll warm up under the covers. My eyes are closing. It's light outside.

My eyes are opening. It's dark outside. And it's still so darn cold on the other side of these blankets. The good angel, on my right shoulder, says, "Get up."

The bad angel, on my left shoulder, says, "Naw. Go ahead. Wallow in warmth and softness. Stay where you are."

I agree with the bad angel. Who wrote the rules about having to be up freezing my buns off in a cold house? The good angel is losing patience. "You're being ridiculous. Get up. Act like a grown-up."

All right, already. I throw back the covers, dash to the closet, and grab a sweater. I check my email. Someone's forwarded photographs of old people looking into mirrors, seeing themselves as they looked sixty years ago. One man says, "It's a universal condition—at some point in your life, you look in the mirror and say, 'Wait a minute, how did I get this old?'"

Someone else adds, "I need to go lie down for a while."

For crying out loud. I think the bad angel sent this email. Be forewarned, bad angel. I'm not getting back into bed. I'm going to look at myself in the mirror. What reflection will I see? I'll probably see a bear, an old scruffy bear, scratching her butt on a redwood tree and about to curl up in a dark, toasty cave.

JANUARY 5, 2014

MY TO-DO LIST

It's a new year. People make New Year's resolutions. I don't. Instead, I'll make a short list of things I want to get done. It's my little ritual of visualizing goals to make them happen. Last year, my list included the following:

1. Get Pat into permanent housing.
2. Sell the golf cart.
3. Install storage cabinets in the garage.

Check. Check. And check.
What's on my have-to-get-done list for 2014?

1. Update my living trust.
2. Sign on with a personel trainer at our community gym.
3. Plan something for my 70th birthday.

The first item doesn't need explanation. The second item's because, if I don't have someone waiting for me to show up, I won't make it to my workout.

Last week, I bought two three-pound barbells at the thrift shop. These two purple bell thingies were sitting, side by side, on a small table, when one of them picked itself up and threw itself onto the floor. I'm not kidding. It didn't roll off the table. It flew off the table. It landed with a loud thud. No one was standing nearby. The three of us in the shop froze. We looked at the barbell. We looked at each other. Whoa. What just happened here? How did that barbell move? A big sign.

GO TO THE GYM.

The third item on my to-do list is about my birthday. Here's the thing, the only birthday party I ever planned for myself was when my then-husband and I turned 40 at the same time. When I was married, I waited, hoping something would happen on my birthday. Often, whatever happened was last-minute. "You want to go to dinner or something? It's past six o'clock. We could go to the club."

I should have been less self-negating. I should have taken the bull by the horns. I should have stormed the barricades. I should have drawn my sword and shouted, "Carpe Diem!"

My birthday's coming up.

My birthday's this year.

My birthday's next month.

My birthday's next week.

My birthday's tomorrow.

My birthday's today and we have reservations for dinner at Scoma's in San Francisco.

I should have left notes around the house. "I want a 22-inch, dark blue, beaded, single-strand necklace with a decorative clasp, to wear with the light-blue dress I bought for my birthday. Thank you very much."

I should have been obnoxious.

At any rate, my birthday's in a few months—my seventieth birthday. How many times have I mentioned this? Am I being obnoxious?

In the past year, I've lost four friends who didn't make it to 70. I want my turning 70 to be meaningful. I want turning 70 to be an expression of gratitude. I don't know, yet, what this commemoration will look like—a party, a trip, a house full of family and friends, a silent retreat? But I have it written down on my to-do list for 2014. And if something's written down on my list, it generally comes to pass.

Patrick's Facebook Post: California weather update for my East Coast friends: 58 degrees and cloudy.

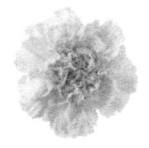

JANUARY 7, 2014

THE BRIAR PATCH

Back working at the thrift store. It's received so many donations in the past month—people cleaning out closets—that we're having a sale to move merchandise.

ALL CLOTHING AND SHOES IN THE STORE ARE $1
THE SALE CONTINUES UNTIL JANUARY 21.

Starburst, an orange kitten, is in the adoption room. He's six-months-new to this world and he's got attitude. "I'm here. Listen to me roar."

Starburst's two siblings have been adopted and he doesn't like being alone. His cries are loud and demanding. Guests in the store take turns playing with him. Pick him up and you press a purr button. Never mind he doesn't know you. He likes you.

One little girl wants to adopt Starburst. "I have to ask my dad. I'm going to go home and draw two kitty pictures. One for my house and one for the store."

"Wonderful. We'll put your drawing on the bulletin board."

Last week, the same little girl wanted to buy a s'more maker. Her mother told her to go home and ask her father. The next day she was back. "Dad said 'yes' to the s'more maker."

This time her mother tells her, "It may not work the same way when you ask for a kitten."

People are taking their time shopping. They don't want to overlook a good buy. I offer assistance. "Can I take those clothes out of your arms while you shop for more?"

Folks head out the door with 20 pieces of clothing each—dresses, shirts, shoes, winter jackets, leather jackets, children's outfits, sweaters—for $20 plus tax. A woman buys a long violet evening gown. She's not planning to wear it. "This dress will make lots of doll clothes."

Another woman buys a card maker. A new lady enters looking for an egg plate. We don't have one anywhere, but we do get them in. She'll check back. It's for an art project. An elderly woman is hunting for tap shoes. She's signed up for tap lessons.

People, with bits and pieces of their stories, file in and out the door. In and out the door. I feel like Br'er Rabbit in the Uncle Remus tales. Someone's thrown me in the briar patch.

Patrick's Facebook Post: One of the great things about being the son of a doctor was that you could always get a prescription when you needed one. I called the Kaiser advice nurse and reported my sore throat and congestion and was advised to "do a saltwater gargle." I might as well have called my grandmother.

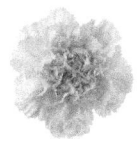

JANUARY 9, 2014

WTF

Pat calls. "I met with the bankruptcy attorney this morning. All the paperwork is turned in. We're waiting for a court date. Probably in February. I saw a program at Sierra Junior College for library tech certification. I think I'd qualify for a loan. It's about $10,000 per semester for two semesters, but I'd need help with the registration fees and books."

"Why is it so much per semester?"

"Well, it covers living expenses like housing and food."

"But you have housing and food."

"Barely. It would be nice to have things not be so tight."

"You're filing bankruptcy. It's not time to take on new debt. Go to some libraries in the area. Talk to the head librarians. Find out if they're hiring and what skill sets they need. You may end up getting a certificate for a job that's being eliminated with budget cuts."

"I knew I shouldn't have told you about this. I'm trying to do something constructive and you're being negative. Bye."

I need the wisdom and patience of I don't know WTF who.

Just hung up the phone with my new personal trainer, Deanne. She made me feel good. "I have clients in their late eighties. You're just a kid."

I may be a "kid" but I'm an out-of-shape kid. Deanne has her work cut out for her. I do, too. My first session will be next

Tuesday, and we'll work on strength, balance, and flexibility. My goals are to feel less stiff in the morning, to be able to stand up from a squatting position without help, and to have more muscle strength in my arms and legs.

Deanne will give me some exercises to do with my new purple weights. That should keep the spirits in the thrift store quiet. Let's hope Pat's bankruptcy and my strength-training go well.

JANUARY 10, 2014

OUR SUPPORT GROUP

At the Family Mental Illness Support Group, ten people show up, including two new people. Random comments at the meeting:

"I'm here to support my twin sister."

"I found a new psychiatrist to help me with anxiety issues about my bipolar son."

"Things seem to be revving up with my daughter again."

"Well, we're here because we come every time. Our son is homeless."

"My daughter lives clear across the country but I still need support."

"Our son is back home with us. The housing he was in foreclosed and he had nowhere else to go. It's driving a wedge between my husband and me."

I tell the group, "We've been offered an opportunity to get a little funding from the local foundation. We could use the money for books, speakers, and programs. Do you want me to pursue this?"

There's a unanimous "Yes."

"What are some of the topics you'd like to have addressed?"

"Housing."

"Denial."

"Legal issues."

"Special Needs Trusts."

"Okay. I'll look into the application process and get it started. Have a good month everyone."

Patrick's Facebook Post: Top ten books that have had pivotal influence for me:

1. *Letters to a Young Poet*, Rainer Maria Rilke
2. *Franny and Zooey,* J.D. Salinger
3. *The Great American Novel,* Philip Roth
4. *Fear of Flying*, Erica Jong
5. *Storming Heaven,* Jay Stevens
6. *On the Road,* Jack Kerouac
7. *A Confederacy of Dunces*, John Kennedy Toole
8. *The Collected Poems of Joseph Brodsky*, Joseph Brodsky
9. *The Phantom Tollbooth*, Norton Juster
10. *Autobiography of a Yogi*, Paramahansa Yogananda

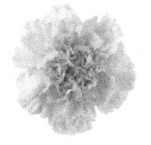

JANUARY 11, 2014

THAT'S ALL FOLKS

Yahoo. I played duplicate bridge this morning and my partner and I came in second. It's a puzzle. When we think we've played well, we come in last. When we think we've played like fish, we come in first. It keeps one humble. But oh, on days like today, coming in second felt marvelous.

Now I'm cleaning floors like Miss Happy Homemaker in a TV commercial—sans the ruffled apron and dark red lipstick. I have a smile on my face and a trill in my voice. Jazzy's running for cover. I don't know if she's afraid of the vacuum cleaner or the spirited woman pushing it.

Tomorrow, friends I met on Guam 41 years ago are coming for the night. All in all, a good weekend. That's all folks. Yabba daba-doo.

Patrick's Facebook Post: I guess I should take my Christmas tree down but thinking about leaving it up for the rest of the year.

JANUARY 12, 2014

OLD FRIENDS

I'm waiting for my friends, Bill and Bette, to arrive. I've popped a cranberry pie-cake in the oven. I've licked the batter in the bowl. Eggs, flour, sugar, butter, and almond flavoring. Yummy.

Bill and Bette ring the doorbell. They walk in and we start chatting where we left off two years ago. Bette and I share Instagram photos on our smart phones. Bill dithers with his smart tablet. We're three old farts, sitting in my living room, trying to use technology. Glad no one's watching.

I make tuna sandwiches for lunch. We watch the 49ers win their football game. We drive to dinner at a southern ribs place. Bill orders deep fried okra as an appetizer. I wrinkle my nose but then eat my fair share. We watch *Downton Abbey* and cut into the cranberry pie and wash it down with homemade Irish cream.

All of us turn in at the bewitching hour of 10 p.m. Bill plugs in his breathing machine for his sleep apnea and wraps it in a towel to muffle the noise. "It bothers Betty," he says. These folks generally get up early—like 5:15 a.m. For my sake, Bill sleeps in until 6 a.m. and Bette starts getting dressed at 7 a.m. I join them to make breakfast.

Bill and Bette have attended exercise classes at 5:45 a.m., three times a week, for 20 or 30 or some ungodly number of years. I'm in awe. Nothing, and I mean nothing, is important to me at 5:45 in the morning except to stay warm under the covers. Guess you could say I'm not a morning person.

Bill ambles out to get the newspaper. His back is hurting—he has arthritis in his spine. Several neighbors are out walking dogs. "They saw me," he says. "Maybe they'll start a rumor about a man spending the night at your house." Bill's sprouting horns. "Let's sneak Bette out the back door so no one sees her. They'll only see me."

It's 9 a.m. Bill's pulling out his maps. Who uses maps anymore? Bill uses maps. He loves maps and he spreads them out on the kitchen table. He's marked two routes home—a direct route and a longer, more scenic one. He's trying to decide which to take. He'll decide on the road.

"Let us know if you want to travel someplace with us. Come visit us in Medford."

I wave as Bill and Bette back their grey SUV out of the driveway. It's good to keep in touch with old friends.

Patrick's Facebook Post: A poster. "Relax. Nothing is under control." And all this time I thought the opposite.

JANUARY 14, 2014

WORKING OUT

I'm at the gym with Deanne. She's my new personal trainer. She's young and pretty with a long, brown ponytail, dark brown eyes, and a toned, healthy-looking figure. If I pursue this fitness program will I look like Deanne?

Deanne asks about my health and has me check off boxes on a form. "Looks like you're pretty healthy," she says.

Pretty healthy and out of shape. We get right to it. I'm lifting weights over my head and to the sides. I'm pushing handles on weight machines. I'm leaning on chairs, crossing my legs and stretching my hamstrings. Hamstrings, biceps, triceps, quadriceps—I hear Deanne using these words.

I do two sets of 12 of each exercise. I try to remember to breathe. Is it exhale on exertion or inhale? "Don't worry," Deanne says. "It's most important to keep breathing. If you mix up inhaling and exhaling sometimes, it's okay."

The half hour flies by. "You'll be sore tomorrow," Deanne says as a matter of fact.

I leave the gym and go to Snap It Up. The manager asks if I can hold down the fort for a few minutes on my own. I assure her I'll be fine. It's busy. People are aware of our "all shoes and clothing for $1 sale." Two hours into this shift and, oh my, I'm feeling a tad sore. Three hours in and I'm feeling worse. I sit down at the cash register when there's a lull.

Now I'm at Lori's salon getting a haircut and highlight. In addition to being sore, I'm getting stiff. I fall into Lori's chair. I moan and groan when I have to move to the shampoo bowl.

I'm wondering what it will be like getting out of bed tomorrow morning. Maybe I should sleep in a chair. It might be easier to lift my body out of a chair than out of my bed. And Sonia will be here at 8 a.m. sharp to clean. I better set my alarm for 6 a.m. It might take me a while to get up, showered, and dressed. I may get slower before I get faster.

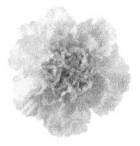

JANUARY 16, 2014

ROSE

My friend Rose and I are meeting for lunch. She's 75 and such a trooper. She's still fighting the exhaustive fight for a competent mental health system. She's one of three co-authors of California's Prop 63, the Mental Health Services Act.

Disappointed in its implementation, Rose lobbied for an audit by the California State Auditor. The auditor reported that it wasn't possible to determine whether Prop 63 programs had been of benefit to those served, had improved community mental health delivery, or whether programs had complied with the requirements of the law.

In addition to the appalling number of untreated mentally ill, Rose, based on her continuing research, believes eighty percent of those in the system are not receiving adequate care. "Parity," she says, "we still don't have parity for physical and mental health."

"Would you be willing to come speak to my support group? I'm applying for some funding so we can reimburse speakers for their gas and give them a small honorarium for their time."

"Yes, I'll speak to your group."

Rose's husband and son always come up in our conversations. They both ended their struggle with mental illness by suicide. Two grandsons—one is living with her—also deal with the illness. We agree. If all the parents and grandparents housing their mentally ill children and grandchildren were to dump them on the street, there'd be major socio-economic fallout. Our health and welfare programs would be more overwhelmed than they already are. These family members, who've given up on the mental health system, are a hidden, unappreciated population.

I ask about a mutual friend's thirty-something son. County mental health hasn't helped him. He has schizo-affective disorder and is in Napa State Hospital for the seriously mentally ill. Rose says, "He was charged with a crime after he got into a fight with another patient. He spent weeks in the county jail and then was transferred to the 'other side of the wall.' He's in the forensic unit of the hospital under horrible conditions with chains on his legs and wrists. He has a good attorney, but the whole process is really outrageous."

I can't imagine what this is like for my friend. My mother-heart shudders for her. We change the subject. We talk about Rose's 75th birthday party. We talk about my mother, my children, and grandchildren. We try to talk about everyday things like average folks. We hug goodbye and remind each other, "Take care of yourself."

Patrick's Facebook Post: It's been said that you always get screwed at the drive-through but lately I've been getting screwed every time I buy cottage cheese. Something about it doesn't taste right.

Mark: Sounds like it tastes like cottage cheese.

JANUARY 17, 2014

AMERICAN HUSTLE

My friend Grace and I are at the movies to see *American Hustle*. The theater's sold out. We end up sitting in different rows. It's a good movie with good actors—Bradley Cooper, Amy Adams, and Jennifer Lawrence. I'm enthralled watching Jennifer Lawrence. She's 22 or 23 and she's amazing. It will be interesting to see how her acting career progresses.

After the movie, Grace and I buy salads from the deli at Nugget Market. We catch up. Among other things, we talk about Governor Brown's announcement today. "It's official. California's experiencing a severe drought, the worse in 100 years."

The governor's requesting a 20 percent reduction in water usage. Folsom Reservoir is so short of water that a ghost town, submerged by the lake, has become visible. The American River is at a two-decades low. The water shortage threatens, among other things, California's Central Valley agriculture and the supply of water sent to Southern California.

Water is always political. Ongoing fights continue between Northern and Southern California about water rights. With this drought, water will become even more political. In the hours after Governor Brown's announcement, opponents of fracking repeated their call for a moratorium on the process of extracting oil by using large amounts of water. They called for more water storage and more dam construction.

In the movie this morning, some 1978 congressmen were caught accepting bribes in exchange for supporting private interests. They were sent to prison. My guess is that today, behind the scenes, there's an "American hustle" going on among California's special water interests.

What's that saying? "The more things change, the more they stay the same."

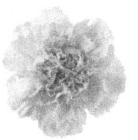

JANUARY 18, 2014

SORRY STATE OF MENTAL HEALTH CARE

An email message today from NAMI California is quoting an article in the *Wall Street Journal*.

"According to the US Department of Health and Human Services, almost 91 million adults live in areas where shortages of mental health professionals make obtaining treatment difficult.

"A departmental report to Congress earlier this year said 55% of the nation's 3,100 counties have no practicing psychiatrists, psychologists or social workers, a combination of budget cuts and doctors leaving the profession.

"Such shortages are expected to grow now, as the federal healthcare law goes into effect and allows more people to seek help. Indeed, according to the National Association of State Mental Health Program Directors, some 6.8 million uninsured people with a mental illness will gain coverage after federal and state health insurance exchanges implement the new law.

"More people will be chasing after scarce resources, an influx that will 'overwhelm if not inundate the field,' said Dr. Jeffrey Lieberman, president of the American Psychiatric Association."

Patrick's Facebook Post: The cough syrup with codeine the Doc gave me triggers hyper-REM sleep. Very intense dreams.

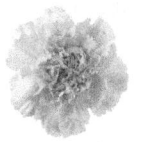

JANUARY 19, 2014

LEARN AND LIVE

This quote appears in an advice column in today's newspaper. "We have two lives. The life we learn with and the life we live with after that." Bernard Malamud

The writer to the advice columnist signs her letter "Just Sick." She says she lied to her date about using birth control and now she's pregnant. She's in her 40s with no husband and no support. She's realizing she doesn't know how to undo the mess she's made.

The adviser, Carolyn Hax, admonishes "Just Sick." "You've become rudely acquainted with what a bad person you're capable of being. Arguably everyone will, or should, have that awakening over the course of a lifetime—but it's still tough to live with."

Hax advises J.S. to get therapy to help her use this lesson to become a better person than she was pre-deceit.

When does the life we learn with end, and the life we live with begin after that? My life is like a grocery cart still filling up with assorted mistakes and lessons learned. All the more reason to throw in hefty boxes of humility, cases of compassion, sacks of self-awareness, and cartons of respect for consequences—intended and unintended.

Patrick's Facebook Post: Well, it's officially the marijuana super bowl. Two cities who have legalized marijuana battling it out. The Super Bowl indeed.

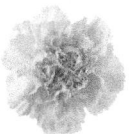

JANUARY 20, 2014

FOOTBALL

Deanne's giving me my Monday morning workout. She's recapping yesterday's football game between Seattle and San Francisco. She's describing incorrect calls by the referees. Deanne's fit, pretty, and nice. And on top of that, she understands football. How long can I keep liking this woman?

Often, I feel like I'm the only person in the hemisphere who doesn't get football. And what's more, I don't care. Football's messy. Football's mean. People get hurt. President Obama said this week, "If I had a son I wouldn't let him play college football. There's too much risk of serious injury—especially life-changing brain injury."

I'll try to remember that it's the Denver Broncos and the Seattle Seahawks who are headed to the Super Bowl. I'll say, "Isn't it sad about the 49ers losing?"

My phone rings. It's Kerry. I can't resist. I don't say, "Hello." I say, "Isn't it sad about the 49ers losing?"

Kerry's laughing. She knows I don't give a fig about the 49ers. You can fool some of the people some of the time, though. To others I'll say what I read on the internet: "The Seahawks started as the favorite in Vegas, but there was early action and the Broncos, within 30 minutes, became the favorite all over town."

I wonder if Deanne knows this?

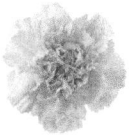

JANUARY 21, 2014

SNAFU

Megan's entry today on her blog.

SNAFU . . . Situation Normal All F*ed Up

"When Aidan fell and lost his baby tooth at two, we were told he would have to wait five or six years for the adult tooth to show up. It broke my heart. He was cheated out of his top tooth for the first eight years of his life, and when the tooth finally showed up, it was sideways. SNAFU!

"Curious people always asked what happened to his tooth and it got to be a really old story. I wanted to snap my fingers and give him the straight tooth he deserved as soon as possible. Fortunately, after waiting six years, an orthodontist aligned the sideways tooth in no time and Aidan's missing, then crooked tooth, is a fading memory.

"Unfortunately, it's Ashton's turn to wait. It's been two years since his osteotomy. The surgery was a hopeful attempt to realign his right hip so that the degenerated femoral head could regenerate and put the Legg-Calve-Perthes diagnosis behind him. We were told that the regeneration phase could take two years.

"Ashton's been patient and here we are, two years later. Unfortunately, we now know that the prognosis isn't in his favor. His femoral head didn't regenerate and it's not aligned for proper growth. Ashton will need a hip replacement, but he has to wait. Hip replacements aren't done on a growing child. "Early twenties," they say, "perhaps late teens."

"Ashton is barely 10.

"This sounds like an eternity to me. I imagine ten more years of stiffness, lethargy, limping, and pain for my son. Again, I want to snap my fingers. I want to see a different X-ray. I want to see the one that shows healthy bones on both sides of his pelvis. I want to see him daily tie his shoes, ride his bike, walk the dog, play any sport he desires, and become a young man with a confident gait. But I can't because the SNAFU is right in front of me, in black and white.

"Listening to the orthopedic specialist, I'm heartbroken, but I don't show it because I'm being watched. My 10-year-old son is watching me to determine what this adult conversation means for him. If I cry, his heart will break, too. So I don't. I play the part of the confident mother. The mother who knows that everyone has a SNAFU in their cards. This is Ashton's. This is ours.

"Like it or not. We got this."

I want to hold my daughter. She will hold her son.

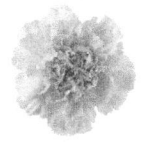

JANUARY 23, 2014

THE PAPERWORK MONSTER

There's nothing on my calendar today except paperwork. I'm paying my bills and Pat's bills. I'm organizing a 2013 tax file and collecting information to take to an attorney to update my living trust and Mom's living trust. I'm completing the application for funding for the mental illness support group. I'm scheduling my annual physical, Jazzy's annual physical, the heater's annual physical, and an eye exam.

The Jazz is as bored as I am. She's pacing back and forth in front of the computer screen. "Do something," she says. "Get out of that chair."

If I get out of this chair, none of the above will happen. It will get postponed until tomorrow or the next day. It won't go away. I see a scary mass of papers spreading out across my desk. It's the Paperwork Monster. It's big and white with blotches of color, irregular edges, and humps and bumps. I can't spray it, shoot it, drown it, or set it on fire—unless I want to burn the house down at the same time.

If the Paperwork Monster could talk it would say, "I've got you. You might ignore me today, but I'll be back tomorrow. I'll be back tomorrow and tomorrow until you have no tomorrow."

Well, that's a sobering thought. Guess I don't want the Paperwork Monster to disappear completely. Unfortunately, we're symbiotic organisms. This fact, frustrating as it is, gives me a modicum of comfort.

Remember this, Paperwork Monster. When I go, you go.

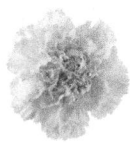

JANUARY 24, 2014

I'M ENGAGED

I'm dreaming and, in my dream, George Clooney's proposing to me. He says, "I know this is the real thing because you have the same placemats as my sister."

I don't remember showing George my placemats. 'Tis of no consequence. I know this is the real thing, too, because we're on a movie set with lots of actors and crew wandering around. George is proposing to me in front of all of them. He gives me three engagement gifts.

The first gift is a candy rosebush covered with dark chocolate roses and edible blinking lights.

The second gift is three pair of long dangly earrings. The first pair has big silver hoops with blue, world globes hanging from them. The second pair has long, wispy, red-and-green parrots made from real feathers. The third pair resembles snowshoes. Miniature snowshoes. I don't wear long dangly earrings. But hey, if George were to give me earrings carved from watermelon rind, I'd wear them.

The third gift is enclosed in an expensive gold box. It's a do-it-yourself necklace—a gold chain with 56 gilded Brazil nuts to string on at my leisure.

We're taking a break on the set. We've about finished filming, but George, as producer, has decided to scrap this screenplay and start over. I give him a copy of my "Manifesto for Mental Health Care Reform." He loves my script. He's making it the centerpiece of the new screenplay. In this story, a determined lady like my friend Rose fights for mental illness parity. It's a musical. I'm in the lead role.

In a few minutes, George is taking me to meet his sister. He wants to show me her placemats. Then darn. I wake up.

JANUARY 26, 2014

ON TO OFF

What a mix of a day. It began pulsating with possibilities.

I've located a writer's group in the Sacramento area. The group is sponsoring a six-week writing course for $60. This is doable. The hitch is the class is in the evening and about 45 minutes away. I no longer like to drive in the dark. I'm hoping Pat might want to join me. He could drive my car and tap into his inner poet. I've invited him for dinner. I'll ask him.

Pat arrives at 10 minutes to six with Lexi in tow. I'm slicing a small loaf of sourdough to make garlic bread. I leave the kitchen briefly and, when I return, several slices are missing. Where's Lexi? She's cowering on the sofa. Pat drags her into the kitchen and shows her the bread.

"Bad dog, Lexi. Bad dog."

"Did you feed Lexi her dinner, yet?"

"I don't remember. I'll check her dish when I get home."

I'm preparing chicken cacciatore. The kitchen throbs with the aroma of chicken simmering in tomato sauce, onion, garlic, mushrooms, and red wine. We sit down to eat.

"So Pat, how was your day?"

"Fine."

"How was the gospel singer at the church service this morning?"

"Good."

"Were many people there?"

"Yes."

"How many?" This takes a few moments. "Fifty? One hundred?"

"About fifty."

The conversation is one-way. No questions or comments are coming back at me. Pat's affect is flat. He's not interested in the writing workshop. "I've done enough of those."

"Recently?"

"When I was in college."

"Okay. Well, think about it. I'd pay for it and I'd enjoy your company." I don't ask, "What are you up to tomorrow?" I know the answer. "Not much."

"Would you like some ice cream?"

"No."

"I have chocolate sauce."

"No, thanks."

"Do you want to take the leftovers home?"

"Okay. Thanks."

I pack up an unopened box of spaghetti, the remaining garlic bread, and the chicken and sauce. "Don't let Lexi get it," I warn.

"I won't. Come on Lexi, let's go home. Thanks for dinner, Mom."

"Thanks for coming, Pat."

Pat hugs me and I hug him back. My son and his dog disappear down the sidewalk into the dark night. I close the front door. I stare at the dirty dishes on the kitchen counter. The pot that was filled with lusty sauce is empty. I feel like an electric candle that someone's switched from on to off.

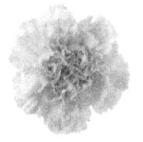

JANUARY 28, 2014

ANOTHER TRAGEDY

A woman from the support group calls to tell me about her friend's son. On January 19, this 20-year-old man jumped to his death from the Golden Gate Bridge. His mother had tried everything to get help for her son's mental illness.

On a balmy San Francisco day, another unserved youth decided he couldn't go on and tossed himself into the bay. How does a mother bear it?

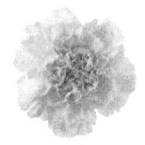

JANUARY 29, 2014

A NEW WRINKLE

Pat has a job. He's delivering automotive parts for a business in Auburn. They'll pay him eight dollars per hour plus four dollars per hour reimbursement for gas. He stops by to tell me about his first day. There's a catch. He doesn't get paid for two weeks. This means he's covering gas costs for this business in advance. He's putting wear and tear on his car.

"Can you front me five hundred dollars until my first paycheck?"

"Why do you need five hundred dollars?"

"To cover gas and pay for lunches."

"Pat, I can't do this. Take your lunch. Most working people don't buy lunch every day. Five dollars per day amounts to one hundred dollars per month. That's money to buy Lexi's dog food and pay for other expenses. This employer shouldn't ask you to cover gas costs the first two weeks. They know you've been out of work."

"Mom, I haven't had work in seven years. I don't want to rock the boat and jeopardize this job."

"Pat, what if they renege? What if they're not reliable? I can't afford to lose five hundred dollars."

I give Pat a check for $40 for gas. "What would you do if I weren't around to help you?"

"I wouldn't be able to take this job."

Pat leaves. He has to get home and check on Lexi, who's been in her crate all day. That's another issue. This poor dog cannot be locked up for eight hours every day. I sit down and take a deep breath. With Pat, there's always a new wrinkle.

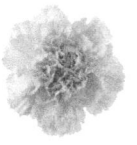

JANUARY 30, 2014

TRADITION AND HERITAGE

I'm immersing myself in an author I've recently discovered. David Mas Masumoto is an organic peach and grape farmer in Del Rey, California—the Central Valley. In his book, *Heirlooms: Letters from a Peach Farmer,* he has a two-generation theory about family. "How many remember our father's and mother's first names? Probably most of us. How about our grandfather and grandmother? Still, most likely, many of us. But how about our great-grandparents? Most have two generation knowledge of our heritage and, within a short time, you and I will probably be forgotten." To Mas, this sounds tragic.

Mas says the things he values include tradition, slow trucks, the culture of fog, home, delayed gratification, memories, thinking, reflection and stories. He means what he says and chooses his words carefully.

Thank you, Mas. I'll try to follow your example. I'll think about tradition and heritage. I'll mean what I write. I'll choose my words carefully.

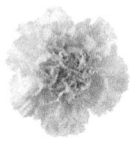

JANUARY 31, 2014

REQUESTS AND SUCCESS

Grants Committee
Lincoln Hills Foundation
P.O. Box 220
Lincoln, CA 95648

Jan 31, 2014
Dear Grants Committee:

Thank you for the invitation to submit a grant request.

I organized this new group—Lincoln Hills Family Mental Illness Support Group—in February 2013. We've had monthly meetings since then.

This is a support group for SCLH family members who have loved ones coping with serious mental illnesses such as bipolar disorder, schizophrenia, personality disorder, clinical depression, obsessive-compulsive disorder, and others.

In many cases, the public mental health system has failed to serve our ill family members, providing inadequate care and poor outcomes. Many in the group, like myself, are the only reason a son, daughter, mother, father, sibling or adult grandchild is not homeless and on the street. Some of us have ill loved ones in prison, unemployed, and in other challenging circumstances.

Our family situations can be unpredictable, chaotic, and heavy financial burdens. Stress levels are high.

Stigma surrounding mental illness is prevalent. Therefore, we meet in the conference room at Raley's. This gives a modicum of privacy removed from SCLH and a safe haven. Our monthly meeting gives us a chance to vent and know that others in the group will understand without judging. We offer support, an exchange of information about resources, and the important knowledge that we are not alone.

To date, we have about 35 members in the group email list. On average, eight to ten attend each meeting. I've promised the group that there will always be a meeting on the second Friday of the month no matter how many are in attendance. They need to be able to count on the meeting routinely taking place.

With a grant, we could purchase books for the group and bring in speakers. Honorariums and speaking fees would determine the number of speakers we could engage in a year's time. With no previous history as a guideline, I'm requesting $1,000 in funding for this coming year. We'll keep you apprised as to the use of this funding and will adjust funding requests, as appropriate, going forward.

Please call me if you need further information. Thank you again for your consideration.

Sincerely,
Dede Ranahan
Support Group Moderator.

Patrick's Facebook Post: After over seven years of unemployment and walking a very precarious financial tightrope which I fell from several times, I started a full-time job on Tuesday as a delivery driver for Millennium Transportation delivering auto parts to mechanics and repair shops. For the first time in a long time I won't be spending my days scouring the classified ads for work. It may be premature to announce this position as I'm finding it hard to believe I actually have a job and hope it lasts but, as of now, I am officially employed full time.

Stephanie: Congratulations!

Keir: Congrats!

Donna: I am so happy for you Patrick!

Meridith: Yeah Patrick!! Congratulations!!!

Amy R.: Good for you! New year, new adventures.

Lara: Way to go!

Cara: Pat, as someone who has also suffered during this crappy economic time, I am so happy to hear this. No one can truly understand the difficulty of submitting thousands of resumes, and going to countless interviews. I am so happy for you and so proud of you for keeping your focus. Congratulations!!!

Amy P.: Congrats Patrick Ranahan. This is wonderful for you!!!

Shannon: Happy for you Pat. I knew you were going to get something soon!

Brandi: That's wonderful!! Congrats!

Pam: Happy driving Patrick!!

Ed: Go Pat Go!!!!

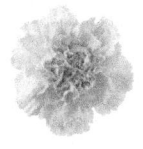

FEBRUARY 1, 2014

DAMN FREUD

While I'm walking home from duplicate bridge this afternoon, a neighbor pulls up and idles her car to say hello. She says, "Weren't those hands difficult today?"

I agree. They were a challenge.

"Something's happened with my fifty-four-year-old son."

Ah. The real reason for her stopping in the street.

"He's in the hospital."

"Is this good news or bad news?"

"Well, he's beginning to recognize when he needs help. His new psychiatrist took him off his medication for schizophrenia and his symptoms came back."

This sounds familiar.

"The hospital's got him stabilized. How can a doctor undo forty-five years of medical history? Where are my son's records?"

Good questions. Serious mental illness is the most challenging illness of this century. Mental illness is the least understood and most devastating illness of this century. Mothers know this. Those same mothers that Freud blames for everything. "Something wrong with your kid? It's your fault."

When will we outgrow Freud and see mothers (and fathers) as mental health allies instead of enemies? When will we move into a compassionate future? A future that will care enough to do research to find answers about our brains and how they can go awry?

That's why my friend and I play bridge. It takes focus. And focus takes our minds off problems that, so far, seem to have no resolution.

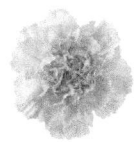

FEBRUARY 2, 2014

SAME OLD SAME OLD

Article in today's paper:

"Mental health hospitalizations of California's youngest residents, 21 and under, increased 39 percent between 2007 and 2012, jumping from 33,000 to 46,000.

"The number of emergency room visits involving suicide attempts among children and teenagers increased more than 20 percent between 2007-2012.

"Some mental health professionals believe that once their young patients commit a crime, they'll enter the juvenile justice system and have much better access to mental health treatments."

Stories and statistics about the failure of our mental health system make the news regularly. That's about it. Nothing changes or gets better. I hope that in 2114 this is no longer true. But, if history is predictive, 100 years may not be enough time to make a difference. Mental health care's been in the Dark Ages forever.

FEBRUARY 4, 2014

"THANKS FOR COMING IN"

I'm working at Snap It Up thrift shop and, as usual, a parade is coming through the door. All clothes are $1 today. The first customer is buying twelve pair of men's jeans. I ask who they're for.

"I'm buying them for prisoners at the jail who are being released. Often, they have only the clothes they wore in. I help stock a closet where they can get a warm jacket or an extra pair of pants to wear out on the street."

Another woman asks me, "Are you having a good day?"

"Yes, are you having a good day?"

"I'm having a very happy day."

Do I leave this statement alone or do I go further? "Why are you having a very happy day?"

"Because my ten-year-old son got placed in a group home and I know he's safe for the moment." This turns into a long story. "My adopted son's real mother was a meth addict when she was pregnant with him. Meth's in his cellular structure and he's always hyperactive. He's on meds for ADHD and oppositional defiant disorder, but they don't have his meds right. He gets violent. He busted through steel doors at the hospital when he saw me on the other side.

"The doctors say his frontal cortex, which is the brain's center for impulse control, isn't developing as it should. If the cortex

294

doesn't begin to catch up in the next two years, he'll probably have to be conserved to a group home permanently."

She continues. "I had serious surgery recently and I'm still recovering. I'm trying to get well and take care of my son. I feel like I'm not setting goals, but my counselor reassures me that I do have goals—to survive and to help my son survive."

This woman has a lot on her plate. I tell her about NAMI. I tell her about the support group.

"Can I join your support group?"

She doesn't live in Sun City. I always try to think about why someone has crossed my path. I'll run this by the group. I get the woman's name and phone number. I'll get back to her.

More clothes are moving out the door. Some with a Caucasian woman for her disabled roommate. Some with a black woman who takes the bus to get to the shop. Some with a Hispanic woman who comes in every week.

I'm working in a thrift shop that could be in Anytown, USA. I like being here when customers find something they need at a great price. I smile, look them in the eyes, and give them an opening. More often than not, they start to tell a story. They're eager to have someone listen. That's all I can do. Listen and be humbled.

I say, "Enjoy that blouse. It looks beautiful on you."

FEBRUARY 5, 2014

WHEN I WAS A CHILD

In preparation for Grandparents' Day, I write a letter for Regan's second grade social studies class.

Dear Regan,

Thank you for asking me to write about my life when I was a child. Time goes by so fast. It seems like yesterday when I was seven—like you.

In second grade, my teacher was Mrs. Quimet. I remember her as I'm about to turn 70 years old. Our teachers are important to us. Somewhere around this time, my father, Pop, surprised us with a black-and-white television. We were the first family on our block to get one. It was like magic. I raced home from school every day to watch *The Mickey Mouse Club*. My favorite Mouseketeer was Darlene. I liked that she had long pigtails and often played the part of a tomboy. I also watched *Sky King* and *Howdy Doody*.

Our family lived in a very small house in San Jose, California. I had to share a bedroom with my little brother, James. I hated the arrangement. I liked dolls and he liked trains. I pushed a dresser into the middle of the room to divide it in two, but this only helped a little. I knew that James was still on the other side of the furniture.

When I was eight, Pop built a hamburger restaurant adjacent to his real estate office. He called it Burgertown. McDonald's didn't exist yet. Most days, after school, I went to Burgertown while Pop and GG cooked hamburgers and waited on tables. Sometimes I peeled potatoes or stocked the candy cabinet with Milky Ways, Snickers, M&M's, and Mounds Bars. I had hamburgers, fries, chocolate milk shakes, and hot fudge sundaes for dinner. It was heaven.

As I got a little older, I discovered that I liked to write poems. I wrote this poem one night while I was in bed.

THE MOON FAIRY

As I lay awake one night beside the window sill,
I raised the shade and took a peek while everything was still.
The moon shone on the house next door, made sparkles in the creek,
And where the purple violets grew, it left a silver streak.
There below my window sill upon a feathery fern,
I saw a wee wee fairy dance about and turn.
He frolicked there the whole night long
and when the moon began to fade,
He looked up and saw me there below the window shade.
He spun around and disappeared into the frosty air,
And many times have I looked in hopes to find him there.
Sometimes when the moon is high and sparkles in the creek,
I raise the shade a tiny bit just to take a peek.
I never see the fairy there who played upon a tune,
But I can hear him playing, still, under the silvery moon.

I'd love to tell you more about when I was child if you want to know more. I wish for you a happy childhood. Don't grow up too fast. Otherwise, you'll soon be 70 years old like me. I love you Regan. I love you lots.

Mim

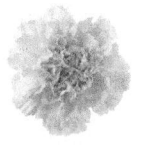

FEBRUARY 6, 2014

STAYING GROUNDED

Finally, It's raining.

I'm at a mentoring session for duplicate bridge. Volunteer mentors coach us on various bridge conventions. Today, we're learning about New Minor Forcing. I read that, except for one or two, no top player has learned to play bridge after the age of 20. There go my chances for the big time.

Meanwhile, two friends died, unexpectedly, this week. One died from the flu. One day my friend was fine, and three days later she was deceased. There's been a higher number of deaths in our area this flu season. The victims include healthy people who didn't get flu shots. This flu strain trips the body's immune response to the point that it overreacts, and the sick person drowns in excess lung fluids. My second friend died from cancer diagnosed a short time ago. Another healthy person felled.

I'm leaving bridge class, walking outside, and letting the rain splash on my face. I'm placing one foot in front of the other, mindful of firm ground. I'm giving thanks for another day. Especially for another wet, rainy day.

Patrick's Facebook Post: I'm posting abstract art by Wassily Kandinsky. Nice! Leave a comment and I will give you an artist to post. The idea is to occupy Facebook with art, breaking the monotony of photos of lunch, selfies and sport. I will assign the name of an artist to whomever likes this post, and you have to publish a piece by that artist with text like this: I was given Rembrandt. Here is his painting—*Christ in the Storm on the Sea of Galilee.*

Shawn: Great choice Patrick Ranahan

Patrick: Lisa, you get Wassily Kandinsky.

Patrick: Nick, you get Willem de Kooning.

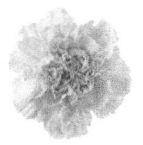

FEBRUARY 7, 2014

THE YOUNG CROWD

Priceless notes from Utah in the mail today.

Dear Mim,

Thank you so much for the birthday and Christmas money! I spent some money on a video game and I'm saving some. I hope you come visit us this year!

Love, Ashton

Dear Mim,

Thank you so much for the Christmas money! I decided to spend the money on books for my Kindle! I bought and read a lot of books with the money! Thank you so much. I can't wait to see you this summer!

Love, Aidan

I'm working out with Deanne. She says, "I can tell you're getting stronger. You're doing this at the right time. Some people say, 'I'm old' and think it's too late. But really, you're getting your body in shape for the next 20 years."

Deanne is gracious.

She hands me ten-pound weights. "I want you to sit, extend your arms down with the palms of your hands facing upward holding the weights. Keep your elbows in. Raise the weights to shoulder height."

She's got to be kidding. My right arm goes up—kind of. But my left arm's a total loser. It can't get the weight past my waist.

"You can do this," she says. "Try for four."

I try. I fail. Deanne switches me to three-pound weights. I can lift three pounds, but I have a ten-pound goal. Now, I know what's expected.

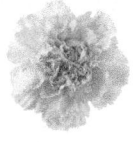

FEBRUARY 8, 2014

LIFE AND UMBRELLAS

I'm headed to Nevada City to attend David's grandmother's funeral. I didn't know Grandma Joyce, but I want to be present at her service for my son-in-law and for his mother, Michele, who is Joyce's daughter.

It's raining cats and dogs—the heaviest rain we've had in a year. I throw on my raincoat and grab my perky black umbrella. It's perky because it has little red, yellow, green, and blue polka dots on it. It looks cheery. And it's easy to spot in a stand full of black umbrellas.

I risk life and limb driving Highway 93 to get to the funeral home. I hang up my raincoat and drop my umbrella onto a pile of black umbrellas. I sign the guest book and give Michele and David a hug.

A family friend conducts the memorial service. He tells the story of a little girl, young woman, mother, and grandmother unfamiliar to me. Kerry presents a video of family photographs displayed in a sequence timed to music. Joyce loved Frank Sinatra. The music swells to Frank's "My Way." I was fine until now. Other people were fine until now. Everyone is pulling out tissues and wiping their eyes.

We have to walk from the funeral chapel to another building behind it for the reception. I slip on my raincoat and pick up my umbrella. That's strange. The button on the handle that opens and closes it is missing. It's difficult to open my umbrella with its button missing. I have to push from the bottom and pull from the top. I don't remember my umbrella being this small in circumference.

I walk to the reception area and try to set my dripping umbrella on the floor. It's a fight to get it to close. The room's packed and warm. Kerry and I wait for the food line to thin. I'm standing with my back to the dessert table. Kerry waves at me from across the room.

"Look behind you," she mouths.

I look. There's a tall man. What's Kerry telling me? Am I blocking someone? She keeps pointing. I turn around, again, in time to see a sweet-looking old lady leaving the reception. She's tucking a black umbrella to her side. Her umbrella has polka dots on it. Her umbrella has an open/close button on its handle. My umbrella. The sweet-looking old lady has my umbrella.

Too late. She's gone. I can't get to her without stomping across a table covered with cookies and cupcakes. Kerry's laughing. I'm laughing. Seems like the thing to do. After pasta salad and sliced ham, I hug David and Michele goodbye. I don't want to be on the road in the dark and with glare on the pavement from the rain. For crying out loud. I have to wrestle this impostor umbrella into my car because it's impossible to close. If someone's watching, they'll call 911. They'll think I'm struggling with an attacker in my front seat.

I'll get a new umbrella. I'll donate this annoying one to the thrift shop. On second thought, it's not good enough for the thrift shop. When I get home, I'll stash the darn thing in the garbage can. A fitting end. In my opinion.

Kerry sends me a text. David's father's umbrella is missing. He's not laughing. Whoever took his umbrella didn't leave a replacement like the sweet-looking old lady who took mine. I hope she enjoys her new, bigger, automatic open and close, perky polka dot umbrella. I hope it helped David and Michele a little that I attended Joyce's service. Life is too short.

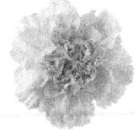

FEBRUARY 10, 2014

STALLING

I'm taking The Jazz for a walk in the cat stroller. It's a warm 62 degrees. No rain. Of course, I run into my next-door neighbor as soon as I push the stroller out the side gate. I was hoping I wouldn't see anyone or they see me.

"I'm taking my cat for a walk."

"That's okay," he says.

"Doesn't it seem a bit eccentric?"

"Look, living here, anything can seem eccentric."

"So you won't say anything?"

He laughs.

I can't tell if The Jazz likes the ride. She's not meowing. She's looking out the back, front and sides. I unzip the stroller's mesh cover on our return. She doesn't leap out right away. May mean she likes this contraption?

I'm in the den, organizing the paperwork for Mom's rental house. She's got all her tax stuff together. She's raring to go. She wants me to set up an appointment with the tax preparer. Now. Walking the cat will not get me off the hook.

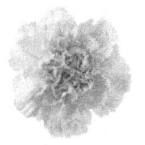

FEBRUARY 11, 2014

LOVE THIS PLACE

Here I am again—at Snap It Up. I love this place. People are grateful and unpretentious. They like to talk.

"I used to have a lot of money. I don't anymore and I'm managing fine."

"I bought a Ralph Lauren blouse here last week for one dollar."

"I make little cat beds. Would you be able to use them if I bring them in?"

"That cat in the adoption room is sweet. I hope someone adopts her soon."

"Do you have yarn? I want to get some for my friend who knits sweaters for the homeless."

"How much is this belt? If it's a dollar, I'll take it."

"I'm going to Weight Watchers. This is the perfect place to buy clothes as I'm changing sizes."

"Keep the change. FieldHaven does good work."

"I love that rubber chicken but it's fifteen dollars. Guess I better wait."

"I found this poster of San Francisco. It's perfect for my mobile home."

"I better stop shopping. My husband's waiting in the car. I'll take these tops because they're a dollar."

I find three tops myself—one from Coldwater Creek, one from J. Jill, and one from Talbots. All are like new. All are one dollar. Like I said, I love this place.

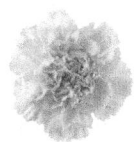

FEBRUARY 13, 2014

A VERY GOOD DAY

The heating and air conditioning man arrives for the annual heater check-up. Everything looks good, but. . . . Here comes the but: "The capacitor that helps the fan is testing below the recommended range of 7.1 to 7.5. It's testing 6.6. As part of our recommended preventative maintenance, you probably should replace it before it dies and causes damage."

"How much?"

"It's one hundred thirty-one dollars, I think. We had a price change yesterday. Also, your drip pan doesn't have a switch to turn the unit off if it's collecting too much water."

"How much?"

"One hundred thirty-eight dollars. It's not code or anything, but when our company installs a new unit, we make sure the pan is equipped with a switch."

Hmm. Everything's been working fine. "You know, I don't go up in the attic. I have to take your word for it."

"You trust me, don't you? I can bring the capacitor down and show you."

"Okay."

The technician, a very personable, pleasant young man, attaches his gismo to the capacitor. It reads 7.0. It reads 7.0 three times. Hmm again. "Thanks, but I think I'll wait on this and see how it is in a couple of months when you come back to service the air conditioning unit."

I may have to rethink this bi-annual heating and air check. I'll clean the filter myself. Thank you very much. If it's not broke, don't fix it.

Pat arrives to do his laundry. Lexi bounds in. She still doesn't know how to walk. I give her a dog biscuit and she runs around the coffee table 15 times. Pat fills out an insurance form to give me power of attorney on his car insurance account. I pay this bill monthly, and it's always getting mucked up because he hasn't completed the power of attorney form. Pat folds his last load of laundry.

"C'mon, Lexi." Lexi accepts the leash and pulls Pat out the door. She's happy to come. She's happy to go.

I'm at Mom's delivering her very specific staple requests. I give her a new bottle of homemade Irish cream like the one I gave her at Christmas. As I suspected, she has the empty bottle, from Christmas, ready to return to me.

"Have you made an appointment with a tax person, yet?"

"Well, no."

"I really want to get my taxes done and get my money back."

"Okay. I'm on it."

I stop at Kerry's to drop off Ayla's belated birthday gifts—a book about bugs and a birdhouse you attach to a window so you can watch the birds nesting inside. We skim through the bug book. A picture of an ugly scorpion reminds Ayla of something.

"I ate one of these."

"You ate a scorpion?"

"Yes, and it licked me on my cheek."

"Did you swallow the scorpion?"

"No, because it was licking me on my cheek."

Kerry joins us. "Did you know Ayla ate a scorpion?"

"No."

"I didn't eat it, Mim. I was tricking you."

Ayla's a storyteller. "I want to be a bug catcher when I grow up."

"What will you do with the bugs?"

"I'll give them to the birds."

Home again. The heater's humming softly. This morning I saved myself $269 that I didn't spend on my AC unit. This afternoon I caught up with my son, mother, daughter, and granddaughter. All in all, it's been a very good day.

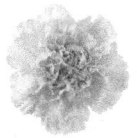

FEBRUARY 14, 2014

HAPPY VALENTINE'S DAY

In the gym with Deanne; she's setting me up in a seated leg curl machine. She's adjusting the weights and the position of the leg rest. The bar that holds my upper legs in place isn't very tight. Should it be?

"It's fine. It's not tight because you have thin thighs."

I catch my breath. Oh my! Stop the presses. Deanne says I have thin thighs. No one's told me I have thin thighs in 40 years. I ask Deanne to say it again.

"You have thin thighs. You're thin."

I knew I loved this woman. She may be my new best friend.

At the Family Mental Illness Support Group meeting, we have a new person in attendance. Each month we have at least one new person. I let the group know that I've been asked to meet with the Lincoln HIlls Foundation grants committee. "Do you have suggestions for what I should present to the committee?"

The group suggests mentioning in-kind donations such as my time and the use of Raley's conference room. We agree that we don't want to spend money simply to be spending money. We want whatever money we receive to be put to work.

There are eight people at the meeting today, each of us making a difference for each other. A small group impacting a small group. What's that Margaret Mead saying? "Never doubt that a small group of thoughtful, committed citizens can change the world; indeed, it's the only thing that ever has."

Happy Valentine's Day.

Patrick's Facebook Post: Happy S.A.D. (Singles Awareness Day). I celebrated by taking myself out to lunch and enjoyed a mushroom burger among all the paired-up sweethearts.

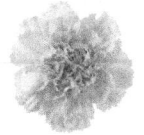

FEBRUARY 15, 2014

GETTING ORGANIZED

The Jazz is ensconced in a basket on top of a trunk in my closet. Her from paws stick out over the basket's edge. She raises her head so she can see over the side. Nothing moves but her eyes. I'm being watched.

I'm sorting through my clothes and have filled up three large bags with pants and tops that no longer fit. There are a half dozen mistakes in the give-away stuff—what-was-I thinking garments that I've never worn. This sorting process will help me be more focused when I'm clothes shopping. As I decide what to keep and what to get rid of, I remember five getting-dressed rules I picked up from Andy Paige in her book, *Style on a Shoestring*:

1. Use lipstick.
2. Wear outfits that give me shape—clothes that define a middle in my torso.
3. Carry a statement-making handbag. I'm weak here. I generally use one handbag at a time—an all-purpose bag so I don't have to switch contents.
4. Select fun shoes and funky socks. I try, but I no longer wear heels because my ankle has a steel plate and six screws in it. My favorite shoes are my sea-blue tennis shoes with white polka dots on them. (What's with me and polka dots?) And I practice sock awareness. I try to match socks to my outfit with color, design, and wit. I like to wear witty socks.
5. Add something unexpected. This is my favorite rule. This can be a pin, a scarf, a pair of earrings. Something that says, "This lady was thinking when she put herself together."

My closet's shaping up. There's still one thing I haven't attended to. Maybe that's why The Jazz is staring at me. "While you're in this mode, ahem, there's a litter box in the laundry room that needs your attention."

Getting organized can be fun. Mostly.

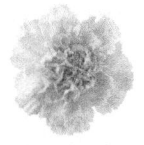

FEBRUARY 16, 2014

STUFF

Continuing my spring organizing, I'm at Target picking up a few things—hangers, storage containers, makeup, hand towels, pillows for the guest room, and a wallet. Somehow this adds up to $121.82. How do a few minor items cost this much?

Mom calls. "Have you set me up with tax person yet?"

"No, I didn't call anyone today because it's Sunday."

"What about the bank? Did you look into CD rates?"

"No, not yet."

Mom's getting antsy. "What if the tax person has steps into her office? I won't be able to go up the steps. What if she charges too much to come to my place? Or to your place?"

I better get on this.

Well, the good news is the wallet doesn't work. Once you put coins, cash, and credit cards in it, it won't close. I'll take it back and knock $14 off the $121.82 bill. My old wallet is good enough. I'll go back to getting rid of things instead of acquiring things.

Who needs all this stuff, anyway?

FEBRUARY 18, 2014

CONFLICT

I'm at the movies to see *The Monuments Men*. It's the story of US and British soldiers charged with retrieving European art stolen by the Nazis during World War II. Critics aren't giving this movie top reviews. The theater, however, is packed.

When the credits roll at the end, the audience has reflected on artwork and culture as evidence of humanity's collective soul, and a time when humanity seemed hell-bent on self-destruction.

World War II combat in Europe ended in May 1945. Since then, the US has engaged in wars in Korea, Vietnam, the Persian Gulf, Iran, and Afghanistan. Today, as we withdraw from Afghanistan, we're witnessing uprisings around the globe—in Egypt, Syria, Ukraine, Thailand, Venezuela, Libya, Sudan, Somalia, and Congo.

Conflict is the ongoing human drama. Each of us has our own hot buttons. Familial dysfunction is the stuff of storytelling. Countries are macrocosms of individuals and families. Why does equilibrium—personal, tribal, global—forever elude us?

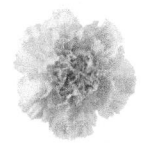

FEBRUARY 20, 2014

INTERVIEW

The Lincoln Hills Foundation grants committee is asking about my application for $1,000 for the Family Mental Illness Support Group. They're exercising due diligence.

"What's your background and professional experience?"

"I'm a family member and retired policy director for NAMI California."

"What is the group's geographical outreach?"

"Lincoln Hills."

"What are the group's expenses?"

"We have none. We'd like to buy some books for the group and pay for a few speakers."

"What is your main purpose?"

"To provide support for family members who have someone coping with serious mental illness."

I have a few questions, also. "People from outside Lincoln Hills have asked if they can join the group. Do you have any objection?"

"No."

"What kind of expense reporting do you need?"

These retired volunteers explain their process and give me an hour of their time. They're trying to make a difference in our community. Whether or not they decide to give us a grant, I respect the work they're doing and the responsible way they're making funding decisions.

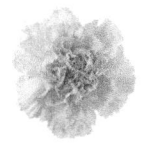

FEBRUARY 21, 2014

MISSING

A photo's missing. I found it a few weeks ago as I was rifling through some files. It's a candid snapshot of me when I was about 36. I don't know who took the photo. I think I was at a writer's conference. I'm wearing a name tag, a dark silk blouse, and a white blazer.

I like the way I look, at this moment in time, captured on black and white film. The skin on my face appears soft and moist. My features aren't as angular as they are now. My lips are full. My eyes have an intelligent, I'm-listening-to-you gaze. They're big and brown. I have thick, dark-brown hair in a stylish short cut. I look like someone I'd like to know.

I'd planned to make copies of this two-by-three-inch photo and give one to each of my children. They have no pictures of me as a young woman. I tucked the photo into the corner of a framed photo on my bookshelf. Now, it's not there.

This is troubling me more than I want to admit. An irreplaceable little keepsake of what I looked like once has vanished. I think I'm mourning my own disappearance. A time when not only my photo but I will be missing.

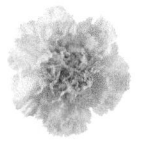

FEBRUARY 22, 2014
CONGRATULATIONS, AIDAN

Aidan's done it again. His latest poem's placed in the student Chaparral Poetry Contest. An award ceremony will be held March 20 in the opera house in St. George, Utah. The top six winners in each category will read their poems.

DISTANT FUTURE
—AIDAN MACE

As we approach our landing,
I move toward the window to get a good look.
I see the beautiful landscape approaching,
This landscape is red and filled with little clusters of buildings.
Soon our ship captain calls for everyone to get off.
As I exit the ship I begin to float in the low gravity environment.
I look around.
What I see is amazing.
I see a civilization beginning.
I can feel the red dust blow past my cheek,
and envelop my pores,
Then I feel a strong breeze.
It seems to blow some sense back into me,
and I realize,
I have just set foot on an astounding place,
MARS.

Patrick's Facebook Post: Got a late Christmas present from my Dad. An all expense paid trip to Nashville to buy a guitar.

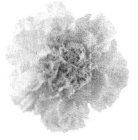

FEBRUARY 23, 2014

WATER

On this day in 1948, Mom gave birth to a little girl, Loretta Marie. She lived for four hours. I hope my little sister knows I'm thinking of her.

I'm on my walk. It's 71 degrees and not a cloud in the sky. To me, it feels like spring. My nose thinks so, too. It's itching and twitching.

Me and my nose aren't the only ones who're confused. Roses are leafing out. Yellow daffodils, blue periwinkle, purple pansies, crimson fringe flowers, and pink-blossomed flowering plum trees are bursting forth. Birds twitter and flit from tree branch to tree branch.

The National Weather Service reports there is a 1 in 1,000 chance that this season will conclude with average rainfall. Cuts in water allocations will affect rice, tomato, and corn production. Reduced rice planting also means less habitat for migratory waterfowl and other wildlife. One climatologist observes that this winter represents a different world compared to anything since 1895.

In my own backyard, I've got some serious plant damage. I'm waiting to see if bottlebrush, podocarpus, citrus trees, and an African sumac tree are able to rally. They look pretty distressed from the dry, cold winter. All my potted plants have croaked.

Outside, my sprinkler system is turned off. Inside, I'm careful not to let the faucet run when I'm brushing my teeth. I run the dishwasher and washing machine with full loads. A couple of droopy houseplants won't be replaced. I'm taking short showers and using a shower bucket to catch water as it falls. Small measures. Hope they add up.

FEBRUARY 24, 2014

NEWS

Pat calls. I ask, "How's the job?"

"It's going well."

"Thanks for the check, Pat." Pat mailed me reimbursement for the $40 I loaned him for gas.

"Did you cash the check yet, Mom?"

"No, why?"

"Can you wait until Friday? I need the money for gas."

Pat laughs at himself.

"Okay, but I'm cashing the check Friday afternoon."

I laugh at myself.

"I talked to Dad. He says he's been thinking about a Christmas present he hasn't given me, yet. He's getting me an electric guitar."

"Really?"

"He says we should fly to Nashville and buy the guitar there."

"Really? When are you going?"

"I don't know. I have to get a few days off work. Meanwhile, some Tibetan monks are coming to the church. I'm going to ask them to call on GG for her 96th birthday."

"Really? Will you tell her in advance?"

"I'm thinking of surprising her."

"What will they do when they see her?"

"I don't know. Pray, I guess."

I hope the father-son trip to Nashville comes to pass. I hope the Tibetan monks are well-received. I hope, when they're praying, they say a prayer for Pat. And for me. I never know what the next news will be.

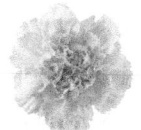

FEBRUARY 25, 2014

OVERDOING IT

While Deanne is on vacation, I decided to use my three-pound weights here at home and practice some of the exercises she's shown me. Yesterday, I worked out for half an hour.

Today, I can hardly move. The muscle in my lower back is unhappy and it's letting me know. It hurts to lie down. It hurts to sit. It hurts if I have to cough or sneeze.

Maybe I was too cocky thinking I'm getting myself in shape. This twinge in my back is a good reminder to go slow with my workout routine. I'll tell Deanne about this when she returns.

I hope, in a week, my back muscle will have relaxed. My body will say, "Okay, let's try this again. No bad feelings."

Literally.

FEBRUARY 27, 2014

HOME

I'm at the vet's office with The Jazz. We're here for her annual rabies shot and general check-up. A woman pushing a little blond, blue-eyed girl in a stroller comes through the door. She's followed by a dark-haired, dark-eyed little boy. And, of course, by an animal on a leash—a tiny, wiry haired, white terrier. We start up a conversation.

"The puppy's about 13 weeks old from a rescue center. My eldest daughter is 20 and she's from China. When she was small, she had a little white dog. Then an earthquake wiped out her home and her village. Someone ate her dog."

My reporter self kicks in. "How did you get connected with your daughter?"

"Through our church. We're in the process of adopting her even though she's legally an adult. She's in touch with her family in China, but it's a complicated relationship and it probably won't get better. My daughter's been through so much and she has major trust issues. She wants us to adopt her. She needs that kind of commitment."

The little boy gives a green squeeze toy to the little girl in the stroller. His mother continues.

"I surprised my daughter the day we went to see the puppy. She was nervous about the house where it was being fostered along with her doggy mother and four puppy siblings. She thought we were shopping for a dresser for her bedroom. She said, 'This doesn't look like a store. I don't want to go in.' I told her she'd have to trust me—that it was okay to go into the house. The foster mom handed the puppy to my daughter and said, 'This puppy needs a mother.'"

I'm never disappointed. Start a conversation with someone, anyone, and you're apt to hear an amazing story.

"My daughter began sobbing. She couldn't stop crying. She wanted the puppy, and yet it brought back many sad memories for her. It was one of the most emotional days of my life."

The woman and her little group leave. A man and woman come in together with another wiry little dog. A brown one. I smile and say, "Good morning."

The man says, "No, but I'm working on it."

As they disappear into an exam room, the receptionist explains, "They've been up all night. They came from an emergency animal clinic."

I wonder what their story is. It's our turn with the vet. The Jazz is good for her exam and her shot and getting her nails clipped. Afterward, she scrambles, fast as she can, into the blue cat carrier I had to force her into earlier. Like the girl from China and her little dog, The Jazz is adopted and wants to go home.

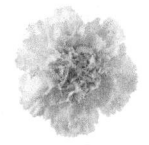

MARCH 2, 2014

HAPPY BIRTHDAY, DR. SEUSS

Theodor Geisel was born on March 2, 1904. In recognition of his mark on children's literature, the National Education Association has declared this day to be National Read Across America Day. In 2114, I predict Dr. Seuss will be as popular as he is today. His words and rhythms make you happy—even when you're out of sorts. Here are some of my favorite Dr. Seuss quotes:

"Today is your day! Your mountain is waiting. So get on your way."

"You have brains in your head. You have feet in your shoes. You can steer yourself any direction you choose."

"Sometimes the questions are complicated and the answers are simple."

"Unless someone like you cares a whole awful lot, nothing is going to get better. It's not."

And my very favorite: "Today you are you, that is truer than true. There is no one alive who is youer than you."

I rest my case. Even Dr. Seuss believes each of us is pretty darn great.

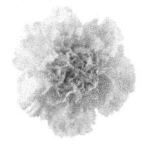

MARCH 4, 2014

AIR RAIDS

In grammar school, I remember air raid drills. Without warning, a siren would begin blasting. We'd dive under our desks, curl into balls, and cover our heads with our arms. As if this would protect us from bombs falling from the sky and exploding all around.

Whenever I heard an airplane overhead, I feared that the Russians were coming to kill us with their communist weapons of mass destruction. We didn't call them WMDs then, but I knew that there was this very bad country, Russia, that wanted to hurts us. They would even hurt us little kids.

In high school, a friend's family dug a bomb shelter into the earth in their front yard. They kept it stocked with food, water, radios, flashlights, tools, books, and other things they'd need in the event of a Russian air attack.

Over time, other countries occupied US attention more than Russia. Today, Russia and the US are again butting heads. Obama has suspended military ties, port visits, planning meetings, and trade talks. If Russia continues to deploy its troops into the Crimean region of Ukraine, other sanctions may follow.

A fragile new pro-Western government in the Ukraine is struggling to get a foothold. Russia wants Ukraine in its sphere. The US has economic and strategic reasons for supporting the growth of democracy in the area. Both countries believe they have a mandate to protect their own interests. Both countries distrust each other. The situation will undoubtedly get worse before it gets better.

I hope my grandchildren don't have air raid drills at school. I hope they're not afraid when they hear airplanes flying overhead. I hope the adults in the room have learned lessons from the past and find a way to get along.

When Pat was in sixth grade, I met with his teacher for a parent-teacher conference. The teacher said, "We had an air raid drill last week. All the kids hid under their desks. As I walked by Pat's desk he said to the boy in front of him, 'If this air raid's for real, you can kiss your ass goodby.'"

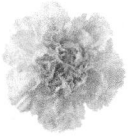

MARCH 6, 2014

MOM'S TO-DO LIST

I'm at Mom's with a tax accountant. Mom's ready. She has her income records rubber-banded together in one file. She has her expense records in another. She has explicit instructions for the tax lady.

"Be sure to deduct my expenses for the purchase of my hearing aids and the thirty-six dollars I spent on hearing aid batteries. Also, remember my sixty dollar renter's credit from the state of California."

With information supplied and collected, we're trying to find a return date for the accountant to come back with the completed tax forms. It can't be too soon.

"I want my money. I want a refund."

The accountant says she never promises anyone a refund. She has to cross all the t's and dot all the i's first. We settle on March 18. The tax accountant leaves. I stay behind to fill out some papers for a money market account we've opened. I give Mom the new attachments she wants for her electric toothbrush.

"How much do I owe you for these?"

"Thirty-two dollars."

"Thirty-two dollars? For toothbrushes?"

"Yep, thirty-two dollars for toothbrushes."

"Well, they each last six months. I guess that's not too bad. There are four in the packet, right?"

"No, there are three in the packet."

"Gads. Only three?"

"Only three. Anything else?"

"No, thanks for your help with the taxes and the shopping. After I get my tax refund, I need to get new eyeglasses."

Okay, Mom. I'll take you to the optometrist to get new eyeglasses. Maybe that's the secret to your long life. You always have a next project on your to-do list.

MARCH 7, 2014

WINDOWS

A little girl asked her mother about death. "What will it be like?"

Her mother thought and said, "Do you remember what it was like before you were born?"

The little girl said, "No."

The mother said, "That's what it will be like when you die."

But really, none of us knows what death will be like. A window of time. That's what each of us has—a window of time. My window is from May 22, 1944 to ????

In some ways, we have more than one window. My immediate window is my front kitchen window. I have a bigger "window" by telephone, email, and local activities to observe what's happening in my neighborhood. Through television, the internet, newspapers, and other media, I have windows to the bigger world. Through recorded history and family stories handed down, I have windows into the past. I have no window, except through speculation, into the future.

No one else, ever, will see, hear, and experience exactly what I do. That's a critical reason why I'm writing—to try to realize the life that is unique to me. I could be breathing but unconscious. My life is my one chance to be fully awake. Then, when I die, I can more peacefully sleep. I mean this to be comforting. It is, to me, at least.

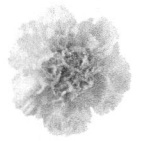

MARCH 8, 2014

MY BOOK

What a nice surprise. I check Instagram this morning for new posts. I see two posts from Marisa—a photo of my book, *Contributions of Women: Medicine*, is in one post. A photo of me, on the back page of the book, is in a second post. Marisa writes:

"When I was eight years old, my mom's book was published as a part of series on contributions of women. What a wonderful role model I have. Happy International Women's Day!" To the photo, in the second post, she adds, "My Mom."

As a parent, you never know what makes a lasting impression—good or bad. I know I made lots of parenting mistakes. I cringe thinking of some of them. But you have to hope that, on balance, your parenting turns out okay.

Writing that book was a lifesaver. A lifesaver because, as a young mother of four children, I needed something adult to wrap my mind around. Kerry was two. She'd sit in my lap at the typewriter. I'd punch a key. She'd punch a key. I'd punch a key. She'd punch a key. White-out everywhere. What a friggin' mess. It took me three years to write a one-hundred-seventeen-page book. One-hundred-seventeen pages with big print.

I remember the day my copies of the book were delivered by UPS. I opened one of the books and studied its Table of Contents. I ran my fingers across the cover. And, yes. I checked my photo in the back. I was in awe of myself. I'd actually written a book. I'd visualized the book in my mind and, now, I held a hardbound copy in my hands. I'd achieved a goal. I didn't know, yet, that my book would win the 1982 first prize for nonfiction books from The National League of American Pen Women, Inc. Thanks, Marisa, for taking me back to that moment. I hope you read my book. I hope you liked it.

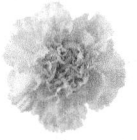

MARCH 9, 2014

A BIRTHDAY INVITATION

Hi Everyone,

You're receiving this email because Evelyn Moon, better known as Mom and GG Moon, is celebrating her 96th birthday on April 8. As the calendar falls, we're hosting her "official" birthday dinner on Saturday, April 5th. You're all invited and, if you're too far away and can't attend, you're welcome to call and wish the lady of the day, Happy Birthday!

Michael's preparing an arugula salad and a Cassoulet D'Artagnan. I didn't know what this fancy-sounding concoction was either. It's a hearty dish of duck sausage and beans. Very French. I'm offering sardines, with sun-dried tomatoes, garlic, onions, and capers as an appetizer and a lemon-rosemary layer cake for dessert.

The above-mentioned dinner will be at my home around 6 o'clock. Please RSVP. Hope to hear from you, one way or the other.

Love, Dede

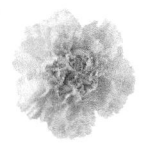

MARCH 10, 2014

A NEW DILEMMA

Pat calls. He's still delivering auto parts. The church gave him a going-away party. He quit his Sunday job there.

"How's Lexi?"

"She's being a bit of a problem at the moment."

"How?"

"Well, she pretty much chewed up the shutters on an upstairs window. And she's peed a few times in the upstairs loft."

This is not good. Poop would be gross but dog pee? It sinks into the carpet padding and you can't get rid of the odor. We consider a few solutions. Pat's thinking of shutting Lexi in the downstairs closet when he's gone. I don't like this idea. The closet's bigger than her crate, but still.

"You can't leave her in the backyard?"

"No. She howls and digs out under the fence."

"What about the upstairs bathroom? It's bigger than the closet and has a window to let light in."

Pat doesn't like this idea.

"I know you love Lexi, but is this a fair arrangement for her? Do you think you should give her back to the dog rescue?"

"Give her back? No, I'm not giving her back."

"Well, something has to be done."

"I know."

Silence on the other end of the phone.

"Could she ride along with you in your car when you're making deliveries?"

"No, Mom. She can't ride along with me."

Silence on my end of the phone.

I'm concerned. I won't worry Mom with what's happening in her rental house. A "real" landlord wouldn't allow the dog to stay. I remind myself I can't fix everything.

"Well, let me know what solution you come up with."

"I will."

"You saw the email about GG's birthday dinner?"

"Yes, I'll be there. Talk to you later."

"Bye, Pat."

This situation needs a remedy. It can't continue as is. I'll let it churn a bit. I hope Pat will think of something he can live with—an accommodation that's good for Lexi and good for the house. I hate that getting a job means he may have to give up the dog he loves.

A chat with Pat. A new dilemma.

MARCH 11, 2014

PERSPECTIVE

Cosmos, a new television series, is premiering. The reviews compare it to an updated Carl Sagan program. I'm watching the first episode. It includes computerized graphics and animated storytelling. The narrator talks about space and time in terms of trillions and billions of galaxies and light years. He says, "According to a cosmic calendar, human beings didn't appear until 11:59 p.m. on December 31." He mentions a space probe we've sent that broadcasts a message in different languages. "Hello, we're from earth. Is anybody out there?"

The message includes quadrants and specific directions to our address in the solar system. Stephen Hawking, the scientist, doesn't think this probe is a good idea. He says, "The universe is big and weird. Would you call out in the jungle to let others know of your whereabouts?"

The TV story takes us out to the edge, to the moment before the Big Bang—a time before time, when nothing existed. And then, from one explosion, came worlds upon worlds upon worlds. It's hard to get your head around. Our home, our earth, isn't even a speck. It's a speck on a speck. We're specks on a speck on a speck.

Have to keep this in mind as I worry about dog pee.

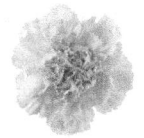

MARCH 12, 2014

EMPTY BOWLS

My friend Grace and I are at the Sacramento Convention Center. The River City Food Bank is holding its annual fundraising luncheon, Empty Bowls. Local artists and art students donate their pottery. A lunch ticket costs $40. It includes soups prepared and donated by local restaurants, and the choice of an empty art bowl to take home.

We worked at last year's event, which raised $100,000. This year's goal is $125,000. One-third of the meals, provided by the food bank, goes to children. One of four children in the Sacramento area lives in poverty. The food bank also serves seniors and families.

Grace and I are dressed in black pants, white tops and black aprons imprinted with the words, "Empty Bowls." We're serving soups—chicken and artichoke, pozole rojo, and lentil. The soups rotate a pot at a time until the pot is empty. The favorite, year after year, is a crab bisque.

Empty Bowls is simple, elegant fundraising. Everything's donated. Volunteers staff all the stations—check-in, pottery tables, information tables, and soup lines. High school students clear tables and replenish table settings. When the event ends at 1:30 p.m., volunteers get to select a bowl from the ones remaining.

I choose a small, light-green bowl that I'm putting on the dresser in my guest room. It's a perfect receptacle for car keys, earrings, or spare change. My multi-colored bowl from last year decorates the table in my entryway. It's filled with jelly beans for Easter. Sometimes it holds candy hearts or candy corn or red-and-green-wrapped chocolate kisses.

My event souvenirs are year-round reminders to give thanks for my full pantry, and to remember that there are hungry folks out there—many in my own neck of the woods.

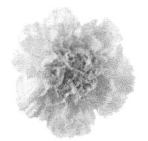

MARCH 13, 2014

A REAL LIFE MYSTERY

Where did Malaysia Airlines Flight 370 go?

The plane disappeared six days ago on a routine flight from Kuala Lumpur, Malaysia, to Beijing, China. The Boeing 777 aircraft is one of the largest and safest in the world. The plane reached its maximum known altitude, 35,000 feet, and speed, 539 mph, twenty minutes after taking off. It disappeared, without a warning or a distress message, twenty-two minutes later. Forty-two ships and thirty-nine aircraft from 12 countries, including the US, are searching the Gulf of Thailand and the South China Sea.

Everywhere I go—in line at the bank, in the check-out line at the grocery store, in the bridge room—people are speculating about this missing plane. Theories abound. Mass electrical failure, sudden decompression, pilot suicide, terrorism. One man predicts that the plane will be found empty. "The passengers and crew have been kidnapped by aliens."

Everyone's pointing fingers. China's criticizing Malaysia's handling of the situation. Bloggers suggest the Malaysian military shot the plane down and then covered up their mistake. Chinese citizens complain their government isn't doing enough to help find the aircraft. In Iran, because two Iranian passengers with false passports were on board, one lawmaker calls the entire episode a form of psychological warfare by the US to sabotage relationships between Iran, China, and Southeast Asia.

Meanwhile, families and friends of the 239 people on board wait, in limbo, to learn the fate of their loved ones. Just when I've been pondering the relative, minuscule size of our earth in the universe, our world seems very large again. Where is this airplane?

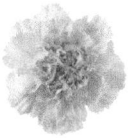

MARCH 16, 2014

OF ANTS AND ME

I've been battling ants around the kitchen sink for two days. The pest control person comes. He traces the ant pathway from inside my dishwasher, across the entryway, down the hall, through the laundry room, and out the door to the garage. He spies a hole in the door frame, at the garage floor level, where the ants are trailing in and out.

I like ants. Maybe "like" isn't the correct word. I respect ants. They're industrious and social. They eat insects and do other good works. I search the web for ant info.

- Ants can lift 20 times their body weight. In other words, if a first grader were as strong as an ant, she could pick up a car.
- There are various jobs in an ant colony—taking care of eggs and babies, gathering food, and building mounds.
- At night, caregiver ants move eggs deep into the nest to protect them from the cold. During the day, they move the eggs to the top of the nest for warmth.

- Some birds put ants in their feathers to eat parasites.
- Ants are clean. Worker ants take rubbish from the nest and put it outside in "rubbish bins."

When I was little, I'd pick up ants crawling around the bathtub and take them outside. They're living things, I thought. I hated to kill living things, except maybe aphids on rose bushes. Mom says, "I never had to hire a pest exterminator because I had you."

So, here I am, hating to kill ants. I know I can't share my house with them. They'd be pushy, overbearing roommates. I let the pest control guy spray. He says, "You'll see strays for a couple of days."

I squirt the stray ants around the sink with window cleaner. They don't make this easy. I'm watching one ant, pacing back and forth, trying to comprehend the dead bodies all around him. Oh, shit. He's carrying a sick comrade on his back. This is too much. I can't kill this hero ant. He gets a reprieve. I coax him, still carrying his buddy, onto a napkin and carry them outside.

For the rest, I hope this window cleaner kills you right away. I hope you're all, mature, two-year-old ants who've enjoyed good ant lives, with weekends off and comprehensive medical coverage. I hope your colony gets the message to stay out of this house so we can live in peaceful co-existence.

I must share all this ant stuff with Ayla, the little girl who loves bugs. I'll tell her the story of ants and me.

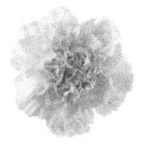

MARCH 17, 2014

NO INVADERS, NO DRAGONS, NO TROLLS

I'm with Regan and Ayla at their house. Kerry and David are down the street at a neighborhood get-together. Regan's playing "Home on the Range" on the piano. She's concentrating on the notes on the sheet music. She's learning.

"Do you like playing the piano?"

"Yes, I also like having different members of my family babysit us. It's good to get to know other family members besides Mommy and Daddy. You, and my other grandma, Michele."

Ayla adds, "And Papa."

Regan says, "Yes, Ralph. Ralph and Michele."

We shift gears. Regan pulls a game out of the closet. The three of us sit at the dining room table playing Operation. As usual, I'm losing. Ayla makes a statement I've heard before. "Let's play a game that's easy for Mim."

Regan and Ayla begin assembling plastic tunnels and runways for marble races on the entryway tile. I'm still trying to get down on the floor. I do what I'm told. "Hold this piece." "Remove that section." Regan reminds us, "We need to work together as a team. Mim, as a team member, would you like a Girl Scout lemon wafer?"

Sounds good to me. Regan and Ayla want lemon wafers, too, but there's a hitch. Regan asks, "What if Mommy and Daddy notice that three lemon wafers are missing?"

Not to worry. I say, "If they notice, I'll explain that I ate all three lemon wafers myself." Problem solved.

We head upstairs to the playroom. It's a disaster. It looks like, well, a well-played-in playroom. Toys and princess dresses cover the floor. I offer to hang up the dresses in their special princess wardrobe. One by one, all the dresses are off the floor.

Hmm? Regan's formulating a plan. "Let's clean up the playroom and surprise Mommy and Daddy." In short order, everything's being restored to its proper place. If I don't know where something goes, Ayla tells me where to put it. Regan says, "This is exciting. Mommy and Daddy are going to be so happy."

We dump a jar full of beads onto the pristine, cleaned-up floor. For twenty minutes, our team pops beads together in a long string. We're building a giant worm. The worm's finished. We're looking for a measuring tape to measure how long it is, but we can't find one.

We put on pajamas and brush teeth. We watch a video about Wally the Troll, his pet dragon, and Bad Gremlin Bob. Bad Gremlin Bob has captured the castle. He's nailing signs across all the castle windows and doors—NO INVADERS, NO DRAGONS, NO TROLLS. This becomes our mantra. We march around the family room chanting.

"No invaders. No dragons. No trolls."

"No invaders. No dragons. No trolls."

David checks in. It's 9:30 p.m. and Regan has an early morning to get to a ski lesson. Regan climbs into her bed. I climb into bed with Ayla to read three books The last book, about a caterpillar, is her favorite. I ask Ayla if she's sleepy. She is. "When Mommy and Daddy come home, I'll ask them to cuddle me. When they're not here, I like to fall asleep by myself."

Got it, Ayla. I turn off the light in Ayla's lavender room. "Good night, Ayla. I love you."

I check in Regan's pink room. She's sound asleep. "Good night, Regan. I love you."

How do you freeze time?

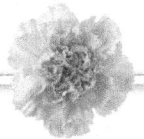

SPRING 2014

Spring has returned.
The Earth is like a child that knows poems.
Rainer Maria Rilke

INTERNAL DRUM

Those footsteps beneath my window
came and went so fast. The ground,
still frozen in spots, begins
its long thaw. The boy passed by
without incident, just the sounds
of his feet, a mud-sucked heartbeat.
When I think about my heartbeat,
its patterns and palpitations, windows
and valves busy with blood, the sounds
of circulation and murmur, the ground
pulses right along with me. It works
by pure magic, this internal drum,
begins anew every moment, always beginning
another push, another pump. Heartbeats
seem to be generated by superhuman force.
I asked the window what it thought.
It said, "there's the ground, trees point to the sky,
I hear no sounds.
But if you can hear the gift of sounds,
place them on the page as evidence of what began
and ended in an instant." A survey of the ground
complete, a military jet maneuvers, its heartbeat
hushed, into its inland cavern, its window-

less womb, where tools clang when dropped by
the uniformed hand. States away, traffic rushes by
the dancing cop, his frantic hands, the short sounds
of whistle and clap. A broker puts his nose to the window
on the thirtieth floor, mutters, "I must begin
my day," clutches his chest and drops, his heartbeat,
tired of his refrain, shows him the ground.
Out in a suburban field, a child squats upon the ground,
runs his fingers through the mud, listens as cars race by.
Today in school he learned the subject heartbeat,
he held his wrist and counted as the sounds
came through his ears by stethoscope. "Begin,"
the teacher said, the children obeyed. The window
took on the fog of nervous youth, and the ground began
its long stretch from the window to the sounds
of the eastern sea, all of this by way of heartbeats.

—PATRICK RANAHAN
Published in
Latitude on 2nd
Cool Waters Media, Inc., 2012

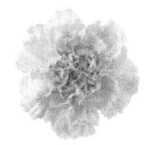

MARCH 19, 2014

A BOUT OF SELF-DOUBT

Here I sit at the computer, staring at the screen. The monthly cleaning crew is dusting and vacuuming and I'm trying to stay out of their way. I'm trying to stay out of my own way. Pesky thoughts flit across my mind. Why am I writing? Do I really think my life could be of interest to someone, sometime, somewhere? Some days I think I'm leaving a "gift" for my descendants. I'd love to find letters my great-grandmother wrote 100 years ago. Other days, I fear I'm becoming a self-absorbed old woman.

A writing teacher once told me to write what I want to read. I've always preferred nonfiction over fiction. I've always favored history and peeks into days gone by. In that sense, I'm writing what I want to read. I can't be the only who'd love to read a grandmother's diary.

Or am I?

Patrick's Facebook Post: Monsanto is not banned in America because in America if you make something that is bad for you but tastes fucking great and makes you feel good, you are going to make a fortune.

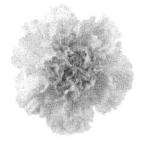

MARCH 20, 2014

A PARADOX

I write I'm not writing anything today.

MARCH 21, 2014

WHAT TO KEEP AND WHAT TO DISCARD

When I think about the past, I remember specifics—images, sounds, scents. I see dimples in a smile, drops of water, my Rottweiler's big brown eyes. I hear train whistles, lawn mowers humming, and the white noise of clothes dryers spinning clothes. I smell pink bubble gum, apple cider vinegar, and pine Christmas trees.

I think about the life that's been unique to me. I remember the ordinary. I reflect on the struggle that life can be, even when it's good. I bow to the everyday challenges of climbing up, sliding down, and climbing up again. I admit to the ways things came out differently, many times, than I'd imagined—or hoped. I deliberate about the friend who wasn't a friend, and the person

I ignored who was. I acknowledge decisions that turned out wrong and guesses that turned out lucky.

When I look back, I simultaneously see the world as I saw it as a child and as I see it as an adult. From this observation deck, I can choose, with more discernment, what to keep and what to discard. Maybe writing down my daily thoughts, in hindsight, will be an effort that turned out to be a good thing.

I guess time will tell.

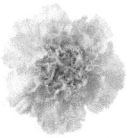

MARCH 24, 2014

THANK YOU

Dear Lincoln Hills Foundation,

On behalf of the Lincoln Hills Family Mental Illness Support Group, thank you for your recent gift of $1,000.

The group is surprised and excited to have this kind of support. I've opened a checking account in the group name with an IRS EIN number. We have two signatures assigned to the account for control purposes. We are in the process of brainstorming a book list for a group library and a speaker list for upcoming meetings.

We will keep you apprised of our activities as you have requested and will acknowledge the Lincoln Hills Foundation at each opportunity.

Please extend our gratitude to the Board of Directors and to your Advisory Board.

Sincerely,
Dede Ranahan
Group Moderator
Lincoln Hills Family Mental Illness Support Group

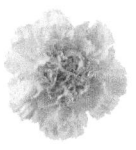

MARCH 25, 2014

ANYTOWN, USA

Back working the cash register in my favorite thrift store. Today, kids clothes are two items for $1.00. Long-sleeved tops are $1.00. Buy a pair of pants and get a second pair free. Repeat customers are beginning to rely on this shop. A regular wants to know, "Are shoes a dollar today?"

"Not today."

"I'll wait then. I'm a single mom. I have to watch my budget."

A woman plops six women's tank tops on the counter.

"Looks like you're getting ready for summer."

"No. I have MS and I spend most of my time at home in my pajamas."

Another woman has a question. "Do you have any long cigarette holders?"

"Not that I'm aware of."

"I'm looking for them and they're hard to find."

A woman buys some kitchenware and a plastic nose attached to Groucho Marx eyeglasses.

"Who's going to wear this nose?"

"I am. I teach a class for seniors at the community college. I'll wear this for one of my lectures and see if they notice."

"I'd love a picture of you teaching in your fake nose and glasses."

"Okay. I'll bring in a photo."

A man with long hair comes in every Tuesday. He walks around the store until he senses something calling out to him. Today, he buys a string of costume pearls. "My sister will use these for crafts. I have a room with boxes I'm filling up with the things I buy here. I used to buy and sell stuff. Now I'm stashing it away for my kids when I pass on."

A pregnant woman loads up on baby and toddler clothes. Another regular, a Hispanic woman, returns a pair of black shoes with thick, rounded soles. We don't usually take returns. "The manager said I could return these if they didn't fit my son. They didn't fit."

"Do you have your receipt?"

"Yes, right here."

"Would you like to look around to see if you find something else?"

For 30 minutes the woman picks through clothes, shoes, kids clothing, pots, and pans. "I don't find anything today."

I process her $5 refund. I put the returned shoes back on the men's shoe rack. As the woman goes out the door, a man walks in. In short order, he stacks three men's tops on the counter and spies the newly returned shoes. "Those are really interesting shoes. Looks like you could rock back and forth in them."

"Would you like to try them on?"

"Yes, I would." The man walks around the store with his old shoe on the left foot and the new shoe on the right. "Yep. These are interesting shoes."

"Would you like to try on the other one and make sure they feel good?"

"No, I know I want these shoes."

He makes his purchase. Three winter shirts and one pair of shoes. $8.

Items of all sizes and shapes come in, go out, come in, go out. People of all sizes and shapes come in, go out, come in, go out. Another ordinary, extraordinary day in the thrift store.

Patrick's Facebook Post: My dog just set the world record for most urgent shit ever taken.

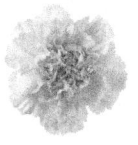

MARCH 28, 2014

GRANDPARENT'S DAY

Today is Thomas Jefferson Elementary School's 10th Annual Grandparent's Day. Regan's teacher says, "This kind of day is what makes me love teaching. Keep your fingers crossed, as we're losing other things to 'core' curriculum, that we don't lose this day."

I take a seat in the multi-purpose room. I'm getting teary perusing the program—Flag Salute and Pledge of Allegiance. Out of five classes of second graders, Regan's been selected to lead the 200 visiting grandparents and her classmates in this pledge. When it's finished, Regan, holding the microphone in hand, says, "Thank you. Please be seated."

Her little voice is clear and steady like she does this every day. Later, Kerry will tell me, "Do you know how much this means to me? I mean, she's shy and it's taken a long time to get her to this point."

Five second grade classes proceed to sing nine songs. The program builds to a climax and ends with one of my favorite songs from Sesame Street—*My Name is You*:

> *I come from everywhere*
> *And my name is you.*

There's hope for all of us. The next generation, Regan's generation, will be fine. They have good parents and grandparents and teachers. Why shouldn't they be fine? Listening to these pure, sweet voices I'm coming undone.

Grandparent's Day continues. It's quite a production. We take a break and the kids serve the grandparents treats. Regan brings me a cup of strawberry lemonade. "Is this okay or would you rather have raspberry lemonade?"

"This is perfect."

She gets her own strawberry lemonade and a plate of cookies for us to share. I ask her how she was chosen to lead the Pledge of Allegiance. "Some of us tried out. I had the loudest voice."

Hmm. I suspect a wise, caring teacher here.

Back in the classroom, grandparents share stories of branding irons, sewing their own clothes, ice trucks, and war medals. The kids are attentive. The teacher asks the children what they've learned from their grandparents' stories. They all agree. Life is very different now. One little girls says, "I like hearing what grandparents have to say."

Regan and I leave for a quick lunch off campus. She orders a cheeseburger, fries, and a chocolate milkshake. I seem to make a good grandma move when I say "yes" to the milkshake.

I drop Regan back at the school office. Later today, I'll pick her and Ayla up at their house for an overnight at my house. Stay tuned . . .

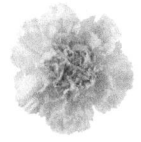

MARCH 28/29, 2014

LOVE IS ALIVE

I'm not in charge of this overnight. Two little redheads outline the program. It's nonstop activity from drawing, to picking out the right color jelly beans, to dressing up, and dancing to made-up songs and cheers.

In the kitchen, Regan's wearing her mother's high school cheerleading outfit and brandishing ostrich feathers for pom-poms. Ayla's twirling in a pink princess dress from the thrift store. The floor is littered with discarded clothes.

> *"We are the feather eggs."*
> *"We are the feather eggs."*
> *"We will beat the dogs."*

Ayla shakes plastic eggs, filled with pebbles, to Regan's beat. At the end of their cheer, they both take a bow. Of course, Grandma Mim applauds with wild enthusiasm.

We're hungry now, and we chow down boxed macaroni and cheese shaped like Sponge Bob characters, and a couple of strawberries. We settle in on my red sofa, under my red blanket, to watch *Frozen*. Regan and Ayla have seen it three times. It's their favorite movie.

I say, "I'm excited. I haven't seen it yet."

Ayla assures me, "Mim, if you need something, we'll get it for you because we've seen the movie before and you haven't."

We enjoy the voices, the heroines, the animation. When all seems lost, as it always does somewhere in a Disney movie, the heroines discover that "love is the answer." We like Elsa because she has magic powers. We like Anna because she's spunky and has red hair.

It's time for vanilla ice cream drumsticks with caramel centers and chocolate on top. Regan picked them out at the store. "They're the best."

In the pull-down wall bed, the three of us snuggle together for bedtime reading. One of the books is *When Did I Meet You Grandma?* The last page is to be filled in.

"I call my Grandma, 'Mim.'"

"My favorite thing about my Grandma is . . ."

I'm holding my breath.

"She gives us candy."

"My Grandma is wonderful because . . . she gives us candy."

"I love my Grandma because . . . she gives us candy."

Every question ends with the same answer. This is very funny. So much for my dreams of "wonderfulness." Ayla asks, "When did I meet you, Mim?"

"We met each other in the hospital when you were born."

"Can we have another jelly bean?"

"Umm, no, you've brushed your teeth. Good night, Regan. Goodnight, Ayla."

I'm writing this down, hoping that sometime Regan and Ayla might remember this day. And this overnight.

Patrick's Facebook Post: For those of you who don't believe in love, love is the sound of a man tightening his lug nuts on his wheels with a drill before heading off on a long journey with his wife and child. Love is alive.

MARCH 31, 2014

PACING MYSELF

I'm gearing up for the big 96th birthday dinner this Saturday. Today, after my workout with Deanne, I vacuum, change the beds, wash two loads of clothes, pay some bills, and make a to-do list for the rest of the week.

I promised myself, when I began writing about this year, my subject matter would be organic—my recordings would spring up from real events, not from contrived drama. My premise was most any day, and most anything, could be interesting. Sometimes, in describing a quotidian event, I find a gem. Like watching a lowly corn kernel transform itself when it pops.

When I was in high school, I collected an anthology of poems about little things. I wish I could find that anthology now. I had an early intuition about what's important and I want to nourish that intuition again.

In this week that will be one of busyness, I'll factor in time to reflect. In the moments between doing and doing more, I'll listen for the cadences, the soundtrack that would rise and fall, if my life were a movie.

This is one of the gifts of aging. Things don't have to be as exciting as they used to be. I'm pacing myself.

Patrick's Facebook Post: Lunch has become my favorite word.

APRIL 3, 2014

GETTING READY

I'm cleaning toilets, cutting dead leaves off plants in the outside entryway, and grating lemon peel for the cake I'm baking tomorrow. Michael's package of French sausages and duck legs arrived, and I've put them in the fridge, along with three batches of homemade Irish cream I blended this afternoon.

I'm nervous about the lemon layer cake since I've never made it before. If it looks like a flop, I'll call Kerry and ask her to pick up a cake at the market. I'm hoping my cake will come through, though.

My to-do list, in addition to the cake, includes clean the litter box and make Saturday's prepare-ahead breakfast. Probably, clean the litter box is the most important. Don't want the house reeking. Ah, the things we wind ourselves up about.

Patrick's Facebook Post: People playing music together is the polar opposite of people fighting. I know I posted this photo a while ago, right around the time it happened. Wanted to revisit this remarkable luncheon hosted by Michael Bayard celebrating a recent healing journey I made. This is the group of sound heal-ing musicians who became a pivotal support group in a time of great distress. Thanks again!

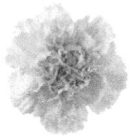

APRIL 4, 2014

LIFE GOES ON

My Kansas City cousin calls. She wants to know what time to send two dozen roses for GG to my house on Saturday. She also wants to let me know she has a blind date coming up.

"How old is he?"

"He's 82. His wife died a year ago."

"Where are you going?"

"He's taking me to dinner and picking me up at my house. I want him to see who I am and where I live."

"Please call and let me know how it goes."

"I will. Danny told me, 'Have fun, Mom.'"

Yes, have fun and go find a person who needs to find you. This is not always easy to do. May the Force be with you, my Kansas City Cuz.

Patrick's Facebook Post: This whole missing Malaysian jet-liner thing just goes to show that, though we claim to be highly evolved, we really have no idea what we are doing.

APRIL 7, 2014

96TH BIRTHDAY

A birthday whirlwind weekend. I drove Jim and Sharon to the airport this morning after nonstop eating Saturday and Sunday. Michael prepared a delicious arugula salad with candied walnuts and pears poached in sauterne and, of course, his French bean, sausage, and duck cassoulet. David made Brussels sprouts in a Dijon mustard sauce. The lemon layer cake with rosemary and whipped-cream and cream-cheese frosting was a success. Sunday morning was Michael's quiche and more of the poached pears.

Thirteen adults and three children joined GG for her 96th birthday fete. Kerry hung 12 gold helium balloons over the dining room table. She tied double-sided family photographs to the end of each balloon string. Cousin Annette sent two dozen pink roses from Kansas City.

Mom beamed. "It's the best birthday party I've ever had."

She blew out two candles on her cake—a nine and a six—and made a wish. "Can I tell everyone what I wished?"

"Mom, you can do whatever you want."

"I wished that all of you will come back here, in four years, to join me for my one-hundredth birthday."

"We will. We will."

Happy 96th Birthday, GG Moon.

Patrick's Facebook Post: The great thing about walking your dog in the park on a leash is that, if you get caught up in an awkward conversation with your neighbors, the dog will drag you away and you don't have to excuse yourself from the conversation.

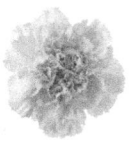

APRIL 8, 2014

YAY FOR OUR TEAM

Annette calls. She wants to make sure her roses arrived. She also wants to tell me about her blind date.

"How did it go?"

"It went well. Jim picked me up, opened car and restaurant doors, showed me around his beautiful white-everything house, and kissed me goodnight. He's invited me to dinner again next Thursday. He wants his friends to meet his girlfriend."

"Wow. His girlfriend?"

"That's what he said on the phone."

This gentleman owns several houses, a boat, and flies his own airplane—at 82 years of age. Annette says, "I'm not ready to go up in the air with him."

Yay, Cousin Annette. At 75, you're a spring chicken and a fine catch.

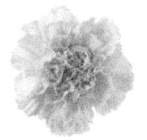

APRIL 9, 2014

LET THE CELEBRATION BEGIN

I'm going to Bend, Oregon, on Sunday. This is a surprise trip from Marisa and Kerry for my 70th birthday. A little early, but it's Easter break and they can get away for a couple of days. Kerry, Regan, Ayla, and I will drive from Lincoln to Bend. Marisa, Sam, and Elise will drive from Seattle to Bend. Marisa has reserved a craftsman-style house in the center of town.

I'm adjusting my calendar—canceling dentist appointments, bridge dates, my shift at Snap It Up, and arranging a cat sitter for Jazzy. This morning I wake up with a scratchy sore throat. Drat. I have to will this sore throat away. I'm happy and excited to be preparing for this unexpected Oregon excursion with my daughters and grandchildren.

Let the 70th birthday celebration begin.

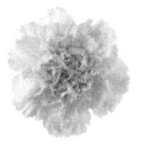

APRIL 12, 2014

THELMA AND LOUISE

I'm running around, getting ready to go. I've been laid up with this cold and I'm catching up. I hate colds. You feel like you're not really sick but you're really not well, either. Actually, you feel like shit. I'm drinking orange juice, using nose spray and eye drops, and taking antihistamines and cough syrup. Probably, all together, they're a lethal combination. But I don't have time to fool around. We're leaving tomorrow morning at 6 a.m. on our road trip to Bend, Oregon.

Lay in cat food and kitty litter. Check. Water houseplants and outside potted plants. Check. Print off a map. Check. Fill the gas tank. Check. Buy birthday favors for the grandkids. Check. Sounds like I'm leaving for four weeks instead of four days.

This will be a Thelma-and-Louise adventure with a seven-year-old and a five-year-old, I'm raring to go.

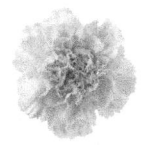

APRIL 13, 2014

ON THE ROAD AGAIN

On the road again. Can't wait to get on the road again. Kerry, Regan, Ayla, and I are settled into my 2006 Prius. Kerry's driving. I'm assigned the passenger seat and the role of navigator. Kerry's phone is programmed to Siri for directions. My old-fashioned printed directions are a backup in case we lose cell phone contact.

Regan and Ayla, still in pajamas and buckled in their car seats, sit surrounded by blankets, pillows, stuffed animals, and kid-size electronic gadgets. Kerry and I agree on some ground rules:

- The driver's always right.
- The front seat passenger is allowed to scream once. Only once.
- What happens in the car, stays in the car.
- Because I'm the Birthday Queen, Kerry and Marisa can't call me out—for anything—for the duration of the trip.

According to my Google map, the distance to Bend is 424.3 miles, or seven hours and five minutes not counting pit and food stops. Ten minutes out of town we run into a dead end. How did we get off the main road? Was it the driver or the navigator? Oh, boy. This could be a long trip.

Back on track, it's a clear day with blue, cloudless skies. We pass a reasonable mix of green and brown grasses, given the drought situation. Lake Shasta is low. A wide swath of black, muddy earth rims the perimeter. Halfway to Bend, Kerry and I realize we haven't turned on the radio. We've been "banterizing." Kerry makes up this word. We're laughing and teasing each other. We're having a good time.

The girls are getting restless. Now I'm driving and Kerry's navigating and directing car yoga. Ayla throws her feet up over her head in her car seat. Regan's a swirl of hair flying from one side to the other.

We pull off the road in Weed. Kerry sees a photo op in front of a "Welcome to Weed" sign. She asks Regan to run as fast as she can to get an action shot and to use up some of her kid energy. Back on the road, we're driving through northern California outback. We pass an adult superstore. Gun shops and signs for certified NRA instructors appear like Golden Arches—with predictable regularity. Looking for lunch, we pass a restaurant that advertises, "We now serve good food."

Hmm. Think we'll keep looking.

As we approach Bend, we call Marisa. We're a little bit ahead of her and will arrive at the rental house first. Marisa gives Kerry the code to gain access to the house key. Our get-away is about to begin for real.

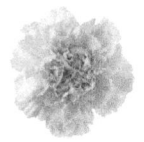

APRIL 14, 2014

HELL-O-OH

NW Federal Street is our Bend address. The owners live in Cleveland, Ohio. This house will be their retirement home, along with an East Coast home in Florida.

I claim the downstairs bedroom. It's not the master bedroom, but it means I don't have to climb the steep, narrow stairs to the second floor. Marisa and Kerry are sharing the master bedroom. A third bedroom, on the second floor, has a single bed for Sam and a double bed for Ayla, Regan, and Elise. The kids want to be together. This morning, the four of them are up at 4 a.m. There's too much excitement for young cousins to stay asleep.

Marisa and Kerry walk to the Back Porch Coffee Shop to buy coffee and breakfast treats. I brought ground Yuban, my coffee of choice for many years, but it doesn't meet M & K's minimum standards. It comes in a plastic container from the grocery store. It's not tall or short or blended. My cup of "real coffee" from the coffee shop doesn't impress me. I like my Yuban better.

The unexpected magic, though, is in the breakfast rolls that Kerry and Marisa bring home to all of us—Ocean Rolls, a Bend exclusive from the Sparrow Bakery. Oh, my. This is a true discovery. A cross between a breakfast roll and a croissant and flavored with cardamom. The seven of us share two of them. We all agree these are among the most wonderful, delicious concoctions we've ever tasted. Kids and grownups fight over the last few crumbs.

I don't eat breakfast rolls and I'm not a fan of croissants, but these Ocean Rolls are over the top. Why they're called Ocean Rolls isn't clear. Bend is far from the Pacific ocean or any ocean. Cardamom is native to the evergreen forests of Southern India. Nomenclature is of no significance, however. The roll is the roll is the roll.

At lunchtime we pull in at the Ten Barrel Brewery a few blocks from the house. The day is much warmer than we were expecting. We sit outside at a polished picnic table. Crayons and coloring paper are provided. Halfway through our meal, the drinks for the kids haven't arrived. I spy our waitress across the yard. In an instant, in Bend, my life changes forever.

"Hell-o-oh," I yell in a high pitch. "Hell-o-oh!"

The waitress turns around. Marisa and Kerry duck down. Customers at other tables are staring at us. Sam and Elise are laughing. What did Mim just do? This is so embarrassing. The waitress comes to our table. "We're still waiting for the kids' drinks."

"Oh, right. I'll get them for you."

"Hell-o-oh" becomes the vacation catchphrase. I remind everyone of the trip rule. No one can criticize the Birthday Girl.

This afternoon we hike in Shevlin Park, which has level walking trails, lots of big and little sticks, and water running over rocks and logs. Perfect. "Hell-o-oh" everyone shouts through the forest. We stop at a covered bridge for a group photograph.

Back at the house, the evening's filled with games like "I'm going camping and I'm bringing . . ." Everyone has to guess the secret code to be allowed to come on the camping trip. The kids love this game. They take turns making up the rules. After a while, the game deteriorates into knock-knock jokes involving butts and poop. Butts and poop are as funny as "Hell-o-oh" and all are mentioned, often, to fits and giggles.

The walls in this house on NW Federal Street are blushing. They've never heard such goings-on. It's a good thing the owners live far away. In Cleveland.

"Hell-o-oh."

APRIL 15TH, 2014

70TH BIRTHDAY PARTY

My 70th birthday party continues. Everyone's up before me and there are more Ocean Rolls this morning. About one quarter of an Ocean Roll is left for Mim. That will teach me to get up last.

We pile into Marisa's white Honda Odyssey mini-van. We're driving to Sisters, a little tourist town about half an hour from Bend. Turns out it's not a good time to walk the main drag. The streets and sidewalks are all torn up for a major renovation. The make-over will be finished in a month for the summer tourist season, but right now, walking is a pedestrian's nightmare—plenty of opportunities for tripping and stumbling. I watch my feet and where I put them.

We head to a restaurant famous for its fish and chips. The girls order from the kids menu—their third meal of mac-n-cheese. Sam joins M & K and me in sharing an order of fish and chips. The fish and chips come and they're good. We order another basket. Kerry orders a diet Pepsi for the second time as it has not yet arrived.

Our chatty waitress says, "I used to live in Seattle. I lived there seven months. I didn't like it."

"Was it the weather you didn't like?"

"No, it was the traffic."

M & K take the receipt to the cash register to pay for lunch. I sit with the kids. And sit with the kids. This is taking a while. Ayla's upset. She wants her mom. The woman at the cash register rings up three baskets of fish and chips instead of two. She charges $3 for the diet drink that never came. Eventually, all is adjusted and Ayla finds Kerry.

Back at our NW Federal home away from home, I pass out Easter Bunny PEZ dispensers with candy refills. They're received with cheers, thank-you's, and hugs. I had Popeye and Mickey Mouse PEZ dispensers when I was little. PEZ candy was invented in Austria in 1927 as a breath mint. The name comes from the German word for peppermint—"pfefferminz." In 1948, the first PEZ dispenser was designed to resemble a cigarette lighter to encourage people to quit smoking. In 2011, PEZ, Inc. opened a visitor's center in Orange, Connecticut. A true product success story.

With PEZ dispensers in their hands, the kids disappear upstairs. M & K open their laptops on the dining room table. They both have work to do for their jobs for Williams Sonoma. They work from home and away from home.

I opt for some alone time and drive to Bend's main street shopping area where restaurants and clothing boutiques abound. I examine a few items on racks—a blouse, a jacket, a skirt. They each cost the same. $324. Time to move on. At the market, two blocks from our house, I buy cheese, crackers, wine, and the makings for noodles and tomatoes for Sam and the girls. The grownups are having Happy Hour for our last evening in Bend.

We open the wine and drink a toast to my birthday. We play Simon Says and Sorry with Sam and Ayla. Regan and Elise are upstairs. M & K go back to the market for another bottle of wine. I pick up dirty dinner dishes and load the dishwasher. The grandchildren are dueling each other with the long, plastic tubes their PEZ dispensers came in. Packaging is always so much fun.

M & K return and there's a commotion in the dining room A sparkler's blazing on top of a cupcake. My two daughters and their four children are singing "Happy Birthday." We have a choice of chocolate cupcakes with chocolate frosting or vanilla cupcakes with vanilla frosting. And, if we're good, we can have one of each.

This birthday celebration is my best, ever. Marisa and Kerry have gone above and beyond—making the plans, renting the vacation house, paying for breakfasts, lunches, and dinners. I'll pull this memory out of my memory box and relive it again and again.

"I love you Marisa, Kerry, Sam, Elise, Regan, and Ayla. Thank you for sharing this birthday with me."

My 70th birthday road trip is coming to a close, all too soon.

Patrick's Facebook Post: Thank God it's tax day! Now maybe all the idiots who dress up like the Statue of Liberty and stand on the street corner and wave signs and wave at traffic will go away.

APRIL 16, 2014

A WONDERFUL ADVENTURE

This morning we're packing up and getting ready to leave Bend. We walk to a nearby bakery. The first thing Kerry and I notice is the absence of Ocean Rolls. Oh, my. What shall we do? Back at the house, I say, "I have to leave for a few minutes to run an errand."

"How long will this errand take?"

"I don't know. Maybe half an hour. This is still my birthday celebration. I'm still the Birthday Queen."

"Well, okay, but we have to leave pretty soon, you know. It's a long drive home."

I back my car out of the driveway and consult Siri for directions to Sparrow Bakery. Yesterday, Marisa and I stopped by the bakery to check it out. I gathered the necessary information while Marisa used the restroom.

"Yes, you can freeze Ocean Rolls."

"No, we don't have an online site for ordering them."

"No, we don't ship them."

"Yes, you can order them by the dozen."

I ordered three dozen Ocean Rolls to be picked up tomorrow, which is now today. As I pull into the bakery parking lot, my cell phone rings. "Hi. This is Sparrow Bakery. We're holding your order for three dozen Ocean Rolls."

"Thank you. I'll be right there." I don't want my Ocean Rolls sold to someone else.

Heading back to the house on NW Federal, the car vibrates with the smell of warm, baked-this-morning Ocean Rolls, I walk in the house and give a box to Marisa. "For me? All of these?"

"Yes, we each get a dozen."

On the drive home, for an hour and a half, Kerry and I talk about Ocean Rolls. How we'll freeze and reheat them. How we'll try to find a recipe or make one up. How cardamom may be our new favorite spice—ever. An hour and a half. Is this what you call mother-daughter bonding? I don't know. Whatever it is, I want to pack it in a sealed container and preserve it forever.

We arrive back at my house. Ayla and Regan move their car seats from my car to their white Toyota SUV, which is parked in my garage. They're eager to get home. They want to see Daddy.

No matter how wonderful the adventure, it's always good to get home. I'm home. I'm tired. I wouldn't have it any other way.

Patrick's Facebook Post: My official job title is auto parts delivery driver, but a more accurate title would be Sirius Satellite Radio Operator as I scan the dial all day while cruising though the Northern California gold rush communities.

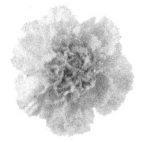

APRIL 17, 2014

THE TREE GUY

The tree guy's here. Over the winter, five of my podocarpus trees have croaked. And the African sumac, in my front yard, is drooping with large sections of brown leaves. When I look at it, I feel like I live in a southern swamp. Maybe it can recover, but there are other issues.

This African sumac tree grows like a weed. It's evergreen yet drops yellow leaves all year long and it's encroaching on my rooftop and gutter line. It's building my case for getting rid of it, even though I hate to remove, okay kill, any plant or tree.

The tree guy says these trees need major pruning every year. Like $300 worth of pruning. Case closed. The dead podocarpus trees have to go. The still-living African sumac has to go. Damn. The other thing is that there's a finch nest in the African sumac with two baby birds inside. I don't know this until the tree guy points it out. He can move it to another tree. I inhale.

"Move it to another tree."

We wait. The mother finch flies to the new tree with a worm in her beak. She's figured out the relocation of her nest. She's found her lost babies. She's on it. "Go, Mother Finch. I'm for you, not against you."

The African sumac comes down. The podocarpus trees come down. Huge holes appear in my yard. I'm having a yard identity crisis. "Wait," says the tree man. "Live with your yard for a while. Think about what new trees you might want to consider."

I need someone to hold my hand in this endeavor. I need a good tree guy. I think I have one.

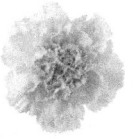

APRIL 20, 2014

EASTER

For me, Easter is about family getting together. We had Easter egg hunts forever when my children were growing up. If not in our own yard, in GG's yard. When my kids were 18, 19, and 20, they still wanted to hunt for Easter eggs, which by then were plastic, and some included five-dollar bills.

I'm at Kerry's house this afternoon watching the custom continue. Two hundred plastic eggs, some with dimes and nickels in them, are hiding in Kerry's backyard. Regan, Ayla, and their friends, Evan and Grant, run around all the bushes and trees. In five minutes the hunt is over. Everyone has a basketful of eggs and a chocolate rabbit. As much as the hunt, sitting down on the entry way floor to count their loot is part of the thrill.

Among our clan is GG, of course, and Doug. Doug is Regan's and Ayla's great-grandfather on their father's side. His wife, Joyce, recently passed away. (My perky polka-dot umbrella story.) Doug, age 85, brings his homemade desserts—a banana cream pie and a lemon pie. I take a slice of the banana cream pie. It's really good. Doug and Joyce were married for something like 65 years. He's making an adjustment. He's hanging in there.

Doug represents what Easter's about—hope and renewal and our individual lives playing out without fanfare. Living, suffering, and living on. It's the best thing about us. We rise up each day no matter what.

Happy Easter, Everyone.

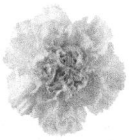

APRIL 21, 2014

HAVING A MOMENT

My daughter posts a photo on Instagram of my ex and his wife with her arms around my grandson. I can try to deny but denial's not good. This photo's stirring stuff up. Shouldn't those be my arms around my grandson? What was wrong with me? How did I let my marriage fail?

"What was wrong with me?" is the question we douse all over ourselves—forever. Maybe nothing was wrong with me. Maybe it was the time or the mores or my upbringing or any number of things. Is it possible I did the best I could?

When it comes to my marriage, I have to start giving myself the benefit of the doubt. I was and am a caring, well-meaning, and intelligent person. If being caring, well-meaning, and intelligent aren't enough, other elements must be in play.

Like luck? Like karma?

I don't know. There's a lesson here I'm supposed to learn. I'll keep working on it but, right now, I'm having a moment.

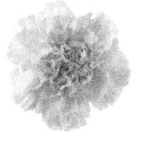

APRIL 22, 2014

KEEPING PROMISES TO MYSELF

I'm huffing and puffing with Deanne this morning. I'm not one of those people who gets high on exercise. I'm one of those people who hates exercise. I'm not enjoying the stretching, balancing, flexing, lifting, and pushing. I know, though, that I need to do this. I need to fight against losing muscle mass. I need to massage the old heart muscle with cardio exercises. Deanne makes sure I cover all the bases.

Home again. I paw through a messy desk drawer to find stamps, address labels, and note cards. I've stopped sending Christmas cards. Instead, I'm sending cards at random throughout the year to say, "Hi," and to let people know I'm thinking of them. Don't know about you, but I love finding cards and letters in my mailbox, and I find fewer and fewer. Like newspapers, written notes are becoming anachronisms.

This morning I've written cards to eleven people and dropped them in the mailbox. I have more cards to write, but I'm taking a break and recharging my batteries. I want my thinking-of-you cards to be energetic, with comments and questions specific to the person I'm thinking about. Otherwise, I may as well send out mass Christmas cards. "Happy Holidays. Love, Dede"

I visualize the recipients of my notes walking to their mailboxes. There among junk mail, bills, advertisements, and political flyers, they find my cards. They sit down at their kitchen tables. They turn the envelopes over, pausing for a second, to wonder what might be inside. They weren't expecting anything from me so what news could this be?

"Surprise. I'm thinking of you and wanted you to know."

Then I imagine that they go about their day with a lighter step, a little glow—someone's thinking, especially, of them. And I go about my day with a lighter step and a little glow because I'm doing what I promised myself I would do.

Patrick's Facebook Post: Nothing like a sign at your favorite watering hole that informs you that you must have been born by today's date in 1993 to legally purchase alcohol to make you feel really old.

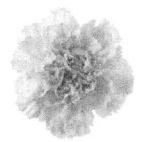

APRIL 23, 2014

MOM

Mom calls.

"Hi, Mom."

"Hi. How's your day?"

"Good. How's yours?"

"Good. What day can I make an appointment with the eye doctor?"

"Well, I'm thinking you better try for something after the week of May five. I'm on call for jury duty that week."

"Okay. How about Tuesday the twentieth?"

"That works if it's after two. Tuesday's my day at the thrift store. And if I happen to still be on jury duty, you'll have to reschedule."

"Okay. The twentieth. You'll pick me up at two?"

"I'll pick you up at two."

"Okay. What about my sheets?"

"I got your sheets."

"You did what?"

"I got your sheets."

"You got my sheets?"

"Yes, a full set that includes pillow cases."

"What color did you get?"

"They're white with a little pattern in them."

"How much?"

"Around sixty dollars for the set."

"Okay. What about my prescriptions?"

"I ordered your prescriptions. You should get them in the mail this week."

"Okay. What about Mother's Day? Do you want to come to the luncheon here?"

"Of course. Sign us up."

"Okay. And I have to tell you something. I had my blood pressure checked today and it was one hundred twenty-one over seventy-seven."

"That's terrific."

"I also got weighed and I've lost ten pounds."

"Wow. Good job."

Mom sounds pretty pleased with herself. She rides her scooter everywhere and walks between her bed and the bathroom with her walker. I know exercise isn't part of her weight-loss regimen. "How did you lose ten pounds?"

"I skipped desserts and cut everything else in half."

"How long did this take you?"

"About three months."

"Well, way to go."

"I'm drinking some Irish cream to celebrate. I have about one-fourth of the bottle left. Bye."

"Bye, Mom."

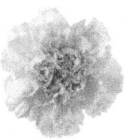

APRIL 23, 2014

IRENE

Irene calls. That's synchronicity. I put a note in the mail to her yesterday. She hasn't received it, yet. "I have a few moments and I decided to call you to catch up."

"It's great to hear from you, Irene. How's everything with you?"

"I'm busy getting our home ready to put it on the market, seeing my doctors, and weeding out what to give away and what to keep. I'm actually looking forward to moving into the assisted living facility in Grass Valley. I want my daughters to get their lives back."

Irene's also preparing for heart surgery and back surgery in addition to managing her progressive MS. "I get really tired and just do a little every day. How are you?"

I tell Irene about the trip to Bend and my mother's 96th birthday. She says, "These sound like wonderful birthday celebrations."

We talk for an hour. Irene is less than a year away from losing her husband, Eddie. She turned 70 in February. "Dede, I think we have to keep positive attitudes and keep moving forward. Let's stay in touch. Okay?"

More than okay, Irene. More than okay.

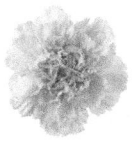

APRIL 24, 2014

DEVIANT NORMAL

I'm not looking forward to this. I'm in for my six-month check at the dentist. The hygienist is examining my tongue. "Have you noticed that the tip of your tongue is redder than the rest of your tongue?"

"Well, no, I haven't noticed." (I don't stand in front of the mirror with my tongue sticking out. Maybe I should.)

"Nothing to worry about. It's what we call 'deviant normal.'"

I like this term, "deviant normal." Shouldn't we all aspire to be deviant normal? To stand out? To not follow the crowd? To sometimes say, "Fuck you?"

"I think I may be deviant normal in more ways than the tip of my tongue. At least I hope I am."

The hygienist laughs. Sounds like other patients haven't told her they aspire to deviancy. She changes the topic. "It's been a year since we took X-rays of your teeth, so we will take X-rays today."

"Stop. Hold on." I'm practicing deviancy. "I've read studies linking dental X-rays to brain tumors. Nothing conclusive, but some experts are recommending receiving X-rays every two to three years instead of annually."

"Well, the radiation level in these X-rays is less than the radiation you'd get spending ten minutes in the sun. They're very safe."

After more discussion, the hygienist offers that I might opt to have X-rays every two years. "You know that X-rays may reveal problems that I can't detect visually."

"If you see something that concerns you, you'll let me know. Then, we can still take the X-rays, right?"

"Right." The dentist sits down next to me. I've never met this dentist and I don't know why she's not the same dentist I saw six months ago. The dentist concurs with the hygienist."You realize I can't see what X-rays might show."

"Yes, I realize. Let's take that risk."

The dentist pokes around in my mouth for less than three minutes. "I agree with the previous dentist. You should have treatments in four areas with receding gum lines. The teeth in these areas aren't protected by enamel. They can become infected."

"Are these fillings covered by insurance?" I know they're not covered by insurance because I asked this question six months ago. I'm testing the waters. I'm being deviant.

"I don't know anything about costs and insurance. I simply make recommendations on what's needed. The woman at the front desk can tell you about price and coverage."

Hmm. I've heard doctors say the same thing. "I don't know anything about costs or insurance coverage." Maybe medical/dental knowledge and knowledge of patient costs should be more integrated. Maybe health care personnel would think twice about recommending less critical, expensive procedures. Again, maybe they wouldn't. Maybe these procedures provide welcome, additional revenue. This is the new culture of health care—impersonal, corporate, pricey.

The hygienist cleans my teeth. "You're good to go."

The young woman at the from desk double-checks for me. "No, the recommended fillings would not be covered by insurance. Yes, they would cost twelve hundred dollars."

I schedule my next six-month appointment. Deviant or not, I'm not looking forward to it.

Patrick's Facebook Post: Overheard at work: "Are you gonna go to the gun show, the fishing derby, or the rodeo this weekend?"

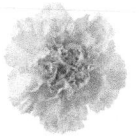

APRIL 26, 2014

ALL THE MEANING IN THE WORLD

Pat calls. "Mom, would you like me to take you out for a birthday dinner tonight?"

"Tonight?" It's not even my birthday month. My birthday celebrating will be over before my birthday.

"Do you like that fish restaurant in the Fountains?"

"It's good, but it's a little pricey."

"That's okay. It's your birthday dinner. Meet me there at six thirty."

Here we are sitting in a cozy booth. The restaurant's busy. Rustling prom dresses and black tuxedos fill the chairs. There's lots of girlish giggling at the tables. The waiter brings us the menu. At the top it says, "Happy 70th Birthday!!!"

I'm impressed. "Thanks for the personalized menu."

"You're welcome. Would you like something to drink—wine or from the bar?"

I order a glass of Chateau St. Jean chardonnay. Pat orders the same. "Good choice." Waiters always say that. Pat decides to order a bottle—two glasses for each of us. I worry about his budget, but this dinner is as much for him as it is for me. Today's his payday. He hasn't had paychecks in a long time.

There were days, in the past, when I hoped and prayed my son would survive. He was often missing, in jail, 5150d to a psych ward, or living on the street. I remember one night in the middle of yet another crisis. I was home alone in my big house on a hill. I felt like a mother animal—any mother animal—lion, tiger, bear, elephant, cat, dog—whose offspring was in mortal danger. I felt primal, obliterating emotional pain. I started crying in my kitchen. The crying turned to screaming—a someone-is-being-murdered kind of screaming. The screaming wouldn't stop. I wanted to smash every glass, cup, saucer, and dish in my cupboards. I wanted time to start over without the bipolar/schizoaffective disorder or whatever illness it was that no one could pin down, without the illness that was kidnapping my son and holding him hostage.

It's been a long road from that night to this night. For the first time in seven years Pat has a job. Thanks to my mom's generous rental policy he has a roof over his head. Thanks to me he has a car, and his monthly utility, phone, internet, and car insurance bills are covered. We talk about this.

"I want to start paying these bills myself, Mom, but can we wait until next month? My car's flashing a 'maintenance required' light on the dashboard. I don't know how much it might cost if the problem isn't under warranty."

"Take care of the car, Pat, then we'll revisit your finances."

Pat's bankruptcy filing was finalized March 22. Since then, he's been bombarded with letters from car companies congratulating him on his responsible decision. They're offering him deals on cars that don't require a down payment. He's also receiving new, pre-approved credit card applications. This should be illegal. It's corporations preying on consumers who have a hard time managing their income and outgo. These letters and enticements are placing a bug in Pat's head. "I'm thinking I should get a new car before I have to put a lot of money into the one I have."

The car Pat drives, and I own, is a 2006 Ford Focus. It's the same age as my Toyota Prius. I don't plan to buy another car anytime soon. "Pat, I don't think you should be taking on new monthly payments. Your car should be good for quite a while if you take care of it. What if you lose your job? What if unexpected expenses come up?"

My squashing his idea is being ignored. "I'll have to cross those bridges when I come to them."

At 45, almost 46, with an intractable tumor lurking in his brain, Pat's trying to dig himself out of a deep hole. He wants to feel successful. I won't push this conversation further this evening. After all, it's my birthday dinner. It's the first birthday dinner Pat's treated me to. It's probably my best birthday dinner ever. I want the guests at other tables to know what a special dinner the two of us are sharing. I want them to realize this dinner includes, in addition to a side of grilled asparagus, another heaping side:

ALL THE MEANING IN THE WORLD

It's clear that others won't capture this moment. So I must— and I am.

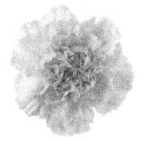

APRIL 27, 2014

MY GEORGE CLOONEY

Well, it was inevitable.

The headlines are screaming it all over the internet. George Clooney, my George Clooney, is engaged.

Maybe it's not true. Maybe there'll be a retraction. Photos, however, don't lie. In the photos, there's something in their faces. They look happy. They look together. George is 52. His fiancee, Amal Alamuddin, is 36. That's a sixteen-year age difference. There's an eighteen-year age difference between me and George. Why her and not me? She is beautiful. And smart—an attorney in international law and human rights who speaks multiple languages.

I get it. George is a human rights activist. She's a human rights activist. I might call myself a human rights activist. On a much smaller scale, of course. Like in my own backyard. I'll take the high road with this. I'll wish the happy couple well. I'll stop having dreams about me and George getting married. I'll start dreaming about getting invited to his wedding to Amal. They haven't set a date. Maybe they have and we're not in on it. Doesn't matter.

It was inevitable. George Clooney, my George Clooney, is engaged.

APRIL 29, 2014

FOR CRYING OUT LOUD

I grabbed the tube of Preparation H instead of the tube of toothpaste and started brushing my teeth.

I left the pot of soup on the stove all night instead of putting it in the fridge.

I walked out the door with my credit card instead of my mailbox key to go get the mail.

I searched five minutes for my purse. It was hanging on my shoulder.

I drove north on the freeway for eight miles when I was supposed to be driving south.

I wore one blue shoe and one black shoe to a block party.

I put a clear earring on my left ear and a black one on my right ear and went to my workout with Deanne. She didn't say a word.

Disclaimer

All of these events are true.
THEY DID NOT HAPPEN ALL IN ONE DAY.

MAY 2, 2014

HAPPY BIRTHDAY, KERRY COLLEEN

Today, my fourth and youngest child is turning 37.

In 1979, the *San Francisco Chronicle* published my article, "Diary of an Unplanned Pregnancy." It was about my unexpected pregnancy with Kerry. Abortion wasn't an option and I felt trapped. I wrote, "I was beginning to dream of time for myself and here I am shackled again." I received dozens of letters from readers who were moved by what I wrote.

Kerry didn't know about the article. I pondered if and when I'd show it to her. Then, out of the blue, this choice was taken away. Fifteen years later, when Kerry was in high school, she and I stood in line at a mother-daughter luncheon. A mother of one of her classmates came up to us and said, "I remember that beautiful story you wrote about Kerry's birth."

Kerry's eyes got big. She looked at me like "What? What is that woman talking about?" There was no way out. I knew, when we got home, I'd have to pull the newspaper clipping from my file and give it to my daughter. Would she understand? Would she be hurt?

Kerry read the article. She said she got it. But really? Could a sixteen-year-old girl relate? Could she believe what I wrote at the end?

"As for you, Kerry, I know I made the right decision. It's hard to believe you once seemed so threatening. Now, I wouldn't give you up for anything. I sit and hold you, brush my face against your soft cheek, and still the tears come. The wonder of you. Of your new life. You and I are going to be fine, Kerry."

Thirty-seven years later, I still wouldn't give you up for anything. And, as I write this, still the tears come.

MAY 5, 2014

JURY DUTY I

I'm sitting in a room on the second floor of the Santucci Justice Center with 60 other people who've been summoned for jury duty. The moderator explains that the trial we're being selected for is a civil law case, a wrongful termination suit by an employee against his employer. This trial will last through the month of May.

Half of the group—students, those with critical medical and dental appointments that can't be rescheduled, and those with personal or business travel already scheduled—are excused. The rest of us are asked to fill out a seven-page questionnaire. The attorneys for the prosecution and defense will review our questionnaires to help them choose the jurors they think will be most helpful to their case. My answers are routine until questions are asked about my opinions.

Would I ever file a lawsuit? Most likely, no.

Do I think civil lawsuits are appropriate? Well, mostly no. I think we have too many lawsuits in our litigious society.

Do I think that punitive damages awarded are usually fair? No, most of the time, I think they're too large.

Do I think I can serve without prejudice on this jury? I think I can in spite of my bias against lawsuits in general.

I call a friend when I get home. I tell her what I wrote on the survey. "Do you think I'll be chosen?"

She's unequivocal. "There's no way you'll be selected for this jury. Trust me."

Well, we shall see. I have to report at 10 a.m. tomorrow morning for more winnowing.

Patrick's Facebook Post: Some people are vibrating at a frequency lower than a burnt bag of microwave popcorn.

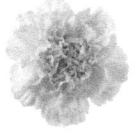

MAY 6, 2014

JURY DUTY II

Another day at the courthouse. I'm sitting in the lobby of courtroom 44. Thirty people are sitting and standing, waiting to be called into chambers. I study a few. A slender brunette, early fifties, says her boss is hoping she doesn't get selected. A heavyset woman, unknown age, reappears from yesterday. She has a puffy white face and puffy white arms. One arm has a wrap-around floral tattoo. A tiny woman with a blond ponytail looks like a teenager. What are their stories? Turns out I'll hear parts of them.

All three are called to the jury box and questioned by the judge. The brunette is a palliative care nurse and widow. She'd like to answer some questions in private quarters. She, the judge, and the attorneys for both sides disappear for a few minutes. Her boss will be disappointed. She returns to the jury box. The heavyset woman is articulate and forthcoming. "Ask me anything. Go for it." She's concerned about dismissal time today because it's her wedding anniversary. The small blond turns out to be a doctor. She specializes in skin cancer surgery.

It's 4 p.m. The judge says jury selection is almost complete. Those of us present in the gallery must return Friday morning at 10 a.m. There's still a chance my name will be called. I'm hoping not. I'd like to serve on a jury but not this one. I'd rather talk with all the people in the room and hear their stories. I'd probably empathize with everyone, including the plaintiff and the defendant. In a sense, I'm mush. No use to anyone. Another day at the courthouse, and I think I can better serve if I'm excused.

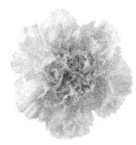

MAY 8, 2014

LADYBUGS

Life is coming fast and furious. I receive two emails. One from a friend whose husband just passed away from the complications of dementia. The second from a friend whose 50-year-old daughter just died from a heart attack. At noon I meet Kerry for a birthday lunch. I tell her about my friends and their losses. She has a story, too.

"Mom, I know you think we use our cell phones too much. But yesterday afternoon, a friend posted a photo on Instagram of a little boy who was hit by a truck and died. Already, the family's received over $40,000 in pledges."

Kerry can hardly tell me this story. She's in tears. Why are we sharing all this bad news? I change the subject. I give Kerry a birthday card and a little gift. She opens the gift bag and smiles. "Live ladybugs. You know who will love this?"

"Ayla. I was worried. The nursery told me to keep them in the refrigerator. When I took them out this morning they looked dead but, one by one, they began moving."

Kerry calls this evening. "Mom, is this a good time to release the ladybugs? Is it cool enough?"

"Yes, it's a good time."

"And do you know where they're from?"

"No. Where are they from?"

"Bend. They're from Bend."

Kerry texts photos of the ladybug emancipation. Regan and Ayla are covered in ladybugs, as are several of their friends. The ladybugs are alive and well.

Patrick's Facebook Post: Dog shit, the perpetual harbinger of the beginning of my day, is my constant companion these days. Its immediate presence after entering the park, courtesy of my dog Lexi, guarantees the day is off to a good start.

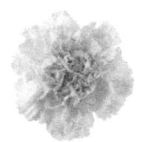

MAY 9, 2014

BEING PART OF IT ALL

This morning I report, again, to the jury room. The jury is chosen, and my name is called as a potential alternate. "Do you have a bias against lawsuits?"

"Yes, I think there are too many frivolous lawsuits."

"Do you have an opinion about unions?"

"My opinion about unions was embedded in my DNA as a young child." The judge asks me to explain.

"My mother and father owned a mom-and-pop hamburger restaurant. I'd sit at the counter after school doing my homework. Every couple of months, without warning, two union men dressed like the Blues Brothers—in dark suits, dark glasses and dark fedoras—would walk through the door and scare my mom and pop to death. They'd poke around trying to find a reason, any reason, to level a two-hundred-dollar fine. I hope things are different now."

The attorney for the plaintiff, a union officer at the time of his termination, takes me off the jury. Good move. I'd have been a terrible juror in this case.

Kerry calls. She's happy to report that, although some died, most of the 1500 ladybugs appear to be thriving in her yard this morning. What a mix of life, death, surviving, and being part of it all.

MAY 11, 2014

MOTHER'S DAY

I start off the morning with a cup of coffee and an Ocean Roll. This is a big deal because, normally, I'd share an Ocean Roll with at least two other people. Not today. I'm eating the whole Ocean Roll myself. It's my Mother's Day present to me.

Lunch is at GG's residence. She's invited a friend, Jean, to join the two of us for the Mother's Day prime rib feast. Jean is an attractive lady—I'm guessing in her late eighties. She has short, shiny white hair, spectacles that make her soft blue eyes look like swimming pools, and a tall, trim physique.

Jean has no siblings and no children. When her husband of many years passed away, a nephew who lives in Auburn insisted that she move from Virginia to the Sacramento region. "Was it difficult to know what to leave and what to bring?"

"Nope. I flew home after I decided to move here, packed six suitcases, and hired an estate company to handle the disposition of everything else."

In her past life, Jean was a housewife, volunteer, cook, vegetable gardener, seamstress, quilter, and travel companion to her husband. They took frequent trips for his job with the government. "I like it here," she offers. "I play games, work on puzzles, and walk an hour every day."

"Where do you walk? Around the neighborhood?"

"No, I walk an hour back and forth on the second floor. It's kind of boring, but I meet a lot of people this way. I keep a book in the sitting area. When I need a break, I read a few pages and then walk some more."

At the end of the main course, the dining room staff person, a pretty young woman with dark brown hair, brings a tray of desserts for us to choose from. I pass and ask for a cup of decaf. Jean orders thin mint ice cream. GG says she wants everything. "I want regular coffee in a mug, not a cup, a cream puff, a banana, and a napkin."

"Wait," our server says, "I'm writing this down. I don't want to forget something."

Still in Mother's-Day-eating-mode, we're at Pat's house— me, GG, Kerry, David, Regan, Ayla, and Pat. Kerry brings the drinks—wine and beer for the adults and juice for the girls. I bring four folding chairs. Pat serves deli potato salad, and ham and beef spiral wrap sandwiches. He passes out white carnations to each of the "girls" including Regan and Ayla. This is Pat's second annual Mother's Day dinner. Last year he served pizza.

Sitting in a circle on Pat's bare wood floor, we make small talk with occasional lulls in the conversation. "Are you taking your car into the shop this week, Pat?"

"Going to try."

Lexi runs in and out. She loves bouncing around all the people. She jumps up and puts her paws on my shoulders. This dog can't get close enough . . . whoever you are. Regan and Ayla, tired from a Mother's Day weekend camping trip, are eager to go home. First, they give me and GG small cactus arrangements in peat moss pots. Kerry gives me a houseplant and a gift card for my Kindle from Marisa and Megan. Soon, we're all saying goodbye and loading GG and the folding chairs back into my car.

Marisa calls from Seattle. Keith's in San Diego to help his parents, Papa and Curly. Papa, at 77, suffers from Parkinson's disease. Curly, his caretaker, wants reassurance that she's doing the right things.

All around me I see courage—Jean, GG, Pat, Curly, Papa. Even Lexi, penned up for many hours while Pat's at work, leaps with joyful enthusiasm. I see Megan and Britt, Marisa and Keith, and Kerry and David being conscientious parents, modeling caring and concern for others. I see Aidan, Ashton, Sam, Elise, Regan and Ayla developing manners and respect, and following their parents' lead.

This is life at full circle—a Mother's Day package wrapped in youth, aging, tough decisions, and topped off with single-stem white carnations. I am grateful.

Note: The carnation is the official flower for Mother's Day. White carnations represent pure love. Pink carnations represent a mother's forever love: "I will never forget you."

Patrick's Facebook Post: Morning—It's time to put on the Hazmat suit and clean my house thoroughly. The mothers are coming! The mothers are coming! Dinner tonight for four generations of women: GG, Mom, Sister Kerry, and nieces Regan and Ayla.

Patrick's Facebook Post: Evening—Well, the 2nd Annual Mother's Day Dinner was a success. GG, Mom, Sister Kerry, and nieces Regan and Ayla all had a good time and left with their bellies full.

MAY 12, 2014

BOOKS AND WOLVES

A Harris Poll asked 2,234 adults, "What is your favorite book of all time?"

1. The *Bible*
2. *Gone with the Wind* by Margaret Mitchell
3. The *Harry Potter* series by J.K. Rowling
4. *The Lord of the Rings* series by J.R. Tolkien
5. *To Kill a Mockingbird* by Harper Lee
6. *Moby-Dick* by Herman Melville
7. *The Catcher in the Rye* by J.D. Salinger
8. *Little Women* by Louisa May Alcott
9. *The Grapes of Wrath* by John Steinbeck
10. *The Great Gatsby* by F. Scott Fitzgerald

Hmm? If I change my initials to J.K. or J.R. or J.D., would I have a chance of making this list? :-)

Good News. It looks like Wolf OR7 may have a mate. His territory stretches north from the California border to Klamath Falls. His name is OR7 because he was the seventh wolf to be radio-collared in Oregon. He became a media star when he traversed the entire length of Oregon late in 2011 in search of a mate. He entered California in December of that year, becoming the first wild wolf confirmed in the state in 87 years. OR7 is now with another wolf in an area protected by the Federal Endangered Species Act. Hope to hear about the pups.

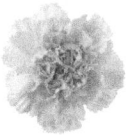

MAY 15, 2014

DEJA VU

A friend's husband is experiencing a psychotic breakdown and is being 5150'd to a psych unit. In California, 5150s are 72-hour, involuntary holds for people whose psychiatric disorders appear to be out of control. My friend's rushing to the hospital to be with her husband. I warn her, "He may not recognize you. He may not want to see you. He may say hurtful things."

"I know," she says. "I know."

When people you love are in debilitated mental states, nothing prepares you for the heartbreak. You watch them barreling toward danger. You cry out from behind soundproof glass. "Stop. Come back. Please don't go." They can't hear you.

This is gut-wrenching anguish. This is raging wildfires in the depths of your soul. This is railing against God, if there is a God. This is wanting to be swallowed up by a giant sinkhole so the pain will stop. At this moment, watching my friend, this is *déjà vu*.

Patrick's Facebook Post: We actually have a thirty-six-year-old guy in Northern California running for Congress who has never voted.

Cheryl: And your point is?

Patrick: My point is, how can a man, who has never participated in our political process, presume to assume a leadership
role in that process?

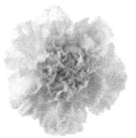

MAY 17, 2014

CALIFORNIA CHROME

I'm channeling Pop. He loved horse races. I'm watching the
Preakness and rooting for California Chrome. He won the
Kentucky Derby two weeks ago. If he wins today, he's two-
thirds of the way to the Triple Crown. This horse is becoming
a California rock star. His owners are from Yuba City.

A horse breeder called them "dumb-ass horse breeders"
because they bought a mare for $8,000 that had only won one
race. They paid a stud fee of $2,000 for a stud at Harris Ranch.
Why would anyone think this parenting would produce a Triple
Crown winner?

One of the two owners had a dream that the coming colt
would win the Triple Crown. The colt was born on his sister's
birthday. She died from cancer when she was 36 years old. It's
been 36 years since a horse won the Triple Crown. This is better than a Hollywood movie. No one could make up this stuff.

The race begins. California Chrome makes a solid start out
of the gate. His jockey maneuvers him into a favorable position
early on. It's looking good, but another horse appears from the

back of the pack and is nudging for the lead. The jockey on California Chrome has to press him into the final push sooner than he intended. Will California Chrome have the stamina, the will to go the distance? He does. He wins.

Pop, I hear ya. I'm so excited. I'm a Chromie. I want a hat. I want a t-shirt. The Belmont, the third race in the Triple Crown, is in three weeks. Go, California Chrome.

MAY 18, 2014

CHECKING IN

I call Mom to check in. She says, "I have something I need to discuss with you."

Uh, oh. "What's up?"

Well, you know my rent goes up a hundred dollars a month every August. Steve, the manager, stopped by to let me know that, this year, they have to raise my rent two hundred dollars a month beginning in August. He wanted to give me a heads up.

"There's a lady here who is one-hundred-and-four. There are two women who are one-hundred-and-two. I may make it to one hundred myself and I've been thinking. If I move into a studio unit, it would cost me five hundred dollars a month less. That's six thousand dollars a year. That's a lot of money. I'm watching my money market balance go down every month. I have to face reality."

"Did you talk to Steve about this?"

"I haven't said anything to anyone. I wanted to run it by you first. I'd have to put my name on a waiting list. What do you think?"

"I think this is up to you. Would you feel comfortable in a one-room unit?"

"I think it would be okay. I'm not using my kitchen anymore. The bathroom would be about the same. I might have to get rid of my sofa and the TV credenza. There probably wouldn't be room for them. But, actually, the closet space in the studio is a little more than I have now."

"Okay. Here's what I think. It won't hurt to put your name on the waiting list for a studio. It may be six months or a year before one becomes available and you can always decline if you change your mind."

"That's what I thought. I'll put my name on the waiting list. We're on for Tuesday, right? You're taking me to the eye doctor. And I need three new prescriptions. Are you ready? They're atenolol, amlodipine, and omeprazole. Did you get that down? And don't forget my shopping list. And don't forget my sheets."

I'm glad I'm checking in. Lots of business to discuss.

Patrick's Facebook Post: I'm in church today, and the congregation is mostly white and elderly, and we're all singing Bob Marley's "One Love" and I realize that this is a really fun group of people to gather with once a week for a conscious party.

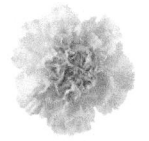

MAY 19, 2014

THINKING YARD TODAY

I've purchased a True Bloodgood Japanese maple to replace the African sumac in the front yard. I've picked up some red, pink, and white begonias for my patio pots, and an amber carpet rose for the biggest pot.

And, for the first time ever, I'm the proud owner of two Sara Bernhardt peony plants. These pale pink flowers are indescribable—all delicate and lacy and multi-layered. Their spicy perfume should be bottled. Where have these peonies been all my life? They're perennials, but they'll die back to the ground, much like hydrangeas, in the winter. The tags on the plants promise that they're easy to grow, and says they need morning sun and afternoon shade. I'm planting them in front of Xylosma shrubs as background foliage for their effusive pink blooms.

My yard's always evolving. I select each shrub, tree, and flower because it speaks to me, and because I deem it worthy to live in my patch of the universe.

There's a slight chance of thunderstorms tomorrow. The dark sky and earthy smell in the air give me hope that rain is coming. I'm thinking yard today.

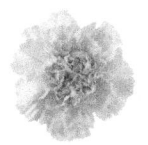

MAY 21, 2014

COUNTDOWN TO 70

7:30 a.m.

I wake up thinking, my God, tomorrow I'll be 70. For some reason, this turning 70 thing is seeming like a big deal to me.

When I turned 40, I wanted to flaunt it.

When I turned 50, I was too busy dealing with life. I didn't have time to think about it.

When I turned 60, I was fighting to regain myself and find a new path.

This morning, turning 70 feels like I'm being force-marched through massive iron gates into the walled city of old age.

11:30 a.m.

A friend arrives with a dozen red roses. Each year, he takes me to lunch for my birthday and we catch up.

2:30 p.m.

My friend and I go for a walk around the neighborhood and take in the blue sky, the Japanese maples and the flowering plum trees. I point out the brown and grey rocks where the little killdeer built her nest.

4:30 p.m.

I post a photo of my red roses on Instagram.

5:30 p.m.

Kerry calls and invites me to dinner, tomorrow, at her house with GG and Pat.

6:30 p.m.

I scan my backyard for daylily and peony blossoms. I note the brown earth and give thanks for it still being beneath my feet.

10:30 p.m.

Lights out.

11:55 p.m.

I wake, suddenly, and check the clock. Five minutes left. I step outside to scan the night sky. No shooting stars. No cosmic omens. I suck in the cool night air and return to bed.

Midnight:

70.

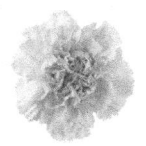

MAY 22, 2014

HAPPY BIRTHDAY

GG calls. "Happy Birthday. Happy Birthday."

"I can't handle this."

"Handle what?"

"Handle being seventy."

"Of course you can. You don't look seventy. You're healthy. You've had a good life. You've lots to be thankful for. You have to think positive."

"Thanks for all the sympathy, Mom."

"You're welcome. Pick me up at four-fifteen to go to Kerry's"

"Yes, ma'am."

Kerry's threading turkey meatballs and fresh pineapple chunks on skewers for the barbecue. She's pairing them with a green salad and bottled dressing and keeping dinner simple. Regan sets the table with white plates and white napkins. She adds knives and forks.

GG's here. David and Pat will arrive after work. I'm turning 70 in the presence of my 96-year-old mother, my youngest daughter, her husband, my eldest child, and two of my six grandchildren. Megan calls from Utah. She and Britt and Aidan and Ashton wish me "Happy Birthday." Marisa calls from Seattle. She and Keith and Sam and Elise wish me "Happy Birthday."

GG's right. I've lots to be thankful for. And to top it off, Kerry serves a chocolate cake with dark chocolate glaze and dark chocolate frosting. The biggest surprise, however, is about to come. A new text on my iPhone says, "Happy Birthday!" It's from my ex-husband—the first message I've received from him since our divorce was final 11 years ago. I'm in shock. My emotions are all over the place. Like a messed up Rubik's cube. Like a chorus line of unsynchronized questions marks.

Eleanor Roosevelt once said, "Beautiful young people are accidents of nature, but beautiful old people are works of art." Maybe I need to rethink this 70s thing. Maybe my 70s will give me the chance to become a beautiful old person. A work of art.

All in all, a wonderful birthday. So, as it comes to a close, why do I know I'm about to go cry?

Patrick's Facebook Post: Happy 70th Birthday to my Mom today. Love you so much.

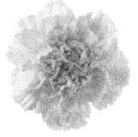

MAY 25, 2014

MAIL

I sent individual notes to Marisa, Kerry, Sam, Elise, Regan, and Ayla to thank them for joining me for my birthday celebration in Bend. Kerry reports that Regan was thrilled. "She loves to get mail." Regan sends me a reply.

Dear Mim,
Thank you for the card. I loved it it was awesome. also, I love the oshon rols. They are so deleshes. I had a lot of fun at Orgen. Bend was so much fun. I rily enjoyed it a lot!!

Love, Regan

P.S. thank you for the doson oshen rols. They wher deleshes.

Regan adds the drawing of a kitten at the bottom of her note.

Like Regan, I love to get mail. I think her thank you card for my thank you card deserves a new card. Have to hurry and send it before Regan outgrows her infatuation with mail.

Dear Regan,

Thank you for your nice note. I really enjoyed your drawing of the kitty cat.

I'm glad that you like to get mail. I do too! I think people feel special when they get a note in the mail. They realize that someone took the time to write the note, address the envelope, add a stamp, and walk the note to the mailbox. It means that the person who wrote the note is thinking of them. I'm thinking of you, Regan. I'm proud that you're my granddaughter. I love you lots!!!

Mim

Patrick's Facebook Post: I have never seen my dog get spooked or scared by anything, but for the last few days on our regular walk, she's cowered and looked very scary and startled in the exact same place on our way to the park. I don't see or smell or hear anything, but she definitely sees something ominous there. She jumped off her collar this morning she was so spooked. I'm thinking of changing her name to Ghost-hunter.

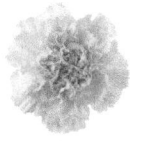

MAY 26, 2014

EMAILS AND BLESSINGS

I send an email to a friend.

"I'm sorry to hear that the mental health system is failing you and your son. It's been 10 years since I worked with you and we had such high hopes for Prop 63. I'm running a little support group here for family members in this over-55 community that I live in. None of them have heard of Prop 63 services.

"As you know, I'm partial to moms of the mentally ill. You are my heroes. Often, you're the only ones fighting for the adult or child no one else seems to care about. Thinking of you. Dede."

My friend emails back.

"My son ran away again tonight with no money and no clothes and he has no friends. He called to tell me it is all my fault, that I do not deserve to live, and that he's suicidal. The police haven't been able to find him. He really belonged back in the hospital last Friday when he tried so badly to be admitted.

"He's somewhere in the city looking for drugs or alcohol and he gets abused by thugs. I think he threw away his cell phone again because he becomes afraid that I will call him. I'm a basket case and have been fighting for 20 years with this. Prop 63 funds are being totally mis-used and no one really understands if they're not one of us. Thanks for your message."

Pat's here to do his laundry and to have some dinner. He's pushed the wrong buttons on my TV remote and we can't get the TV to change channels. Lexi's crashing through the backyard and crapping in my daylilies. She's stealing cat poop from the litter box in the laundry room. Jazzy's hiding under my bed. Thinking of my friend helps me keep these annoyances in perspective. I'm thankful for this day with my son.

Patrick's Facebook Post: I get a fair amount of emails from Barack Obama's organizing for action group asking me for a donation of $3 or more. Similar requests come from many other Democratic organizations. Have our leaders all been reduced to constantly hitting us up for three bucks like they really need to buy a 40 at the liquor store?

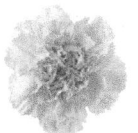

MAY 29, 2014

MAYA ANGELOU

Some of the best perks of being retired are a steaming cup of coffee, the morning sun filtering through my kitchen window, and the unhurried assimilation of the happenings of the day. I admit the local newspaper is not what it used to be. It contains fewer pages, is printed on crackly paper, and is an awkward 22"x11." Its news is often old news thanks to the internet. The morning paper is, I'm afraid, an endangered species. My adult children don't subscribe to newspapers. My grandchildren and great-grandchildren probably won't know what a newspaper is or was.

In my world, this is a loss. Reading the morning paper is one of my rituals. A time to reflect. A place, among all the reports of murder and mayhem, to find pearls. This morning, for instance, the front page is devoted to the passing of Maya Angelou. Somehow I missed her celebrated 1969 memoir, *I Know Why the Caged Bird Sings*, a description of the black experience from the inside. It will be the next book I check out from the library. Meanwhile, a summary of Angelou's life, on the back page of section A, includes her final tweet posted May 23, 2014, the day after my birthday.

"Listen to yourself and in that quietude you might hear the voice of God."

I'm reading and I'm getting goose bumps. It feels like Maya Angelou is whispering to me. "Maya, are you in my kitchen?"

"Listen to yourself and in that quietude you might hear the voice of God."

Writing is how I listen to myself. Every now and then, while writing, I think I do hear the voice of God. This morning, however, I think I hear the voice of God while sitting at my kitchen table. The medium, this time, is Maya Angelou. Maya Angelou in the morning paper.

Patrick's Facebook Post: Rest in peace Maya Angelou. Thank you for your hard work and inspiration.

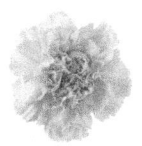

JUNE 1, 2014

ONE OF THOSE DAYS

More and more often I find myself saying, "For crying out loud." Some "crying out loud" examples from my recent past:

A red sock slipped out of my sweater sleeve in front of the checkout clerk at Safeway. I felt better when I recalled, at duplicate bridge, a man shook his pants leg and his wife's undies fell on the floor. I assumed they were his wife's.

I tried on a bathrobe at Target and it left white, clingy lint all over my navy blue sweatsuit. I hurried out of the store looking like a scruffy bird in molting season. A big, scruffy bird.

Which brings us to today.

This morning I scampered around the neighborhood with my t-shirt on backward. And right now, I'm searching high and low for a bag of books. There are only so many places in this house that it can be. I've rifled through every drawer, cupboard, and closet, and looked under every bed three times. I remember thinking, *I'll put the bag here so I'll know where it is.*

The question is, where is "here"?

Gotta get off the computer and get back to the hunt. For crying out loud. It's one of those days.

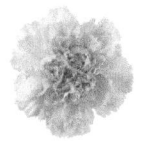

JUNE 2, 2014

MRI SCAN

It's 7:45 p.m. I'm sitting in my car in front of Pat's house waiting for him to come out. I'm here to drive him to Kaiser for his six-month MRI to check if his brain tumor has returned.

We're quiet in the car. Pat gives me directions. "Turn left." "Turn right."

Walking into the hospital, Pat's six strides ahead of me, hands in his pockets. What's he thinking? Is he afraid? He'll take an Ativan, when he checks in, to make himself drowsy through the MRI scan.

I sit in the waiting room. There's one other woman reading a magazine and a young boy occupied with an electric game. The TV's blaring. I'm trying to read, but it's impossible to concentrate in competition with the TV. I get up and ask the woman and the boy if they're watching the television. They're not. I turn the sound off. The new distraction, with the TV off, is the repetitive beeping of a monitor. Do hospital personnel get used to this sound and tune it out? Who and what is being monitored? Is it serious? There's an announcement over the intercom.

"Rapid response team report to 2 North, room 2106. Rapid response team report to 2 North, room 2106."

Again, who and what is being attended to? Is it life threatening? After forty-five minutes, Pat returns. "How did it go?"

"Fine."

As we walk through the hospital's empty corridors, I'm struck by the cold decor—the green and gray walls, the predominance of glass and steel. Feels like a prison, not a place of healing.

Back at his house, Pat get out of the car. "I have to take Lexi for a walk. Thanks for the ride. Talk to you later."

So much unsaid. So much hanging in the balance.

Patrick's Facebook Post: Let's hope that today I can avoid the mistake I made the other day of working for a couple hours in the ninety degree heat with two miniature chocolate bars melting in my pants pocket.

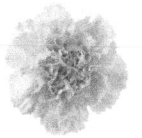

JUNE 3, 2014

SPECIALNESS EVERYWHERE

A woman with gray hair is writing out a check as I arrive at the thrift store. She's ecstatic. She's found a 1980s prom dress with puffy sleeves and yards and yards of pink satin. "It's perfect. I'm Mother Goose for the twenty-fifth anniversary of my hometown library. I used to be Mother Goose there, years ago, and I was afraid I wouldn't find the right dress to turn into a Mother Goose costume."

Another woman, who's joined the mental illness support group, walks in. She gives me a hug. Her young son is coming from his group home to be with her for his birthday. For the last three weeks he's taken a new medication and there's a change. My friend says her son tells her he's feeling more confident. He says, "You know, Mom, how I told you I didn't think I could make it in life? Now I think maybe I can. I'm feeling kind of normal."

I'm tearing up. My friend's tearing up. She buys a coat for $1. She buys a pair of shoes for $2 for the eight-year-old daughter of a friend. "The little girl's in fifth grade, already wears a size eight shoe, and is over five feet tall. The other kids are giving her a hard time. I want to give her some individual attention."

A trim, stylishly dressed woman steps to the counter holding a black, sleeveless dress. "Is there someplace I can try this on?" I direct her to our restroom/dressing room.

A man and his daughter buy Indian jewelry, a boomerang with Indian designs on it, and an Indian doll for $20. "We're from the Central Valley, and every time I drive through Lincoln I've wanted to come in this store."

"What will you do with all the Indian motif?"

"I live out in the country and have a room decorated in Indian decor. Something different for when my neighbors drop in."

During a lull, I poke around. I find a quote on a small plaque. "God put me here to accomplish certain things. Right now I'm so far behind, I'll never die." I buy the plaque for $1. I'll hang it on the wall beside my computer.

The woman with the black dress comes back. "Looks like it worked for you."

"Yes, but I may only wear it one time."

"Is it for a special occasion?"

"My son-in-law's memorial service. He was killed last month in a snowmobile accident. Yesterday, my daughter woke up from a medically induced coma, thank God. Now that she's awake, we can hold a celebration of life ceremony for her husband."

It's hard to find words. "I'm sorry for your loss. I'm glad your daughter's recovering."

With people coming in and out, time goes by quickly. At 2:30 p.m., Pat sends me a text. "MRI results came in. No sign of enhancement or disease in any area."

I text him back. "Awesome!!!!!!"

Another ordinary day. Yet it's remarkable in so many ways.

Patrick's Facebook Post: Got the results from my routine follow-up six month MRI which state: no sign of disease or enhancement in any area. Good news indeed.

Shannon: Awesome news Pat!!

Angie: So happy for you!

Anker: The force is strong within you Pat!

Patrick: Sometimes I feel like I deserve a friggin' medal.

JUNE 4, 2014

TIME IS TICKING BY

I'm almost to the end of my year-long journal. Soon I have to go back to the beginning and read what I've written. I'm aware of the responsibilities inherent in this personal recording. A few of the questions I'm mulling over:

- Which entries need to stay and which need to go?
- Will anyone I've written about be hurt or offended?

- Should these pages stay hidden away until everyone mentioned in them is gone?
- How can I write about my life without including others? Like a vine, I can't tell my story without noting the supporting framework.

Have to sort out the answers to these and other questions. Time is ticking by.

Patrick's Facebook Post:

Midnight housework giving me the blues,
daytime job pays for my shoes,
Eight solid hours of carrying another man's load,
such is the life of a previous toad.
Time at home should be filled with mirth,
but most of the time it dwindles to filth.
What to eat, what to wear,
when to speak, when to care,
these are the thoughts that action the air.
What kind of comedy show is this?

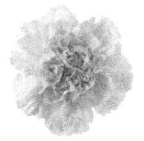

JUNE 6, 2014

D-DAY

Some days should never be forgotten. D-Day is one of them. Today's the 70th anniversary of D-Day in World War II. In 1944, Hitler's forces occupied France, held Poland, and were bombarding England with German rockets. The situation looked grim.

To turn the tide, the largest sea, land, and air invasion in history took place at Normandy, France, on June 6. One hundred and seventy-five-thousand Allied soldiers stormed the beaches. Twelve-thousand soldiers sustained wounds and over four-thousand US and Allied soldiers died. At the end of the day, the assault was proclaimed victorious. It changed the course of the war.

On D-Day, I was 17 days old, fighting a battle of my own. A preemie, born six weeks early and weighing in at four pounds, five ounces, I was clinging to life in a hospital incubator. My little lungs needed time and an assist to fully develop. It would be over a month before my worried mother could pick me up and take me home. A year later, On V-E Day (Victory in Europe), May 8, 1945, my mother would wrap me in her arms and cry as the end of the war was announced on the radio.

I came into the world at the same time many brave American and Allied citizens were leaving it. I wasn't aware of the historic events swirling around me or of the sacrifices of my grown-up countrymen and women. The youngest soldier on D-Day would be about 88 years old now.

I'm pausing to honor the few still living survivors and those who fought and died to make the world a safe place for me, my children, grandchildren, and great-grandchildren. I insert my flag into the metal holder attached to the side of the house by my garage door. I look up and down my street and see one or two flags flapping in the breeze. Shouldn't there be more? Shouldn't the street be decked out like the Fourth of July? Could it be we're beginning to forget a day we should always remember?

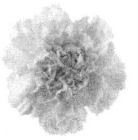

JUNE 7, 2014

THINKING OF YOU, POP

Pop, you've been on my mind a lot in the last few weeks leading up to today's 146th Belmont Stakes. In the past couple of months, California Chrome, a California-born and bred horse, has whipped up new excitement for the fading sport of horse racing.

This muscular, chestnut horse oozes star appeal. He basks in attention and poses for photo ops. He's won the Derby and the Preakness. A win today will give him horse racing's Triple Crown, the first time a California horse has won it.

I can hear you cheering him on, Pop. "Run Chrome, run. Go. Go. Go."

I'm screaming the same words myself. "Run Chrome, run. Go. Go. Go."

But no, it's not to be. Our Chrome has lost his historic bid and tied for fifth place. It's not his day in the sun.

The last time a horse won the Triple Crown was in 1978, six months before you passed, Pop. The Triple Crown was not on my radar then, but you relished watching Affirmed and jockey Steve Cauthen win that day. You talked about it for weeks.

You loved horse racing. Every time you sold a house, you'd stash five $20 bills in your wallet and head for Bay Meadows Race Track. Sometimes you won. You'd burst through the front door with a twinkle in your eye, grinning from ear to ear. "I won five hundred dollars today, Mama." Sometimes you lost. Then you'd slink in the side door like a guilty little kid who'd lifted a pack of gum from the five-and-dime.

The first time you took me to the races, it was at Santa Anita Race Track in Arcadia, California. I was ten years old and too young to bet. You told me to pick a horse and you'd place a bet for me. I studied the racing form in the newspaper. I read about the jockeys and the odds. Before each race, I closed my eyes and ran my fingers up and down the racing program. I was waiting for a sign.

In the eighth race, I opened my eyes and saw my fingers squarely fixed on entry number six. I'd found my horse. For The Best. I knew it. I just knew it. You held two one-dollar bills in your hand, Pop. You'd place the bet or give me the cash. The betting windows were closing. What to do?

I chose the sure thing. I stuffed the two one-dollar bills in my coat pocket. For The Best, a long shot, won easily and paid 40 to 1. The crowd roared. I dropped my head on my knees and curled up in a ball. I wanted to turn back the clock and ask you to place my bet. I wanted to bet on another horse, but I didn't have another hunch. The bitterest blow was still to come.

James said, "Place my bet, Pop," and his horse won. While you pulled our car out of the Santa Anita parking lot, my cocky little brother sat in the back seat counting and recounting his eighteen dollars in winnings. I stared at the cloudy sky out my side window. I was afraid if I looked at James I'd kill him.

California Chrome is kicking up these memories. I'm my deflated ten-year-old self again. I want to turn back the clock, reset today's race, and watch California Chrome bring home the Triple Crown. I want to see Chrome and his jockey, Victor Espinoza, bedecked with roses in the Winner's Circle.

Wherever you are—on a cloud or a star—like me, you're reeling. Another horse-racing broken dream. I'm thinking of you, Pop.

Patrick's Facebook Post: Northern California is going nuts over California Chrome. So as the horse race was about to begin, the parts department became vacant of parts workers. Everyone more or less abandoned their posts and gathered in the aisles of the auto parts store with their necks flexed so they could look up at the live broadcast of the race.

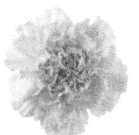

JUNE 9, 2014

PATRICK'S FACEBOOK POST

I'm thinking about what to do with my dog Lexi while I am at the High Sierra Music Festival for four days in July. And I'm thinking maybe about leaving her with my mom or my sister or a friend and then I realize no, this is Lexi, and she deserves a five-star experience. So Lexi has a four-day reservation at the West Roseville Pet Resort where she will play with other dogs, get exercise, eat well, be comfortable, and even be treated to a massage, hot bath, blow dry, and yes, honest to God, an anal gland stimulation before being dusted with a gentle perfume and awarded a brand new royalty bandana.

Cody: I want to stay there.

Patrick: I'm sure that can be arranged, Cody.

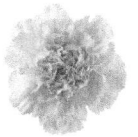

JUNE 10, 2014

PATRICK'S FACEBOOK POST

I know I am on the right track when I encounter pregnant women.

Connie: Please explain

Patrick: I know I'm in the right place when there are pregnant women around. They are the epitome of free, healthy space.

JUNE 11. 2014

PATRICK'S FACEBOOK POST

Bucket List: Play guitar with Tom Petty and the Heartbreakers.

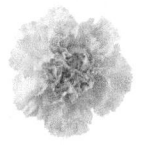

JUNE 12, 2014

WHEN THERE'S A NEED, DO SOMETHING

A little over a year ago, I started a Family Mental Illness Support Group for Sun City Lincoln Hills residents. I put a notice about a first meeting in the local newspaper and in the SCLH magazine. I had no idea if anyone would show up.

Twenty-two people arrived at my house. Some decided the group was not what they needed. Others found regular attendance hampered by complications in their lives. I decided I'd continue posting meeting times and locations in the newspaper until no one appeared. Then I'd give it a rest. Some months seemed iffy. Six people would show up. Other months there'd be ten. Working in the Snap It Up thrift store, I met a woman not from Lincoln Hills. She asked if she could come to the meetings. I ran it by the group and they said, "Of course."

Today is our 14th meeting in a conference room at a local grocery store. There are 12 people in attendance. Five of them are new to the group. The woman from the thrift shop is here. She's telling of her ongoing challenges with her eleven-year-old adopted son. She's a single mom. Her son wants to come home from his group home. She wants him to come home but he has to get through summer school first. A new man asks, "Does your son have a male role model?"

"No, no one seems to want to take on this kid with issues developed in utero. His mom was a meth addict. My son's cells produce meth. Sometimes he has no impulse control. His little body has ballooned from forty-five to ninety-five pounds from all the meds he's taking. He's paying the price for his birth mother's addiction."

She continues. "I'm being christened tomorrow into the Mormon Church. I'm not sure yet about all aspects of Mormonism, but I'm impressed with the young missionaries who keep coming to my house to teach me about their religion. I'm hoping the social network in the church will provide a mentor for my son."

The group moves on to other people while the mom and the new gentleman quietly continue a private conversation. Our meeting ends. On the way out I tell my friend, "I respect your decision to be baptized into the Mormon faith." She says something that blows me away.

"The new couple who came today are Mormon. They're attending my christening tomorrow. The man's offering to spend time with my son. To be his big brother or acting grandfather. Dede, it was my lucky day when I met you in the thrift store."

If nothing else comes from this little support group, it will have served its purpose. You never can tell where one small effort might lead. When there's a need, do something. Anything. Then wait and watch what happens.

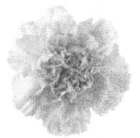

JUNE 14, 2014

ENDING

Right foot. Left foot.
Right foot. Left foot.

Footstep after footstep I configure my life.
Right foot. Left foot.
Right foot. Last foot.
Footsteps and life end so soon.

In May, 2014 I turned 70. I've kept a written record of my milestone year. Today, I feel like I've stepped out of a forest into a clearing free of shrubs and underbrush. I don't know how long I'll idle here or what type of terrain is waiting 'round the bend.

I intend this recounting as a gift for my myself, my descendants, and other wayfarers who catch a resonating echo while wandering in my woods.

It's later than I'd like but sooner than tomorrow.

Maya Angelou said, "There is no greater agony than bearing an untold story inside you."

Let's see.

Patrick's Facebook Post: I currently reside at Latitude: 38.7934560. Longitude: -121.2900540. Elevation: 45.45.m.

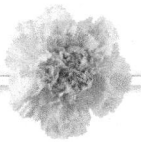

AFTER

After you had taken your leave,
I found God's footprints on my floor.

—RABINDRANATH TAGORE

TAKING A BATH

An intricate hand manipulates the roar
until the spout ceases, providing
only drips, a minuscule rhythm,
and steaming ripples are interrupted
by toes, feet, and then, an entire beast.
Inspiration, expiration: the level
of water shifts with the lungs
and soon sleep overtakes the creature.
Ripples, steam, drips: all continue.
Our man and the window perspire.
Salt-filled beads push through tight tunnels
and emerge from a taut face to soft light.
Released from epidermic passages
they scatter a mandibular stretch to the chin,
dangle, then leap with a microscopic yelp.
They hit the abdominal runway, and sometimes split
before wiggling off to waterline.
It is here that they become something other than alone.
Once submerged, molecular dialogue occurs,

rumors regarding pending demise, lost friends,
and hints of a nexus beyond this container.

—PATRICK RANAHAN
Published in
Latitude on 2nd
Cool Waters Media, Inc., 2012

PATRICK'S FINAL FACEBOOK POSTS

June 17: Have a lunch date today with my 96-year-old maternal grandmother, Evelyn Funk Moon. I treasure these lunches with her.

June 18: Ok, so I caved and did something I swore I was never going to do. I played Candy Crush Saga for like two minutes and now I'm being inundated with Candy Crush requests. Please folks, I doubt if I will every play that stupid game again.

June 21: My schedule doesn't really provide any days off. So six days a week I have to be ready for work. Some days are marked with a B for backup which means that you don't know until morning if you have to work that day until your phone rings. Makes it hard to plan things or get things done. Today is a backup day for me so I am praying that my phone does not ring this morning from dispatch. A day off would be much appreciated.

This is how smart I am: I got up this morning and emptied all of my garbage from the house into the garbage can outside. Then I got in my car and drove to work without putting the garbage can out for collection. So it will sit for another week.

Chris: At least you remembered to get the garbage in the can.

Pat: So I've got that going for me.

June 22: Let the dog in, let the dog out, let the dog in, let the dog out, repeat.

June 23: One of the best lines from the Mother Hips new album, *Chronicle Man,* is, "You can't win, but you can feel good trying."

June 24: Why do I have to leave the toilet seat down, why don't you leave the toilet seat up?
Tanya: What??
Patrick: Girls vs. boys
Brandi: We pee and #2 sitting down, so majority rules.
Patrick: That sounds like a personal problem.
Brandi: So . . . You #2 standing up? You have the problem
Patrick: Equal rights ma'am.
Erin: Plus you had 3 sisters and no brothers. Majority rules again!!! And I guess it's worse to fall into a toilet than to have to lift. But I've wondered about this before haha!
Shawn: Question I've had for years.
Patrick: Yes, Erin, precisely for the reason that I had to suffer through a childhood full of crazy women and no brothers, I am entitled to the privilege of leaving the toilet seat up.
Shawn: I've never understood how anyone sits down on anything, including a toilet, without looking where they are sitting.

June 28: At pre-High Sierra Music Festival meeting last night, learned that our campsite will be equipped with an air conditioned RV with a full kitchen, a full drum kit, numerous guitars, and other percussion instruments.

July 1: If you're in traffic and you have the right of way at an intersection, you're not doing anybody any favors if you wave other cars to go ahead when you're the one who is supposed to go.

July 3: Going offline for a few days at the High Sierra Music Festival. Time to face the music.
Chris: Have a great time Patrick.
Geoff: The Music Never Stopped.
Patrick: For a while it never started.
Lisa: Have fun Pat!!
Beth: Have fun!
Donna: Have a great time!!!

July 6: Just had one of the most restful, refreshing nights of deep sleep I've had in a long while. Outside in a tent and sleeping bag on the cold hard ground.

July 10: My next band is going to be called "Boobs Make the Package."

AFTER THOUGHTS

I had no idea, of course, when I began writing in June 2013, that not only was I recording my 70th year, I was also recording the last year of my son's life. I had no intention of including a "Before" or "After" section of my book. And then events necessitated a change of plan.

On July 9, Pat called about Lexi. "Hi, Mom. I think I have to take Lexi back."

"Why? What did she do?"

"She's destroying the house. She's torn up the bathroom floor. I think the whole thing will have to be replaced. I've got an appointment at four o'clock to take her back to the SPCA."

Pat was crying. This made me cry. "I feel stupid crying," he said.

"No, no. It's okay. This is hard. This is sad. I'd be more concerned if you weren't crying."

"I phoned Dad to see if he could take her on his ranch. He said, "No." I've failed her. I've let her down."

"Pat, you haven't failed her. No one's tried harder with this dog. And it's not fair to her to be cooped up all day while you're at work. She needs to be outside in a big space where she can run around. You're making a really tough decision but it's the right decision. Give yourself credit for doing the right thing."

"I feel like I'm not doing anything right."

"Well, from the outside looking in, you're doing many things right. Do you want me to go with you to take Lexi back?"

"No, I want to do this myself."

"Will you call me when you get home from the SPCA?"

"Yes."

At 5 p.m. Pat called again. "Hi, Mom."

"How did it go?"

"It was awful. I had to fill out lots of paperwork and the lady kept asking me, 'Are you sure you want to do this?' And I found out they're not a no-kill shelter. If they can't place her they'll put her down. The woman asked me if I wanted to be notified if they decide to put her down. At first I said 'no' but then I said 'yes.' I'd have twenty-four hours to try to find a place for her. The lady wouldn't stop with her questions and I was about to break down, so I left."

"Do you want to come over for dinner?"

"No, I think I want to be alone tonight."

"Don't forget to take good care of you."

"I'm trying, Mom."

I was afraid to go over to Pat's house, my mother's property. I suspected I'd find much more damage than Pat had told me about. Whatever damage there was, it could be handled later. My son's emotional well-being came first.

Pat had enjoyed a wonderful weekend at the High Sierra Music Festival, a festival he'd wanted to go to for a long time. On Friday, July 11, Pat stopped by my house. He'd squeezed his money every which way to make it to the festival. "Mom, I mailed a check for my car's DMV renewal. Can you loan me one hundred twenty-seven dollars to cover it until my next payday?"

Pat talked about having trouble sleeping. "I went to the hospital emergency room a couple days ago to get sleeping medication and I had a terrible day at work yesterday. I keep forgetting things. I had to go back to the store three times to pick up the parts I was supposed to deliver. I think it's because I'm so upset about Lexi."

I noticed Pat's slacks were hanging off of him. "Are you losing weight?"

"Yeah, well, I didn't realize how much working full time and trying to take care of Lexi were going to take out of me."

I gave Pat a check and invited him to stay for dinner, but he said he had to get home because a friend was coming by. Later that evening, Pat called. "I meant to ask you earlier, but I forgot. Do you think I should tell my boss at work about my bipolar disorder?"

"Why are you thinking about this now?"

"I don't know. Sometimes I feel like I'm not being honest."

"Do you remember, Pat, the last time you confided to a supervisor about your illness, you lost your job? Why don't you wait and think about it?"

On Saturday, July 12, Pat collapsed at work. An ambulance took him to the hospital where he received anti-seizure medication. In the evening, Pat called to tell me what happened.

"The hospital didn't want to keep you overnight for observation?"

"No, they told me to go home and rest."

"Pat, do you want me to come over?"

"No, Mom. I'm really tired. I want to go to bed."

On Sunday morning, July 13, I texted Pat and asked, "How are you his morning?"

He texted back, "Do you want me to call you?"

"If you want to. I didn't want to wake you if you were sleeping."

Pat never called. Sometime later that day, he was 5150d to the hospital in an agitated state of manic psychosis. The hospital didn't call to let me know about Pat's admission. I found out he was in the hospital psych ward when he called my brother, Jim. Pat had filled out an Advanced Care Directive listing Jim and me as his preferred contacts.

I hired a cleaning crew to clean Pat's house and a carpet cleaner. I wanted to see if something would salvage the carpet, which reeked of dog urine. I picked up Pat's dirty clothes, towels, and bedding and brought them home to launder them. I bought a new frying pan to replace his old grungy one. I wanted everything to be as nice as it could be when Pat got back to his house. And I went to the SPCA to check on Lexi. She'd been adopted, already, by a couple who lived out in the country.

On Thursday, July 17, Kerry and I went to the hospital to see Pat. We didn't know how he would receive us. When we walked into his room, he was sitting up in a hospital bed with his wrists in restraints. He didn't look like the same person I'd seen the week before. His hair hung stringy and unwashed, and his face, pale and thin, was unshaven. His eyes gleamed wildly but he was glad to see us.

"Mom, the nurses don't believe me. You can tell them. Tell them I have a black half-brother."

My heart sank. After six days in the hospital, Pat was still delusional. I shook my head. "Pat, you don't have a black half-brother."

Pat was also upset because he couldn't find his wallet. Although we'd already been in his house to clean it, Kerry was concerned that he'd be angry when he found out we were there without his permission. "Pat," she said, "Do you want us to look for your wallet in your house?"

"Yes, that's a good idea."

The nurses were getting ready to move Pat onto a different floor. Kerry and I waited in the hallway until they wheeled his bed out of his room. As they pushed him away down the hall, I yelled to the back of his head, "I love you, Pat."

427

Without turning around, he yelled back, "Love you too, Mom."

Those were the last words we'd ever hear each other say.

Kaiser told us they'd be transferring Pat to an outside psychiatric facility when a bed became available. It turned out, without our knowledge, they transferred him out of the county to Woodland Memorial Hospital—over 50 miles away. We found out where Pat was when he called Jim again.

Meanwhile, I was trying to get through to a doctor. Jim told a doctor who'd spoken to him that I was also on Pat's advanced directive and it was okay to talk to me. But no one called. I called Kaiser Membership Services. Since Pat was no longer in their care, they said they couldn't help me. I called a number for Woodland Memorial, asking to talk to Pat's doctor. I was told, "The doctor spoke with your brother. He doesn't have time to talk to everyone in the family."

On Tuesday, July 22, a woman called me from Woodland Memorial. She asked, "What is your discharge plan for your son?"

I lost it. "I have no discharge plan. No one has updated me on his status. What's happening with him?"

"Well," this woman said, "your son is very ill and needs long-term housing in a psych board and care facility. Does he receive disability to pay for his care? Do you know what medications have worked for him in the past?"

Now I was sobbing. "I don't know what worked for him in the past," I screamed. "I wasn't given that information. Don't you have his psych records from Kaiser?"

The woman wasn't sure. She said she'd check.

I hung up the phone. I could barely put one foot in front of the other. My legs felt like lead. All we'd worked for, all Pat had worked for, was gone—his dog, his job, his independent living, his mind. How could he face all this loss when he came home?

Tuesday evening, Pat called Jim again. "Uncle Jim, they're killing people here. You have to help me get out of here. I have a car and a driver waiting behind the hospital. Help me get out of here."

Jim said, "Hang in there, Pat. We're working with your doctors to get you home as soon as possible. Do what your doctors say."

When I went to bed Tuesday night, I despaired. I said out loud to the walls, "I give up. I have no idea what to do."

Wednesday morning, July 23, as I sat at my kitchen table, the phone rang. It was a nurse from Woodland Memorial. "We're moving your son to the ICU. A doctor will call you shortly."

The ICU? What was happening? At last, a doctor was going to talk to me. Twenty minutes after the first call, my phone rang again. This time a doctor spoke. "I'm sorry, your son died fifteen minutes ago. We believe he had a seizure. We tried for thirty minutes to save him. I'm sorry."

I froze. My son wasn't hoping to die. He'd told me, when he was admitted to the hospital for a possible seizure that recent Saturday, the doctor gave him a prescription and directed him to go "down the hall that dead ends in double doors to the pharmacy." The phrase "dead ends" rattled Pat. "I couldn't wait to get home," he said.

After going round and round with Woodland Memorial for a week after Pat died, trying to get an autopsy and a toxicology report, the county coroner stepped in and took charge of the process. Six months later, the coroner's report would say the cause of death was inconclusive: "Possible seizure or possible cardiac arrest."

I could write more about the last few weeks of Pat's life, my frustration and anger with our mental illness system (there is none), and the drastic need for change—sooner than tomorrow. I'd make a case for effective, compassionate care for our seriously mentally ill. I'd point out tragedies that could have been prevented and the urgent need for beds and housing. I'd challenge outrageous HIPAA laws that prevent moms and dads like me from giving and receiving lifesaving information. I'd talk about our missing and homeless children and mothers and fathers. I'd tell stories about our sons and daughters in jails and prisons and solitary confinement without treatment and on and on . . . My writing would turn into a tirade, and that rant is for another time. Not here. Not on sacred ground.

When he died, Pat had one dollar and fifty cents in his checking account. The first day I went to pick up his mail, I found a postcard from a student at Hampshire College, his alma mater. The young man thanked Pat for a ten-dollar donation he'd recently made to the college.

On August 26, what would have been Pat's 46th birthday, a certificate arrived in the mail. Per Pat's instructions on his Advanced Care Directive, his eyes had been harvested. The certificate read, "In deepest gratitude we honor and remember Patrick Sean Ranahan. Thank you on behalf of all transplant recipients whose eyes were touched by your generous heroic gifts."

On September 7, over 130 family members and friends attended Pat's Celebration of Life. I put pink, white, red, yellow, and blue Million Bells, their one-gallon containers wrapped in burlap and tied with raffia, on each of 20 tables. Twenty million bells for Pat.

Ten months since Pat's passing, I'm still stuck in disbelief. My grief's raw and, at times, overwhelming. We both tried so hard for so long. In spite of all the ups and downs, I liked the world better when Pat was in it. I miss him and want him back. Some days I feel like I'm suspended in jello and moving in slow motion. This morning, however, I'm heartened on my morning walk.

The killdeer is back on her nest in the same brown and gray rocks as before, one block over. No trees shade her. No bushes hide her from predators. She sits on her four new eggs—faithful, vulnerable, determined. "You inspire me little Mama Bird, and I wish you the best. We mothers have to stick together."

As I'm writing, The Jazz is tromping back and forth in front of my computer screen. "It's time for us to go outside," she says.

Guess I gotta go. I have to end, for now. I'll close with an image from the distant past. An image that—for some reason—lingers in my memory:

Pat called. Out of the blue.
He'd been homeless and missing for over a month.
"Mom, can you come get me?"
Pat was waiting for me at the Pleasanton BART station.
I drove there, immediately, around 11 p.m.
In the dark, I spotted him at the far end of the empty parking lot.
He didn't notice my car approaching.
His attention was on something else.
Standing straight and tall, with his arms at his sides
and his head tilted back,
Pat, my son, was looking up at the stars.

JULY 23, 2014

Kerry Ranahan Joiner: Dear Facebook Friends of Patrick Ranahan, Pat passed away this morning. We miss him so much! We will celebrate his life—details later.

> Marilyn: Kerry, what happened? Please let me know if I can help.
>
> Emma: Kerry, love to you and the entire Ranahan family. You are all in our prayers.
>
> Anna Lynn: My heart is in my throat. I am shocked. Please let me know if there is anything I can do. I send my love to all the family.
>
> Jen: Ron and I are in shock. He just said a few minutes before I read this that he needed to call Pat. So very sorry for your loss. Our thoughts are with your entire family.
>
> Steve: I can't believe this. So very sorry, we had just started communicating again. Wow. My thoughts are with you as well.
>
> Mara: We were so shocked and sad to hear this. Much love from the Johnson family.
>
> Barri: I am so sorry.
>
> Veronica: I'm so very sorry to hear. My thoughts and prayers to the family.

Lara: I'm so heart broken. I'm so sorry for your loss.

Lauren: So sorry for your loss. This is heart breaking.

Chris: So sorry for your loss. I have just announced it to all of our classmates in our Cal High group. He will be missed.

Shannon: We are so very sorry to hear this. Our thoughts and prayers are with you and your family.

Laura: My heart and thoughts are with you and your family. I have enjoyed seeing Pat on FB, his posts and have great memories. Thank you for letting us know though it is sad, sad news. We will celebrate his life.

Paul: I love you Pat. You will always be with me.

Dana: What a shock! He was working and playing, enjoying life, which I know was a tough journey for him. Thank you for informing everyone. How sad.

Angie: So sorry to hear. I am glad to have had this time reconnecting with him through Facebook.

Pam: I am so sorry about Patrick's passing at a time when it seemed he was enjoying life. His creativity and love for music was very compelling and created so much meaning for him. I will always remember his engaging smile and beautiful bright eyes.

Elissa: I'm so, so sorry to hear about Patrick Ranahan. We met in the early 90s, through Deb Matson's husband Steve. Pat was a sweet, gentle soul with a wicked sense of humor. He will be missed. Sending love to his family and friends.

Trent: Sad news to hear. He will be missed.

Tanya: Oh this is so sad.

Merideth: I keep thinking of the posts I saw in the last week while Pat was at the High Sierra Music festival and the absolute joy he was expressing in being surrounded by music. Just heartbreaking to know he is not here anymore, but I know that music will keep his spirit alive.

Dan: Very sad to hear. Our thoughts and prayers are with his family.

Brad: Heavy heart today. Very sad news. His family will be in our prayers. Rest in peace, Pat.

Brandi: I'm stunned and saddened. I enjoyed talking with him about music and politics. He could always make me laugh, even when we would disagree. He will be missed greatly.

Ryan: It was always great catching up with Pat at the Ranahan Super Bowl parties or reading his Facebook posts. Good guy so sad to read about this.

Donna: I am so very sorry to hear this. He became one of my great Facebook friends. My heart is very sad at the news. Yes, even as a young boy he always loved music! My love for you Patrick RIP.

Leslie: Oh no! He was such a sweet guy! What happened? RIP Pat!

Cheryl: Oh no! My thoughts and prayers are with the family. Rest in peace, Pat.

Angela: I am shocked! So sad. He was such a great guy. 1st one to ever buy me room service . . . yeah 10 year old kid got room service steak.

Cindy: So shockingly sad. Prayers for comfort and strength for all his loved ones.

Stephanie: I always enjoyed Patrick's company, his unique sense of humor, his love for music and his perseverance in the face of adversity. My heart goes out to the family at this sad time.

Monica: I am very sorry to hear this. God's blessing to Pat and all his family.

Kerry Ranahan Joiner: As bizarre as it is to tell people over Facebook we couldn't think of how else to reach all Pat's friends. I want to thank you for the kind words. We are finding it comforting to read while we grieve.

Megan Ranahan Mace: One of Pat's final Instagram posts was a sign at the High Sierra Music Festival; "You are the music while the music lasts." He was very happy at the festival sharing the joy of music with several friends. He also loved sharing his prized guitar in a jam session with his nieces and nephews on July 1. It is with heavy hearts that we share the news of his unexpected passing. Dear Pat, will miss you and your music. Love, Megan

Darrell: So sorry to hear of Pat's passing. Our hearts go out to the entire Ranahan family—great memories with Pat that will last forever. What a great human being.

Penny: So sorry to hear this. My thoughts to you and his family.

Mark: I was lucky enough to be at High Sierra with him over the 4th of July weekend. He really enjoyed it. We all did. Glad I have that memory. RIP Pat.

Kate: Megan, so sorry to hear of this loss. So many memories of Pat. He was a good friend and always made everyone laugh. A very kind soul.

Shawn: My goodness. That is sad news. Rest easy Pat.

Angela: Megan, so sorry to hear of this. I have many fond memories of Pat throughout our childhood and adult years. He always made me laugh! My thoughts and prayers are with you and your family. Love and hugs to all!!

Lisa: I'm so sad. I just saw Pat and spent time with him before the 4th at the Tesla concert and horse races. He showed John how it was done at the track. RIP my friend.

Karin: I am so saddened to hear this news. We had such a nice time at High Sierra Music Festival and you were telling me how well you were doing and thanked me for my support through hard times. I thought the hard times were behind you. What a great guy, with a HUGE heart and a wonderful spirit. I will keep your memory in my heart forever. You will be greatly missed my friend! Truly this planet lost a very special person. May you keep shining your light from above.

Tony: One of the few guys everyone liked. So sorry to hear it.

Dennis: I was here in California with my dad the day Patrick was born in Chicago and made him a grandfather for the first time. Dad's Irish eyes glistened with joy at the thought of Mike becoming a father. While the shock of losing this young man is still raw with emotion, I am comforted somewhat with the thought that Pat is now with both his grandfathers and all their eyes are smiling bright in heaven. By the way, because Patrick called his mother's dad, Pop, his beloved grandmother Evelyn, he quickly named Mop.

Jen: I miss you Pat. Thank you for making me laugh countless times over the past almost 30 years. I love that every time I saw you, you always picked up like no time had passed at all. I'm so grateful that I got to see you a few summers ago at Marisa's. I'm going to miss all of your funny Facebook posts. Most of all, I'm sad for your family because they loved you with all their hearts. I truly believe that you're an angel now, so please watch over and take care of them. RIP.

Daryl: So many memories of our friendship Pat. Garcia's, our venture to start Mad Dash Video, we spent so much work on that. I still have a copy of our prospective. We did a great job but too young for anyone to invest in us. Our idea became Netflix! The great times we spent hanging at your house. The Garcia's Christmas party. It was so great we reconnected on FB. I will miss you my friend.

437

Dede Ranahan: Thanks so much to everyone who is posting about Pat. Your comments are very helpful to us. I was retrieving papers from Pat's car and I found this undated, handwritten and signed statement. I'm sharing it with you. Thank you for loving him. Dede (Pat's Mom)

> *I, Patrick Ranahan,*
> *forgive and release and wish blessings*
> *upon all who I have held grudges against,*
> *or have perceived to have done me harm.*
> *I forget all past condemnation,*
> *and wish nothing but the best*
> *and divine fulfillment and inspiration*
> *to all of those I have held*
> *in enmity in my mind and soul.*
> *God bless all beings.*

Chris: I'd like to go into great detail but can't release the flood gates. Patrick was a fantastic friend while he was up here in Oregon; so funny, thoughtful and caring. He had the most entertaining life I could ever imagine.

Roger: So sad that I never got to reconnect. You were a very important person to me in high school. Thanks for everything Pat.

Steve: 4th grade we started to play the trumpet. By the time we went to Pine Valley, Pat was first chair. I was second. The battle was on between Pat, Ron G, and myself. Through 7th, 8th, 9th, 10th, 11th and 12th grades. Cal High had some of the most talented individuals that later became great musicians. Every year at the Reno Jazz festival we won four years in a row. Pat's love for people and music touched everyone he came into contact with. My trumpet that I played with Pat is hanging on my wall in my office. Live to the high potential, treat people with respect, love people and be happy. That was Pat. He never changed. RIP brother. Our condolences to your family.

Anker: I met Pat in 1989 in the first year we both arrived at Hampshire College. He was one of the people I counted on knowing as an old man; tying myself to memories of the beauty and possibility of youth, as only one who has shared the pinnacle of it with you can. The loss of this friendship will leave a hole in me that cannot be filled: Pat's perspective on life and the words he used to describe it cannot be replicated.

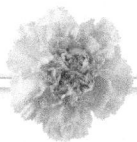

"So," my five-year-old granddaughter Ayla
asks her mom, "we can still talk to Uncle Pat, right?"
"Right," Kerry answers.
Ayla's quiet and then says, as if pointing out the obvious,
"All we have to do is look up."

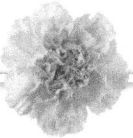

AKAMAI777 MY SON
(Wit, Wisdom, and a Big Hug from the Universe)

I LOVE YOU FOREVER.

MOM

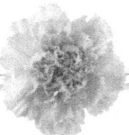

ACKNOWLEDGMENTS

First, thank you to my son, Patrick. Thank you for your poetry, your Facebook posts, and your life. You're the most courageous person I've ever known.

Thank you to my daughters, Megan Mace, Marisa Farnsworth, and Kerry Joiner, for reading *Sooner Than Tomorrow* and giving me permission to put it out there, sharing our family with the world. Your endorsements mean everything to me.

Thank you to everyone I mentioned in the telling of my story. We're all in this thing we call "life" together.

Thank you to early readers: Ann Hedrick, Pat West Guinn, Kathy Hayes, Mary Lyn Rusmore-Villaume, Rosemary Sarka, and Irene Underwood. You gave me the cojones to believe in myself.

Thank you to the cheerleaders, those of you read my book excerpts week after week at soonerthantomorrow.com and sent me emails, text messages, cards, and letters: Joan Andersen, Tama Bell, Chris Biswell, Judy Bracken, Madeleine Cunningham, Bev Chinello, Deborah Fabos, Anne Schmidt Francisco, Heidi Franke, Sheila Ganz, Jeanne Gore, Joyce Herrerias, Swannie Hoehn, Rose King, Nancy Krause, Joan Logue, Grace McAndrews, Jan McKim, Mary Murphy, Fran Neves, Liz Noel, Teresa Pasquini, Den Proudly, Karen Riches, Mary Sheldon, Stace Shurson, Sandy

Turner, Kimberlee West, Annette Williamson, and to so many more of you who left comments, likes, and loves on Facebook. You kept me going, especially on the days when I thought, *what am I doing?*

Thank you to Sharon Lefkov, Kerry Joiner, and Michele Joiner for proofing my pages for spellings and typos. Thank you to my little brother, Jim Moon, for bringing my old photos back to life. Acknowledgments also to Sue Clark, my first editor, who read every page out loud with me and assured me, "Yes, this is interesting." And to the Lincoln Library writer's class who listened in the beginning, when Pat was still with us.

Special hugs to Pat's Facebook friends.

Thanks to Michele DeFilippo and Ronda Rawlins at 1106 Design for your professionalism and guidance.

And finally, thank you to all of you—those I know and don't know—who are reading *Sooner Than Tomorrow*. Readers are the whole point of writing. The *why* in the *what if.*

—DEDE RANAHAN

P.S. Love to my heroes—the millions of mothers of the seriously mentally ill who fight for their children every single day.

April, 2019
Lincoln, California

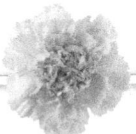

ABOUT THE AUTHOR

Dede Ranahan is a mother, grandmother, and long-time mental health advocate who's worn many career hats. In 1982 she authored a book for young girls that won a national award for nonfiction. In 2001 she established the Institute for Mental Illness Education on the Cal State Hayward campus. In 2004 she served as the Walk Director for the first NAMIWalk in San Francisco. From 2007 to 2010, she worked in the NAMI California office as the Policy Director for the Mental Health Services Act (Prop 63). Today, in her over-55 community, Dede runs a support group for families who have members coping with serious mental illness. She says, "In trying to help our loved ones, we need help ourselves. We need to know we're not alone."

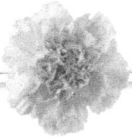

PLEASE SHARE YOUR ONLINE REVIEW OF

SOONER THAN TOMORROW

Like all authors, I rely on online reviews to garner new readers. Your opinion is valuable. Please take a few moments, now, to share your assessment of *Sooner Than Tomorrow* on Amazon or any other book review website you prefer.

If you have a story to tell about serious mental illness, visit my website, www.soonerthantomorrow.com. and read some of the stories already there. Then send your story to me at dede@ soonerthantomorrow.com. I can help you edit your story, if necessary. I'd love to hear from you.

My Facebook author page is https://www.facebook.com/ dederanahan/. My Instagram page is https://www.instagram. com/soonerthantomorrow. And I'm on Twitter, https://twitter .com/DedeRanahan.

Thanks so much.

My best wishes for all your tomorrows. Dede

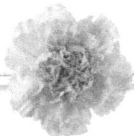

QUESTIONS FOR DISCUSSION

1. Did the author fulfill the expectations she set up for you in her introduction?
2. Did some *Diary* stories make you laugh? Which ones?
3. Did some *Diary* stories make you cry? Which ones?
4. Has *A Mother's Diary* changed your views about mental illness?
5. Pat didn't want to have bipolar disorder or schizo-affective disorder. He saw his sisters and his friends with their families, their jobs, and their homes, and he wanted to be like them. If you knew this about your adult child and that it made him sad, how would it affect you?
6. Pat convinced a psychiatrist (who knew him for one hour) that he didn't have bipolar disorder or schizo-affective disorder. The doctor stopped seeing him. Pat died one year later. Do you think this was a coincidence or a contributing factor?
7. Pat was transferred out of county (without his family's knowledge) because of a lack of hospital beds for the seriously mentally ill. What is known as the IMD (Institutes for Mental Disease) Exclusion—prevents federal payments to mental health facilities with more than 16 beds—is

part of the reason there are not sufficient beds available. Should this law be changed?

8. Three hours after he died, the attending doctor told the author, "There is no suspicion of foul play. We've closed your son's file and sent it to the coroner's office. There's no need to do an autopsy." This comment made the author uncomfortable. She fought for a week to reopen her son's file and to get toxicology and autopsy reports authorized. What would you have done?

9. Do you agree or disagree with these statements? Mental illness is not an addiction. It doesn't respond to tough love. It's not a matter of character or will.

10. Often anosognosia (lack of insight) prevents a person with serious mental illness from recognizing that he or she is sick. How would you suggest a parent/caregiver set realistic expectations and boundaries when anosognosia is present?

11. HIPAA laws often prevent parents/caregivers from inter-acting with mental health professionals and life-saving information is lost. How can a patient's right to privacy and a parent's right to try to get help for their adult child be reconciled?

12. If your child/adult child has a serious mental illness—or any serious illness—what do you do to take care of yourself? What do you do to balance the joy and sorrow in your life?

13. Sometimes, for their own well-being, parents must walk away from their ill sons or daughters. This is like "Sophie's choice." What would you say to a mom (or dad) in this situation to help her cope and to ease her guilt?

14. Do you agree or disagree with these statements? Mental illness is a brain disease and should be reclassified as a

physical illness. We need more scientific research into brain diseases.

15. Has *A Mother's Diary* inspired you to leave a letter, story, diary, song, painting, or poem for your descendants? If so, what are you going to leave for them?

16. If ever in Bend, Oregon, would you stop at the Sparrow Bakery to buy an Ocean Roll?

17. Bonus Question: Should George Clooney have picked Amal or Dede?

Dede Ranahan would love to hear about
your discussions. Please send your insights to her.
dede@soonerthantomorrow.com

Made in the USA
Las Vegas, NV
06 March 2021

19111535R10266